Access of Phonological and Orthographic Lexical Forms: Evidence from Dissociations in Reading and Spelling

A Special Issue of
Cognitive Neuropsychology

Alfonso Caramazza

Psychology Press
a member of the Taylor & Francis group

Copyright © 1997 by Psychology Press,
an imprint of Erlbaum (UK) Taylor & Francis Ltd.
  All rights reserved. No part of this book may be reproduced in any form,
  by photostat, microform, retrieval system, or any other means without
  the prior written permission of the publisher.

Psychology Press
27 Church Road
Hove
East Sussex, BN3 2FA
UK

ISBN 0-86377-960-3 (Hbk)

Printed and bound by Henry Ling Ltd, Dorchester

Contents

1   Access of Phonological and Orthographic Lexical Forms: Evidence from Dissociations in Reading and Spelling
    Alfonso Caramazza

3   Are Reading and Spelling Phonologically Mediated? Evidence from a Patient with a Speech Production Impairment
    J. Richard Hanley and Vincent McDonnell

35 The Independence of Phonological and Orthographic Lexical Forms: Evidence from Aphasia
    G. Miceli, B. Benvegnù, R. Capasso, and A. Caramazza

71 The Autonomy of Lexical Orthography
    Brenda Rapp, Lisa Benzing, and Alfonso Caramazza

105 Further Evidence of a Dissociation between Output Phonological and Orthographic Lexicons: A Case Study
    Jennifer R. Shelton and Michael Weinrich

131 Complex Dynamic Systems also Predict Dissociations, but They Do Not Reduce to Autonomous Components
    Guy C. Van Orden, Marian A. Jansen op de Haar, and Anna M. T. Bosman

167 Reading Comprehension Is Not Exclusively Reliant upon Phonological Representation
    Max Coltheart and Veronika Coltheart

177 How Many Levels of Processing Are There in Lexical Access?
    Alfonso Caramazza

209 Subject Index

Access of Phonological and Orthographic Lexical Forms: Evidence from Dissociations in Reading and Spelling

This special issue of *Cognitive Neuropsychology* is dedicated to a problem of considerable current interest: The role of phonology in orthographic lexical access. The question addressed is whether lexical access in reading and in spelling are necessarily mediated by phonological processes. This question has been the focus of much discussion in the normal literature, but has received only scant attention in cognitive neuropsychological investigations. In fact, most neuropsychological treatments of orthographic lexical access have ignored the problem of phonological mediation altogether. The reason for this seeming indifference is that neuropsychologists have considered the issue long settled: The standard position has been that phonological mediation is not necessary (but may play a role) in orthographic lexical access. Why this difference in the two literatures? The reason seems to be quite simple, if not entirely justifiable. In the case of spelling, for example, the fact that in some brain-damaged subjects the ability to spell is often preserved even though phonological production may be quite severely impaired has been interpreted as indicating that spelling does not require phonological mediation. However, in order to reach this conclusion it would have to be shown that the phonological deficit in these subjects is not at a level of processing subsequent to the point where phonological mediation might take place, and this precaution has not always been faithfully observed. Thus, it is of considerable value to collect in one place reports that purport to resolve the issue of phonological mediation in orthographic lexical access unambiguously.

Seven papers are included in this special issue. Four of them (Hanley & McDonnell; Miceli, Benvegnù, Capasso, & Caramazza; Rapp, Benzing, & Caramazza; Shelton & Weinrich) report case studies purportedly showing that phonological mediation is not necessary in orthographic lexical access. Of these, two focus exclusively on production; the other two address both word recognition and word production. Also in this issue are commentaries by van Orden, Jansen op de Haar, and Bosman and by M. Coltheart and V. Coltheart. Van Orden et al. argue that the evidence presented in the empirical reports does not undermine the phonological mediation hypothesis when it is recast in the framework of "complex dynamic systems." They even go so far as to argue that

© 1997 Psychology Press, an imprint of Erlbaum (UK) Taylor & Francis Ltd

their theory of lexical processing may be immune to empirical falsification. The readers will have to evaluate the significance of this claim for themselves. Max and Veronika Coltheart reach the opposite conclusion from van Orden et al. They argue that the evidence presented by Shelton and Weinrich and by Hanley and McDonnell convincingly demonstrates that the phonological mediation hypothesis of reading comprehension is false. The last paper, by Caramazza, uses the empirical evidence against the (obligatory) phonological mediation hypothesis of orthographic lexical access as the basis for interpreting the patterns of lexical errors produced by brain-damaged subjects in speaking and writing tasks. He interprets the patterns of dissociations and associations of lexical errors in these tasks as providing evidence against the existence of a modality-neutral level of lexical representation (lemma) mediating between semantic and modality-specific lexical forms.

Alfonso Caramazza
Cognitive Neuropsychology Laboratory
Harvard University

Are Reading and Spelling Phonologically Mediated? Evidence from a Patient with a Speech Production Impairment

J. Richard Hanley
University of Liverpool, UK

Vincent McDonnell
Ormskirk and District General Hospital,
West Lancashire NHS Trust, UK

In this paper, we report the case of a patient, PS, who shows excellent comprehension of the meaning of words despite making a large number of phonemic paraphasias on tests of oral reading, picture naming, auditory repetition and in spontaneous speech. In a series of experiments, we attempt to demonstrate that his preserved reading comprehension could not reasonably be explained in terms of the theory of phonological mediation during reading (cf. Van Orden, 1987). Although he is good at comprehending the meaning of written homophones, the critical finding is that PS is unable to produce both meanings of a homophone when presented with the written form of one version of the homophone. That is, he is unable to make a response such as "inherits" in response to the written word "air" (heir). Although phonological mediation may play *some* role in the way in which meaning is accessed from print by normal readers, the results of this study suggest that it is not obligatory (cf. Coltheart, Patterson, & Leahy, 1994). A similar argument is advanced with respect to PS's relatively well-preserved written spelling.

According to the theory of obligatory phonological recoding in reading, it is necessary to generate an internal representation of a word's phonological structure from its written form before the meaning of that word can be accessed. Such a view has a long history of support in experimental psychology, even when reading in a deep alphabetic orthography such as English is being

---

Requests for reprints should be addressed to Dr. J. Richard Hanley, Department of Psychology, University of Liverpool, Eleanor Rathbone Building, PO Box 147, Liverpool L69 3BX, UK (Tel: 0151-7942960; Fax: 0151-7942945; email: JW24@liv.ac.uk).

discussed (e.g. Gough, 1972; Rubenstein, Lewis, & Rubenstein, 1971). At the start of the 1980s, however, there was a growing consensus amongst theorists interested in word recognition that phonological processes play no necessary role in the way in which the meaning of written words is accessed in English (e.g. Ellis, 1984; Humphreys & Evett, 1985; Patterson, 1982). As Ellis (1984, p. 15) put it, "there are a number of reasons why the theory of obligatory phonological recoding cannot be right."

One of the most important of these reasons was data from patients with acquired dyslexia who are very much less impaired at reading aloud words familiar to them before their illness than unfamiliar words and nonwords. This includes patients with deep dyslexia (see Coltheart, Patterson, & Marshall, 1987) and phonological dyslexia (e.g. Funnell, 1983; Patterson, 1982). Their inability to read nonwords suggests that these patients can no longer generate a phonological representation of a word on the basis of sublexical or *assembled* phonology (Patterson, 1982). That is, they can no longer read a word aloud from sounding out its individual letters or graphemes. Despite their problems with nonwords, phonological dyslexics such as AM (Patterson, 1982) are very good at accessing the meaning of familiar words during reading. It therefore appears to follow that reading for meaning does not rely on assembled phonology.

However, there are at least two reasons why such data do not totally rule out the theory of obligatory phonological recoding. The first is that phonological dyslexics may in fact be able to generate a phonological representation of a nonword internally, but may be unable to produce an appropriate response because of a phonological output problem that affects unfamiliar words much more than familiar words (see Patterson & Marcel, 1992, for details of this argument). The second reason is that phonological recoding may involve not assembled phonology, but instead what Patterson (1982) refers to as an *addressed* phonological code. That is, phonological mediation may take place after a familiar visual word form has been identified, but before the word's meaning has been retrieved from the semantic system. Phonological mediation of this kind would occur on the basis of a specific association between a visual word form in the orthographic input lexicon and a representation of the word's phonological form in the auditory input lexicon. Evidence from phonological dyslexia is not inconsistent with this version of the phonological recoding theory, since phonological dyslexics have relatively little problem in generating the appropriate phonological representation of a familiar written word.

There is, however, a further type of patient that has sometimes been used to argue against the phonological recoding theory. These are patients with severe speech production impairments, and include individuals with neologistic jargonaphasia (Caramazza, Berndt, & Basili, 1983; Ellis, Miller, & Sin, 1983), and those who are unable to make any response whatsoever when attempting to produce spoken words (Levine, Calvanio, & Popovics, 1982). The patients described by Caramazza et al. (1983) and Ellis et al. (1983) made a large number of phonological errors when reading aloud both familiar words and nonwords. Patient RD (Ellis et al., 1983), for instance, read *grief* as /prIvd/, and *quilt* as /kwIst/. Despite this, RD's ability to understand the meaning of words that he was unable to read aloud was remarkably well preserved. As he was reading them aloud, RD defined *grief* as "one is sad," and *quilt* as "on top of you on the bed." Levine et al.'s (1982) patient, EB, who could not respond when attempting to read words aloud, showed good comprehension of what he was reading on tests involving the matching of written words to pictures.

According to Ellis et al. (1983, p. 137) and Ellis and Young (1988, p. 219), the ability of cases such as JS, RD, and EB to access meaning from print whilst being unable to say the word aloud are difficult to reconcile with the phonological recoding view. Ellis et al. (1983) argue that RD cannot be accessing the semantic system from print via a phonological representation because of his inability to pronounce words even when he can provide their meaning.

Despite these claims, however, the case of RD does not in fact rule out the obligatory phonological mediation theory. As we said earlier, an advocate of the theory might quite reasonably argue that the meaning of written words is accessed via a pathway from the orthographic input lexicon to the auditory input lexicon. Although a pathway from the orthographic input lexicon to the auditory input lexicon is not to be found in standard dual-route models of reading (e.g. Coltheart, Curtis, Atkins & Haller, 1993), it is present in a recent influential model of reading development (Ehri, 1992). It therefore remains possible that RD is able to generate internally a perfect phonological representation of a word during reading by using a pathway from the orthographic input lexicon to the auditory input lexicon. He may then use this phonological representation as the basis for accessing the word's meaning within the semantic system. The neologistic errors in oral reading might come about as a result of a speech production impairment that occurs *after* the meaning of the word has been accessed phonologically. The recent report by Caplan and Waters (1995), of a patient who appeared to be able to generate the precise phonological forms of words internally, even though he made neologistic errors in oral reading, is consistent with such an interpretation.

Ellis (1984) also claimed that phonological recoding based on addressed phonology is incompatible with our ability to access the correct meaning of homophones in English during reading. Even when reading homophones out of context, we can discern, for instance, that a *tale* is told and a *tail* is wagged. As Van Orden, Johnston, and Hale (1988, p. 379) have pointed out, however, there is a way that the meaning of a homophone might be accessed on the basis of its phonology. It is possible that both meanings of a homophone might initially be activated via phonology when we see either version of it in print, and the inappropriate meaning could subsequently be inhibitied. Inhibition might take place either on the basis of the context, as presumably occurs in speech perception (Swinney, 1979), or else following retrieval of the spellings from the orthographic output lexicon that are associated with each meaning. The meaning of the word whose associated spelling does not contain the same letters as the word being read would then be rejected.

Van Orden and his colleagues have also provided some striking experimental support for phonologically mediated access to meaning during visual word recognition. Van Orden (1987) demonstrated that when normal subjects are asked to respond as quickly as they can, they make significant numbers of false positive errors to questions such as whether a "rows" is a "flower" (see also Jared & Seidenberg, 1991). According to Van Orden et al. (1988, p. 371), such findings indicate that "phonological mediation plays a role in normal reading for meaning." Even Patterson (1992, p. 314) has recently accepted that such findings suggest that "translation of the written word to a phonological representation may play a major role in reading comprehension." There is, however, a crucial difference between the views of Patterson and those of Van Orden. According to Patterson and her colleagues (e.g. Coltheart et al., 1994; Patterson, 1992; Wydell, Patterson, & Humphreys, 1993), direct access to meaning from print and phonologically mediated access to meaning occur in parallel. That is, phonological mediation may play a role in the way in which meaning is accessed from print but it is *not obligatory*. According to Van Orden et al. (1988) and Van Orden (1987), however, meaning is always accessed via phonology during visual word recognition. The existence of a patient who could access meaning without phonology would be compatible with the views of Patterson and her colleagues, therefore, but would appear to be inconsistent with the account favoured by Van Orden et al. (1988).

The present paper attempts to investigate these issues by examining the case of a patient who, like RD (Ellis et al. 1983), can understand the meaning of written words despite making phonological errors when reading these words aloud. Particular attention is given to whether or not this patient might have access to well-formed internal phonological representations of words during reading despite the fact that he makes phonological errors when reading aloud (cf. Caplan & Waters, 1995; Feinberg, Rothi, & Heilman, 1986; Friedman & Kohn, 1990). If he does not have access to internal phonology, then it will be hard to maintain the view that access to meaning is taking place on the basis of a phonological code.

As with reading, the issue of whether or not written spelling of familiar words is necessarily phonologically mediated has long been the subject of debate (see Barry, 1994; Ellis, 1982). Ellis (1984) argued that the inability of phonological dysgraphic patients (e.g. Shallice, 1981) to generate a phonologically plausible spelling for unfamiliar words is difficult to reconcile with the phonological mediation of spelling. As was the case with phonological dyslexics and reading, however, data from phonological dysgraphics do not rule out the possibility that mediation takes place on the basis of addressed rather than assembled phonology. In other words, it might always be the case that, during written spelling, a word's orthographic representation in the spelling lexicon is activated via its representation in the phonological output lexicon rather than direct from the semantic system.

The ability of some patients with anomia (Bub & Kertesz, 1982a; Levine et al., 1982) or jargonaphasia (Caramazza et al., 1983; Ellis et al., 1983) to spell accurately words that they are unable to say aloud has been taken as evidence against the phonological mediation of spelling by Ellis and Young (1988). They argue (p. 166) that "if writing were based on inner pronunciations, then the spellings of patients such as RD (Ellis et al., 1983) and JS (Caramazza et al., 1983) would surely reproduce their mispronunciations, yet they do not." However, it is conceivable that such patients have available an intact phonological representation for use in spelling that they are unable to articulate accurately when attempting to speak. The written spelling of the patient that we will describe in this paper is also relatively well preserved despite severely impaired performance on tasks such as spoken picture naming. Consequently, an attempt will also be made to establish whether or not the process by which he is able to retrieve word forms from the orthographic output lexicon during written spelling could be phonologically mediated.

CASE DETAILS

PS is a man in his late forties who lives with his wife in the north-west of England. In 1990, following a week of severe headache, he left a business meeting after he had difficulty controlling his right hand. He then noticed that his right leg was weak, and that he could not speak. He was taken to hospital, where a CT scan showed evidence of an acute infarct. It revealed a low density area in the left temporal region with a slight mass effect. This took the form of some squashing of the left lateral ventricle. There was evidence of left-hemisphere swelling with effacement of cortical sulci. A Doppler examination revealed very reduced blood flow in the left internal carotid artery. A left carotid angiogram revealed a left internal carotid artery dissection.

PS was treated with anticoagulants, and has made a good medical recovery. His right-sided problems have recovered fully, and his language skills have improved substantially. However, despite speech therapy, which has continued since the time of his illness, severe problems in spoken word production remained 4 years later. He returned to his job as a bank manager 15 months after the stroke, but his continuing problems with speech production made it impossible for him to continue, and he has since retired. Despite his language problems, he achieved a score of 53/60 on Raven's Progressive Matrices, a test of nonverbal intelligence, when tested in 1994. Such a score is associated with the 95th percentile, and indicates that PS continues to function at a high intellectual level. His digit span, however, is only three items forward and three items backwards. Performance was equally poor regardless of whether PS was asked to write or say aloud his answers. These tests and those reported here were conducted during 1993 and 1994, 3 years post-onset.

Speech Production and Comprehension

PS makes speech errors in every situation in which a spoken response is required. This includes tests of auditory repetition, oral reading, picture naming, and spontaneous speech. In an attempt to minimise his difficulties during conversation, PS attempts to keep to a limited vocabulary of words that he can generally produce correctly. These words have been relearnt by PS since his stroke, as a result of practice (repeated articulation) during formal speech therapy sessions, and at home with his wife. He will not attempt to produce other words unless he is talking to his wife or a close friend. This makes him reluctant to initiate conversations with strangers; for instance he will not go to a shop where he has to ask an assistant for the goods that he requires.

Using the criteria employed by Nickels (1995), in which an error is considered to be phonological if it contains at least 50% of the correct phonemes in their correct order, then over 90% of the errors that he makes are phonologically similar to the word that he is trying to produce. Sometimes his errors are nonword responses (e.g. issue → /ɪsʌz/) and sometimes they are real words (e.g. simple → "symbol"). Often, he is aware that he has made an error, and will make repeated attempts to pronounce the word correctly. This occurs in repetition, reading, and picture naming. These attempts terminate either when he has produced the correct answer, an answer that he considers to be correct, or when he gives up after several failures. His attempts terminate in the correct answer approximately 50% of the time. Occasionally, he will continue to make a series of incorrect responses even when he has already pronounced a word correctly. PS always articulates phonemes correctly when he is attempting to produce words, indicating that he does not suffer from a lower level apraxic impairment.

On a test of auditory repetition, he was correct on only 57/80 words from a list of 40 high- and low-imageability words used by Franklin, Howard, and Patterson (1994). His repetition showed a significant effect of imageability (χ^2 = 4.94, $P < .05$), and no significant effect of frequency ($P > .05$); he repeated correctly 17/20 words of high imageability and high frequency, 16/20 words of high imageability and low frequency, 13/20 words of low imageability and high frequency, and 11/20 words of low imageability and low frequency.

Despite his speech production problems, PS's performance appears to be unimpaired on tests of auditory comprehension. On an auditory lexical decision test from the PALPA battery (Kay, Lesser, & Coltheart, 1992), PS was correct on 160/160 trials. When asked to generate a semantic associate to each word from the Franklin et al. (1994) list as they were spoken to him, he was successful with 77/80 of them. For example, he responded "not strong, not brave" to "meek," having repeated it as "meat," and responded "stage" to "debut," having repeated it as "/divʌl/." The only words to which he could not provide an associate were "keen," "idiom," and "moral" (all of low imageability).

TESTS OF READING

Reading Comprehension

On a written lexical decision test comprising 60 nonwords, 30 words of high imageability, and 30 words of low imageability taken from the PALPA battery, PS was correct with 119/120 decisions. Such a level of performance was comfortably within the normal range for this test relative to control subjects, showing that his ability to distinguish written words and nonwords is undiminished.

PS's ability to understand what he was reading was virtually perfect. On the written word version of the Pyramids and Palm Trees test (Howard & Patterson, 1992), PS achieved a score of 51/52 (normal range = 50–52). On a PALPA test where the subject has to match a written target word to one out of four alternative written words according to which is closest in meaning, PS scored 13/15 correct on items of high imageability (e.g. "comb" and "door, *brush*, gate, tweezers"), and 14/15 correct on items of low imageability (e.g. "fraud" and "truth, crime, proof, *deceit*"). Control subjects scored 13.43/15 (SD = 1.26) on the items of high imageability and 12.25 (SD = 1.82) on the items of low imageability. PS was also good on a test of written synonym judgement from the PALPA battery. He was correct on 29/30 decisions about high-imageability items (e.g. deciding whether "gift" and "donation" are synonymous), and 29/30 judgements about low-imageability items (e.g. deciding whether "menace" and "threat" are synonymous). On the written version of Shallice's synonym matching test, PS was correct on 28/29 decisions on easy pairs (e.g. whether "possess" is closer in meaning to "get" or "own"), and 25/29 correct on decisions about difficult items (e.g. whether "peruse" is closer in meaning to "read" or "consider").

When asked to define written words, his performance was perfect even for words of low imageability. On the words of high and low imageability and frequency from the PALPA battery, he produced 80/80 accurate definitions. For example, he defined "tobacco" as "its a smoke," and pupil as "people who go to school" despite having pronounced them as /toækam/ and /piu../ respectively. Even where he made a reading error that was a real word, he always gave a definition that was consistent with the word that he was attempting to read rather than the word that he said aloud.

To investigate further PS's ability to understand written words, he was given the Lancaster/Radcliffe famous names line-up. This is a test of familiar name recognition that has been used in several investigations of the performance of patients with name recognition or name retrieval impairments (de Haan, Young, & Newcombe, 1991; Ellis, Young, & Critchley, 1989; Flude, Ellis, & Kay, 1989; Hanley, 1995; Hanley, Young, & Pearson, 1989; Harris & Kay, 1995). PS was given a set of 60 index cards. Twenty contained the written name of high-familiarity people (e.g. Margaret Thatcher, Harold Wilson, Marilyn Monroe), 20 contained names of lower familiarity (e.g. James Hunt, Anna Ford, David Bellamy), and 20 contained unfamiliar names (e.g. John Lawrenson, Joseph South, Linda Coles). He was asked to rate each name for familiarity on a scale from 1 (unfamiliar) to 7 (highly familiar), and provide the occupation of those names that he found familiar. He recognised 40/40 famous names as being familiar and made only 1/20 false alarms on the unfamiliar items. The mean familiarity ratings that he gave were 6.85 for the high-familiarity faces (control mean = 6.27, SD = 0.63), 6.47 for the lower-familiarity faces (control mean = 5.92, SD = 0.84). He gave the correct occupation for 19/20 of the high-familiarity names (control mean = 19.66, SD = 0.84) and 20/20 of the lower-familiarity names (control mean = 19.16, SD = 1.1). His ability to distinguish familiar from unfamiliar written names is therefore unimpaired, as is his ability to access identity specific information about the person concerned from semantic memory (Bruce & Young, 1986).

PS's ability to understand written sentences was also good on the written version of the PALPA Sentence–Picture Matching test. In this test, the subject reads a sentence and must point to one of three pictures according to which picture matches the meaning of the sentence. For example, for the sentence "The man is kicked by the horse," the distractor pictures showed a man kicking a horse, and a man sitting on a horse. PS was correct on 59/60 items. Such a level of performance placed him comfortably within the normal range compared to control subjects.

Oral Reading

Despite his excellent comprehension of written words, PS's ability to read words aloud is severely impaired. He read correctly only 34/80 of the words of high and low imageability and frequency from the PALPA battery that he had defined faultlessly. When PS was asked to read aloud the names of the people from the Lancaster/Radcliffe set, he was able to read only 3/20 unfamiliar names and 5/40 famous names correctly, despite his unimpaired ability to identify the celebrities concerned.[1]

---

[1] The errors that PS made in reading these names aloud are shown in Appendix 1. It can be seen that the type of errors that he makes are qualitatively similar to those that he makes in reading ordinary words, in that they are phonologically similar to the correct name.

The incorrect responses that PS made while reading the PALPA list are shown in Table 1. The nature of his reading errors on this test and on a set of high- and low-imageability words devised by Shallice, in which the items fall into four separate imageability ranges each matched for length and frequency, are summarised in Table 2. It can be seen from Tables 1 and 2 that the overwhelming majority of the error responses that PS made were nonwords that are phonologically related to the target word. None of PS's responses on any of the lists that we have asked him to read could be categorised as a semantic error. Many of the paralexic errors that PS made were morphemic errors. In virtually all cases, these involved PS pluralising the target word (e.g. "season" → "seasons", "denial" →"denials").

The remaining real word errors could be classified as either visual errors or phonological errors (e.g. "mouse" → "mouth", "popular" → "poplar"). Of these, eight appeared to be more likely to be phonological errors than visual errors. This was because they shared more phonemes than letters with the target word, or because they contained an incorrect phoneme that was close to the target in terms of its phonetic features. These were "ancient" → "asian"; "broad" → "brawn"; "build" → "bill"; "effort" → "ever"; "great" → "grave"; "knife" → "night"; "needle" → "kneel"; "wide" → "while". Only three of the paralexias could be said to be closer visually than phonologically to the target ("cult" → "could"; "length" → "lent"; "thou" → "though"). We therefore take these errors to reflect the problem with spoken word production that affects PS's repetition and picture naming performance; we do not believe that he makes visual errors of the kind that are commonly observed in deep or phonological dyslexia. Consistent with this, even when he made a paralexic error in reading PS always defined the word correctly whenever this was requested of him.

As in his auditory repetition, PS read correctly significantly more words of high imageability than low imageability ($\chi^2 = 7.37$, $P < .01$), but there was no effect of frequency ($P > .05$). He read correctly 16/20 words of high imageability and high frequency (control mean = 19.94, SD = 0.25), 7/20 words of high imageability and low frequency (control mean = 19.94, SD = 0.07), 5/20 words of low imageability and high frequency (control mean = 20.0, SD = 0.25), and 6/20 words of low imageability and low frequency (control mean = 19.52, SD = 0.68). On the set of words devised by Shallice, PS read correctly 23/40 words with an imageability rating between 5.5 and 6.5, 22/40 words with an imageability rating between 4.5 and 5.5, 14/40 words with an imageability rating between 3.5 and 4.5, and 11/40 words with an imageability rating between 2.5 and 3.5, the effect of imageability being significant ($\chi^2 = 10.67$, $P < .05$). It appears, therefore, that PS's ability to read words deteriorates quite suddenly once the imageability of the words drops below about 4.5.

The other variable that affected PS's reading significantly was word length ($\chi^2 = 43.23$, $P < .01$). On a list devised by Howard (1989), PS read correctly

TABLE 1
The Reading Errors that PS Made on the 80 Words from the PALPA Imageability x Frequency List

Word Type	Real Word Errors	Phonological Nonword Errors	Other Nonword Errors
High Imageability High Frequency		church > /čuz/ hospital > /apIskɑl/	student > /sönt/ audience > /ali/
High Imageability Low Frequency	feather > fetter cart > car wheat > weeks gravy > gravies	potato > /pʌtɑto/ tobacco > /toɑkʌm/ monkey > /mʌnki/ slope > /splo/ elbow > /hɛlpo/ pupil > /pUlpIl/ alcohol > /ælkal/ funnel > /fʌmnl/ elephant > /ɛlʌfʌlz/	
Low Imageability High Frequency	length > lent character > char purpose > purrs theory > thing principle > prince	opinion > /o..pIn..yʌn/ crisis > /kr/ay/sIz/ effort > /ɛfʌz/ system > /sIstUnz/ session > /sɛtan/ quality > /kaviti/ attitude > /ætIcud/ concept > /kamsɛps/ moment > /momʌnt/	
Low Imageability Low Frequency	bonus > bone...us	gravity > kræbIti/ treason > /riz../ realm > /rIlm/ valour > /væl / miracle > /mIlriækl/ mercy > /mɛrsi/ wrath > /ræb/ episode > /ɛpsto/ dogma > /dagmʌz/	satire > /tɑsə/ irony > /ɑro/ tribute > /tuplu/ analogy > /ænilaŋ/ deed > /diʌnt/

20/20 words of three letters (e.g. ear), 11/20 words of five letters (e.g. grass), 4/20 words of seven letters (e.g. chicken), and 1/20 words of nine letters (e.g. chocolate). PS also showed a significant effect of word length when he was given this set of words in a test of auditory repetition on a separate testing session.

TABLE 2
The Number of Reading Errors that PS Made on the Imageability × Frequency Lists as a Function of Imageability and Frequency

Word Type	Correct Responses	Real Word Errors	Phonological Nonword Errors	Other Nonword Errors
PALPA Set				
High Imageability High Frequency	16	0	2	2
High Imageability Low Frequency	7	4	9	0
Low Imageability High Frequency	5	4	11	0
Low Imageability Low Frequency	6	1	8	5
Shallice Set				
Imageability				
6.5–5.5	23	7	8	2
5.5–4.5	22	6	10	2
4.5–3.5	14	9	12	3
3.5–2.5	12	5	20	3
High Frequency	38	14	25	3
Low Frequency	33	13	25	7

PS showed no significant effect of grammatical class of spelling to sound regularity on reading ($P > .05$). On a list of words from the PALPA battery in which the nouns, verbs, and adjectives are matched for imageability, he read correctly 7/20 nouns (control mean = 19.87, SD = 0.43), 7/20 adjectives (control mean = 19.97, SD = 0.18), 7/20 verbs (control mean = 19.97, SD = 0.18), 5/20 functors (control mean = 19.93, SD = 0.37). On a list of words produced by Parkin, McMullen, and Graystone (1986), in which the regular and exception words are matched for frequency, length, and orthographic regularity, he read correctly 14/24 regular words (e.g. "mint"), and 19/24 exception words (e.g. "pint"). None of the errors on the exception words were regularisation errors.

PS's ability to read nonwords was extremely poor. On PALPA test 36, he read correctly 3/6 nonwords of three letters (control mean = 5.77, SD = 0.71),

0/6 nonwords containing four letters (control mean = 5.89, SD = 0.43), 1/6 nonwords of five letters (control mean = 5.57, SD = 0.90), and 0/6 nonwords of six letters (control mean = 5.65, SD = 0.85). Thirteen of his 20 errors were lexicalisations (e.g. "cug" → "cub," "snite" → "snake"). Four of his errors were a different nonword (e.g. "ked" → "keb". On two of his responses, the nonword was split into two (e.g. "dusp" → "dus...p"). There was one failure to respond ("squate" → "I can't do it"). Although we have not directly compared PS's nonword reading with his reading of real words, the number of nonwords containing three and five letters that he read correctly is markedly lower than the number of real words of this length that he read correctly on the Howard (1989) list.

PS was given a further test of nonword reading in order to discover whether he was better at reading pseudohomophones than nonhomophonic nonwords (cf. Patterson & Marcel, 1992). On a set of nonwords taken from PALPA test no. 27, on which the two sets of nonwords were matched for both length and for "N" (a measure of "word likeness"), PS read correctly 6/15 nonhomophonic nonwords and 8/15 pseudohomophones. PS also read correctly 7/46 nonhomophonic nonwords and 15/46 pseudohomophones from a set devised by Howard and Franklin (1988). When the data from these two sets are combined, there is an effect of homophony that just reaches statistical significance ($\chi^2 = 3.94$, $P < .05$). The superior reading of pseudohomophones suggests that PS's speech production problems make some contribution to his poor reading of nonwords (Patterson & Marcel, 1992).

PS's poor performance on tests of nonword reading, and his failure to show any advantage in reading regular words over irregular words, suggest that his ability to use assembled (sublexical) phonology in reading words aloud is extremely limited. This, together with the fact that he also shows a significant effect of imageability in reading, would be consistent with the claim that PS is a deep dyslexic. However, PS's unimpaired ability to comprehend words of low imageability is not consistent with recent models of deep dyslexia (e.g. Plaut & Shallice, 1993). Moreover, PS does *not* make semantic errors in reading, which are generally seen as being the hallmark of deep dyslexia (Coltheart et al., 1987). In addition, few, if any, of the errors that he makes when trying to read words aloud appear to be visual errors. Instead, they appear to be phonologically related to the word that he is attempting to read. This, along with his intact reading comprehension, suggests that PS's oral reading problems reflect, to a great degree, the speech production impairment that also affects his spontaneous speech, picture naming, and oral repetition. The effects of imageability suggest that the routes that PS uses when reading and when repeating familiar words go through the semantic/cognitive system. If he was able to read successfully via the direct link between the orthographic input lexicon and the phonological output lexicon, then his reading should not have been affected by imageability.

PHONOLOGICAL RECODING IN READING

Although it is clear that the ability of PS to read aloud words and nonwords is severely impaired following his brain injury, his ability to understand what he reads appears to be entirely preserved. This applies to the reading of single words, to the reading of proper names, and to the reading of meaningful sentences. Impressive written comprehension despite the production of spoken errors in oral reading has been observed previously in other patients (e.g. Ellis et al., 1983). These authors have asserted that it is difficult to see how the appropriate meaning of a word might be accessed during reading on the basis of such a corrupted representation of the word's phonological form. Perhaps even more strikingly, the incorrect responses that PS makes when reading aloud are sometimes real words (e.g. "wheat" → "weeks"). If PS were accessing the meaning of these words on the basis of phonology, one might expect that he would define "wheat" as if it meant "weeks." This never occurred, however. PS's definitions were always consistent with the meaning of the word that he was reading rather than with the meaning of the word that he said aloud.

As was pointed out earlier in the article, such a pattern of performance is not necessarily incompatible with the theory of obligatory phonological recoding in reading. This is because a patient such as PS might have access to appropriate, intact *internal* phonological representations of words during reading. This is a particularly important issue since Caplan and Waters (1995) have reported a patient, RW, with preserved comprehension of visually presented words who appears to have access to well-formed internal phonological representations of words despite making phonological errors in oral reading, auditory repetition, and picture naming tasks. The problems that PS encounters, therefore, may occur because he is unable to produce an overt phonological code that matches the phonological representation that he can generate internally. The alternative view is that PS, although he can perceive spoken words well, is quite unable to generate an internal phonological representation of a word from print, despite his excellent comprehension. If this latter account turns out to be true, then severe problems would be posed for the theory of obligatory phonological recoding.

Tests of Written Rhyme and Homophone Judgements

Experiment 1

In the first of our experimental investigations, we examined whether PS was able to distinguish pseudohomophones from nonhomophonic nonwords on a silent reading task. Although PS is severely impaired at reading nonwords aloud, it remains possible that he can generate a well-formed internal phonological representation of an unfamiliar letter string on the basis of assembled phonology even though he is unable to produce it accurately when reading aloud. PS's superior reading of pseudohomophones over nonpseudohomophonic nonwords is consistent with such an interpretation (Patterson & Marcel, 1992).

PS was given a list comprising 15 pseudohomophones and 15 nonhomophonic nonwords, and was asked to put a tick next to any that sounded like real words. He ticked 1/15 nonhomophonic nonwords and 3/15 pseudohomophones. He was therefore correct on only 17/30 items (14 correct rejections and 3 correct acceptances). When given these same 30 items as an auditory lexical decision test on a subsequent testing session, his performance was 100% correct. Such a level of performance indicates that PS's problems in reading nonwords do not merely reflect a difficulty in phonological output processes. His inability to detect pseudohomophones suggests that he is unable to generate an accurate internal phonological representation of a letter string on the basis of subword level orthographic to phonological conversion. This suggests that he *cannot* generate a well-formed internal phonological representation of a letter string on the basis of assembled phonology (cf. Patterson & Marcel, 1992).

Experiment 2

Despite the results of Experiment 1, however, it remains possible that PS can generate accurate internal phonological representations of *familiar* words on the basis of *addressed* phonology. For example, he may be able to activate a representation of the word's phonological form in the auditory input lexicon on the basis of a direct association from a representation of the word's visual form in the orthographic input lexicon. If a patient does have access to preserved internal phonological representations of this kind, then it might be expected that he or she would be able to judge whether or not two written words rhyme or are homophonic with one another (Friedman & Kohn, 1990). PS was therefore given a list of 40 pairs of words, half of which rhymed with each other, and half of which did not rhyme with each other. In 10 of the rhyming pairs, the rime segments were spelled the same way (calf half), and in 10 the rime segments were spelled differently (hole coal). In 10 of the pairs that did not rhyme, the rime segments were spelled the same (fear bear), and in 10 the rime segments were spelled differently (sprout shoot).

The results showed that PS was correct on only 29/40 decisions. His errors comprised seven false alarms and four misses. This score was significantly better than chance ($z = 2.85$, $P < .01$) but was well outside the normal range (control mean = 38.5/40, SD = 1.3, range = 36–40). On an auditory version of the same task, PS scored 38/40. This finding contrasts with the results that Levine et al. (1982) obtained with EB, who was equally impaired at auditory and written rhyme tasks. PS's relatively good performance on the auditory rhyme test indicates that the poor performance he shows on the written version is not because he no longer understands the concept of rhyme.

Experiment 3

It appears from Experiment 2 that PS lacks adequate phonological representations of written words. There is, however, an alternative explanation of PS's poor written rhyming performance. According to Besner (1987), written rhyme judgements make particularly heavy demands on phonological short-term memory (Baddeley, 1992). PS's limited digit span suggests that his phonological short-term memory capacity is relatively small. His poor written rhyme performance might therefore reflect an inability to manipulate the phonological representation of a written word within the phonological loop, rather than an absence of adequate phonological representations altogether. In contrast, Besner claims that written homophone judgements, compared with rhyme judgements, make relatively few demands on the phonological loop.

PS was therefore given a list of 40 word pairs, half of which were homophonic and half of which were nonhomophonic. On all of the nonhomophonic pairs, one of the two words contained a rime segment that could be pronounced in a way that would make the two words homophonic when it appeared in another word (e.g. clown-clone, cf. mown; height-hate, cf. weight). PS scored only 25/40 on this task, which was not significantly better than chance ($z = 1.58$, $P > .05$). His errors comprised nine false alarms and six misses. These results are consistent with those that Levine et al. (1982) obtained with patient EB, who performed very badly when asked to decide which two words were homophonic from a set of four written words. Since the strategy used by Levine et al.'s patient on this task was to find the two words that had the most letters in common, it would have been interesting to see whether he would have been able to complete an auditory homophone matching task. When PS was given an auditory version of the homophone test, he was correct on 38/40 trials. This indicates that PS's poor performance with the written homophones did not come about simply because he does not understand the concept of homophony.

PS's performance is very different from that observed by Caplan and Waters (1995) with their patient RW, who performed extremely well on a test of written homophone judgement that was virtually identical in form to that used with PS. The performance of Caplan and Waters' patient shows that it is possible for a patient to have access to the phonological form of a word during reading even when they make phonological errors in oral reading.

Experiment 4

It follows from the performance of PS on the homophone task that he does not have available the correct phonological form of written words when he accesses their meaning. Nevertheless, we devised an even more sensitive test of the theory of obligatory phonological mediation that did not require PS to compare two separate word forms explicitly.

In this critical experiment, PS was given a list of 20 written homophones (e.g. air, symbol, sweet), and was asked to write next to each homophone a semantic associate not of the word that he was reading, but of "the other word that has exactly the same sound as the word you are reading." A correct answer for "air" would therefore be "inherits" (heir), a correct answer for "symbol" would be "drum" (cymbal), and a correct answer for "sweet" would be "furniture" (suite). If PS is accessing the meaning of written words via addressed phonology, then it should be possible for him to access both meanings that are associated with that phonological word form and thus to provide the required definition.

The results of this test showed that PS found the task to be very difficult. He was correct on only 6/20 items. The correct responses that he wrote were *symbol*: → "band, drum" (cymbal), *chute*: → "football" (shoot), *rain*: → "queen" (reign), *cereal*: → "TV" (serial), *ale*: → "sick" (ail), *flour*: → "bunches" (flower). The only other response he made was "stay" in response to weigh. Full details of PS's performance in this experiment can be found in Table 3.

Could PS's poor performance on this test have come about because he did not know the meaning of the other version of the homophone? In order to rule out this possibility, PS was next given a sheet of paper containing the alternative version of each homophone. He was asked to supply a semantic associate of each of the words that he saw on this list. PS scored 19/20 on this test. It is also conceivable that PS did not recognise the visual form of the homophone that he was reading. In order to discount this possibility, PS was next given a fresh sheet of paper containing the original version of the 20 homophones. He was asked to provide a semantic associate of each of the words that he saw on this list. Once again, PS performed well, scoring 20/20. Overall, therefore, PS's score of 6/20 on this test appears quite incommensurate with his excellent ability to comprehend both written versions of each homophone (see Table 3).

It seems to us that the only reasonable conclusion that can be drawn from this experiment is that PS is able to access the meaning of written words despite being unable to generate either an accurate internal or an accurate overt phonological representation of them. It is difficult to reconcile this finding with the claim made by Van Orden and his colleagues (Van Orden, 1987; Van Orden et al., 1988) that, during normal visual word recognition, the generation of a phonological code is a necessary first step that must be accomplished before the meaning of a word can be accessed. If such a stage is obligatory, then a patient who cannot make this first step should surely encounter grave difficulties when attempting to access the meanings of written words during reading. In the remainder of this paper, we investigate whether PS's *written spelling* shows any evidence of phonological mediation.

TABLE 3
A Summary of the Responses Made by PS in Experiment 4
(*= Incorrect Response)

Homophone	What Does the Other Version Mean?	What Does This Version Mean?
symbol (cymbal)	band, drum	badge, band
groan (grown)	NR	sick, tree
way (weigh)	stay*	route, food
root (route)	NR	teeth, road
bough (bow)	NR	tree, tree*
soar (sore)	NR	plane or bird, fall
colonel (kernel)	NR	army rank, nut
chute (shoot)	football	coal bunker, football
bury (beret)	NR	dig, hat
sweet (suite)	NR	cake, sitting
quay (key)	NR	docks, door
rain (reign)	queen	weather, king
earn (urn)	NR	money, tea
scene (seen)	NR	play, eye
air (heir)	NR	amtophose *(atmosphere)* queen
dough (doe)	NR	bread, deer
cereal (serial)	tv	breakfast, tv
ale (ail)	sick	beer, sick
flour (flower)	bunches	bread, bundle
jewel (dual)	NR	ring, sword

INVESTIGATION OF SPELLING

Written vs. Spoken Naming

PS's written spelling of familiar words is impaired relative to control subjects. Nevertheless, he is much less severely impaired at written word production than at spoken word production. The fact that he is better at writing words than at saying them aloud provided the starting point for our attempt to demonstrate that PS's relatively well-preserved spelling of words was not phonically mediated.

PS's ability to understand the meaning of pictures remains unimpaired. On the picture version of the Pyramids and Palm Trees test (Howard & Patterson, 1992), he was correct on all 52 trials. He also performed well on a PALPA picture–word matching test. Despite this, his ability to name pictures orally is severely impaired. On a simple test of picture naming ability (e.g. "comb," "bear") from the PALPA battery, PS named only 23/40 pictures correctly. Mean performance by 29 control subjects was 39.80 (SD = 0.35). When he was asked to write his responses, however, he was correct with 36/40 pictures. This difference was significant ($\chi^2 = 10.91, P < .01$). Two months later he was given the same words to spell, but this time in a spelling-to-dictation test. PS again spelt 36/40 words correctly. His spelling errors on the dictation test were anchor → anocher, elephant → elanphant, scissors → scirros, lemon → lemmon. His errors in response to the pictures were elephant → elanaphant, scissors → scirror, swan → swann, fork → no response. Nevertheless, even though it was significantly better than his oral naming score, PS's written spelling score of 36/40 on this test was impaired relative to controls, who correctly spelt 39/40 of the words (SD = 1.33). Consequently, a series of tests was undertaken to discover the precise nature of PS's written spelling impairment.

PS showed no evidence of being able to spell regular words better than exception words. On a list of words taken from Hanley, Hastie, and Kay (1992), PS spelt 34/45 regular words correctly, and 35/45 exception words correctly. PS was also given 70 words from a list devised by Kreiner and Gough (1992), in which half of the words contain a schwa vowel (e.g. s*a*lute), and half of the words contain a corresponding nonschwa vowel (e.g. c*a*ndid). PS spelt correctly 29/35 of the nonschwa vowels, and 26/35 of the schwa vowels. This difference was not significant ($P > .05$). If PS were using spelling rules, he would have been expected to find the predictable nonschwa vowels easier to spell.

Consistent with this, his ability to spell nonwords is very poor. On a test from the PALPA battery that manipulates the letter length of nonwords, PS spelt only 1/24 nonwords correctly. Control subjects achieved a mean score of 5.43/6 on the three-letter items (SD = 0.88), 5.25/6 on the four-letter items (SD = 1.14), 5.25/6 on the five-letter items (SD = 1.24), and 4.96/6 on the six-letter items (SD = 1.45). PS's errors comprised 10 lexicalisations and 13 nonword errors. The only nonword that PS spelled correctly was "lat" spelled as "latt." *Latt*, however, is a word commonly used in Lancashire to refer to a piece of wood.

PS's spelling showed a smaller effect of imageability than his reading or auditory repetition. When given the set of words of high and low imageability and frequency from the PALPA battery (test 31) to spell, he was correct on 18/20 items of high imageability and high frequency, 16/20 items of high imageability and low frequency, 16/20 items of low imageability and high frequency, and 13/20 items of low imageability and low frequency. On

Shallice's graded set, he spelled 74/80 words with imageability values between 4.5 and 6.5, and 66/80 words with imageability values between 2.5 and 4.5. The effects of imageability reached statistical significance only on the Shallice list ($\chi^2 = 3.66$, $P < .05$). The effect of imageability was significant ($\chi^2 = 5.40$, $P < .05$) when the data from the two lists were combined. There is also a significant effect of frequency in PS's ability to spell the Shallice set; he spelt correctly 76/80 words of high frequency and 64/80 words of low frequency ($\chi^2 = 8.23$, $P < .01$).

When given the list of words from the PALPA battery that manipulates part of speech to spell to dictation, PS spelt correctly 18/20 nouns, 16/20 adjectives, 17/20 verbs, and 8/20 functors. The effect of word class was statistically significant ($\chi^2 = 16.21$, $P < .01$). As the functors in this set are of lower imageability than the nouns, verbs, and adjectives, PS was also asked to spell the words from PALPA test 33, in which the nouns and functors are matched for imageability. A deficit in spelling functors was again observed; PS spelt 16/20 nouns and 10/20 functors correctly. These differences were significant ($\chi^2 = 3.96$, $P < .05$).

This problem with functors also emerged when PS was asked to look at a picture and write a sentence to explain what was happening (the pictures were taken from PALPA test no. 56). Only 4/10 sentences were syntactically correct. For example, he wrote "The lady is brush his dog" instead of "The lady is brushing her dog," and "A lady is look in the fridge" instead of "A lady is looking in the fridge." When he was subsequently asked to say aloud a sentence to describe the picture rather than write it, all of his sentences were syntactically well formed. The effect of modality was significant ($\chi^2 = 8.57$, $P < .01$). Conversely, his spoken sentences contained the same sort of phonological errors that characterise his spoken single word production (e.g. staring → stirring, kicking → kissing). Errors of this kind were not observed in his writing of these sentences; *kick* and *stare*, for example, were both spelt correctly. When asked about his problems in writing function words, PS responded that he "can see" in his mind's eye the letters of the nouns, but that the letters for the function words do not appear.

Written Spelling Errors

A list of the errors that PS made while spelling single words can be found in Appendix 2. These fall into *three* basic categories. First, 52% of them were errors in which the response was a nonword that contained several letters in common with the target word. These included transposition errors, in which a letter appeared out of position (e.g. virtue → virute), insertions, in which an additional letter was inserted into a word (e.g. mustard → mustmard), substitutions, in which an incorrect letter replaced the correct letter (e.g. span → spay), and deletions (genesis → gensis), in which a letter was omitted. There were also errors that showed a combination of these error types (e.g. salute → slatutle). For this first type of spelling error, it is clear that PS has the correct word in mind but has misspelt it. These errors might be seen as being errors of partial lexical knowledge (Ellis, 1982). They might alternatively reflect an impairment at the level of the graphemic buffer (e.g. Hillis & Caramazza, 1989).

The second major type of spelling errors were real word errors (29%). They were correctly spelled words that were either related to the target morphemically (justify → justice, potato → potatoes), visually (e.g. severe → service), or semantically (anyone → else, ballot → electer, beyond → behind, enough → again, yourself → one else). Finally, 14% of his errors were either partial responses or complete failures to respond. The real word errors and failures to respond would seem to occur when PS was totally unable to access the correct word and either wrote down instead the spelling of a similar word, or else failed to respond at all.

The poor spelling of nonwords, and the failure to find any advantage in spelling regular words and nonschwa words over less predictably spelt words, indicates that PS has deficits in subword level orthographic to phonological conversion, and that he might be a phonological agraphic (e.g. Bub & Kertesz, 1982a; Shallice, 1981). However, the fact that he also shows a significant effect of imageability, shows a function word deficit, and made five errors that could be considered semantic errors, suggests that he might instead be classified as a deep dysgraphic (e.g. Bub & Kertesz, 1982b).

IS WRITTEN SPELLING PHONOLOGICALLY MEDIATED?

The critical question in terms of the phonic mediation of spelling is whether access to the orthographic output lexicon in spelling occurs via an indirect link between the semantic system and the phonological output lexicon (as an advocate of obligatory phonological mediation must claim), or whether access occurs via the direct link to the orthographic output lexicon from the semantic system (a link that must be denied by an advocate of obligatory phonological mediation). It is intuitively unlikely that PS could be using the phonological output lexicon because his written word production is so much better than his spoken word production. Nevertheless, it remains possible that PS is able to generate the phonological form of a word internally from its semantic representation even though he cannot say it aloud.

The issue of whether patients with speech production impairments have available an intact internal phonological representation for use in spelling has been investigated in the past by asking such patients to make rhyme judgements about pictures. In some cases of conduction aphasia, remarkably good performance can be observed on tasks such as this (Feinberg et al., 1986). The patients reported by Bub and Kertesz (1982a), Levine et al. (1982), and Caramazza et al. (1983) all had severe difficulties when they were presented with a set of pictures and asked to indicate which of the pictures had names that rhymed with each other, however. Such findings are consistent with the view that these patients are unable to generate internally a phonological representation of words on the basis of a semantic representation. In none of the studies, however, was the patient also asked to write the appropriate picture names. We therefore investigated the ability of PS to make picture–rhyme judgements, and also examined the accuracy of his written spelling of these items.

PS was given a rhyme judgement task from PALPA (test no. 14) in which he was presented with pairs of pictures and was asked to indicate whether or not the pictures had names that rhymed with each other (e.g. hat, cat; comb, coat). In this test, the subject is not allowed to say the words aloud. After he had made his decision on each trial, PS was asked to write down the two words that were represented in each picture. Performance on the rhyming test was at chance levels; he was correct on only 21/40 decisions. He spelled correctly 75/80 of the picture names, however. Occasionally, when he could see what he had written, he would ask if he could change his rhyme decision. When the 35 trials on which PS spelt both items correctly were considered alone, his rhyme decisions were still only 19/35 correct.

The finding that he cannot perform rhyme decisions accurately even when he can spell the items in question is consistent with the view that PS does not have access to a well-formed phonological representation of a word even when he spells it accurately. Nevertheless, as was argued in the corresponding section of this paper that examined PS's reading, rhyme judgements may require intact phonological short-term memory processes, as well as an intact phonological code (Besner, 1987). It is also important, therefore, to examine PS's performance on homophone tasks.

Experiment 5

In the critical experiment that we designed, PS was given a set of 20 definitions of homophones one at a time written on a sheet of paper (e.g. "To bend the head before the Queen to express greeting or humility" [bow]; "There are 24 of them everyday" [hours]; "to measure how heavy an object is" [weigh]. PS was told that all the definitions applied to homophones. In Phase 1, PS was told to write down the spelling, not of the word that fitted the definition, but the spelling of the word that sounded the same as the word whose definition he was reading. The correct answers for the three items given above would therefore be "bough," "ours," and "way." He was given some examples to clarify the nature of the task. He provided the requested written version of the homophone on only 8/20 trials. As soon as he had finished this task, he was asked to go through the set once again, this time writing down the correct spelling for the word referred to in the definition (Phase 2). The correct answers for the items just given would now be "bow," "hours," and "weigh." This time, he was correct on 19/20 items. Thus, PS's poor performance on Phase 1 could not have come about because he failed to generate the original version of the homophone from its definition. In Phase 3, Phase 1 was repeated, but this time with the experimenter saying the word aloud as PS read the definition. PS was now correct on 17/20 items. Performance in Phase 1 was significantly lower than in Phase 2 ($\chi^2 = 13.79$, $P < .01$) and Phase 3 ($\chi^2 = 8.64$, $P < .01$). Therefore, PS's poor performance in Phase 1 could not have come about because he did not know the correct spelling of the version of the homophone that he was supposed to produce in Phase 1. Table 4 summarises his performance on the three phases of this experiment.

Table 4 also demonstrates that when PS does not get the answer correct, his answer is not simply the version of the homophone appropriate to the definition. This makes it unlikely that his problem in performing this task was due to a difficulty in suppressing the homophone appropriate to the definition.

We believe that this result has strong implications for the processes that take place when PS is spelling. If PS were accessing the spelling of a word in the orthographic output lexicon via the phonological output lexicon, as the theory of obligatory phonic mediation holds, then he should have performed at a similar level on all three phases of this task, instead of being impaired only in Phase 1. If his spelling were mediated by addressed phonology, then both versions of a homophone's spelling should have been available from the definition of either of them. This is because the same phonological representation would be used to access both spellings of the homophone. Since PS performs so badly on this task despite the high level of spelling that he shows for the same items on standard spelling tests, it is hard to see how the theory of obligatory phonic mediation of spelling can explain his performance. Of course, these results do not indicate that no phonic mediation of spelling takes place in normal spelling; what they indicate is that accurate spelling can take place without it.

The conclusion that PS is not using the phonological output lexicon during spelling is also consistent with some of the other facts about his spelling performance that were reported earlier. The imageability effect, and the fact that he does make some semantic errors in spelling, suggest that in the terms of the model of Patterson and Shewell (1987), PS is spelling auditorily presented words via the cognitive/semantic system. The fact that he appeared to perform at a similar level when writing/spelling picture names to dictation as when writing/spelling the names of pictures is consistent with this. In fact it suggests that PS's spelling relies exclusively on the lexical semantic route. If PS was able to spell any words via a direct link between the auditory input lexicon and the phonological output lexicon, then he might have been expected to perform better at writing picture names to dictation than at writing the names of pictures.

TABLE 4
A Summary of the Performance of PS in Experiment 5

	Write the Other Version	Write this Version	Write the Other Version with Auditory Presentation
A female deer (Doe/dough)	+	+	+
A gem or precious stone What a diamond or ruby is (jewel/dual)	NR	+	+
A Frenchman's hat (beret/berry)	+	+	+
Rank in the army above Major and below General A French word (colonel/kernel)	kernl	+	+
White powder used to make bread or cake (flour/flower)	+	+	+
It turns to open a lock (key/quay)	+	+	+
Brass part of a drum kit, hit with a drumstick (cymbal/symbol)	NR	+	+
A settee and chairs (suite/sweet)	NR	+	+
To bend the head before the Queen to express greeting or humility (bow/bough)	+	+	+
To measure how heavy an object is (weigh/way)	wait	weight	wait
What a tall adult has done when they got bigger (grown/groan)	g	+	+
Belly button (navel/naval)	+	+	navy
Wild pig (boar/bore)	+	+	boar
Seven of them in a week (days/daze)	NR	+	+

(Continued)

	Write the Other Version	Write this Version	Write the Other Version with Auditory Presentation
You climb them to reach the 1st floor (stairs/stares)	NR	+	+
A female monk (nun/none)	+	+	+
There are 24 of them every day (hours/ours)	NR	+	+
To be certain (sure/shore)	suit	+	+
Wooden platform over the sea Every seaside resort has one to stroll on (pier/peer)	pear	+	+
Next in line to the throne (heir/air)	hair	+	+
Total correct	8/20	19/20	17/20

Although the results of the present study suggest that phonological mediation is not necessary for the way in which content words are written, a similar claim cannot be made for the writing of sentences and the writing of function words. PS's impairment in writing sentences in the context of preserved writing of content words is reminiscent of the results that were obtained by Bub and Kertesz (1982a) with patient HM, who also had a severe speech production deficit. Taken together, these results suggest that phonological codes may play a critical role in the way in which syntactic information is written. Since it seems unlikely that function words are associated with semantic representations, the spellings of these items may not be accessible via a direct link from the semantic system to the orthographic output lexicon. The poor performance of patients such as PS and HM when writing function words may therefore occur because the spelling of these two patients is so heavily dependent on a link of this kind.

CONCLUSION

Phonological Mediation of Reading and Spelling

The key theoretical issue that we have investigated with PS concerns the nature of the functional processes that are involved in silent reading and spelling. The speech production impairment that PS experiences, together with his excellent written comprehension, means that he is an ideal individual with whom we can investigate the issue of whether or not reading and spelling are phonologically mediated. Preserved reading comprehension in a patient of this kind has often been taken as evidence that reading could not be phonically mediated (Ellis et al., 1983). However, it remains possible from previous studies that access to meaning is occurring on the basis of a preserved internal phonological code generated from print, despite the problems with spoken word production. Consistent with this, Caplan and Waters (1995) have shown that inner phonology can be preserved in a patient with preserved reading comprehension who makes neologistic errors in speech.

A detailed investigation of the extent to which PS retains the capacity to generate an internal phonological code from print was therefore undertaken. This revealed that PS was unable to make written rhyme and homophone judgements. This suggests that PS does not have access to any internally generated phonological codes during reading. The critical finding was that PS was unable to access both meanings of a homophone from seeing one version of the homophone in print. When looking at a homophone such as "rose," PS was unable to indicate the other meaning that is associated with that phonological word form. If PS was activating the phonological code /roz/ as a precondition for determining that it meant flower, he should be able to activate the meaning of "rows." If Van Orden et al. (1988) are correct in arguing that both meanings of a homophone are activated bottom-up during reading, then PS should be equally able to access either meaning when he is reading a homophone.

If meaning is always accessed from print via phonology, then the inability of PS to generate a phonological code from print should undermine his ability to comprehend what he reads. In fact, though, his reading comprehension seems to be entirely preserved. Such findings do not indicate that no phonic mediation takes place in the comprehension of visually presented words; what they reveal is that normal comprehension can take place without it. Such an outcome is much better explained by the weaker theory of phonological mediation put forward by Patterson and her colleagues than by the views of Van Orden (Van Orden, 1987; Van Orden et al., 1988). Patterson's position is that direct access to meaning from print and phonologically mediated access to print generally occur in parallel in normal readers (Coltheart et al., 1994; Patterson, 1992; Wydell et al., 1993). This view is also consistent with other recent theories of visual word recognition (Coltheart et al., 1993; Jared & Seidenberg, 1991; Seidenberg & McClelland, 1989). So long as it is acknowledged that access to phonology is not necessary for successful written comprehension to occur, Patterson's position is consistent with both the findings from PS and with Van Orden's findings that normal subjects sometimes make comprehension errors when reading homophones.

A similar conclusion regarding whether or not *spelling* is phonologically mediated can be made from an examination of the way in which PS spells familiar words. When presented with the meaning of a homophone, PS is able to generate the spelling that is consistent with the meaning he has been given. He is not, however, able to generate the spelling that is associated with the alternative meaning of the homophone. That is, when shown a definition such as "to bend the head...," PS can write "bow" but not "bough." If PS were accessing the spelling of words via the phonological output lexicon, then he should have been equally able to generate both spellings, as the phonological representation /b/æw/ in the phonological output lexicon should access b-o-w and b-o-u-g-h with equal fluency. The conclusion must be that PS is spelling via a direct link (that bypasses phonology) between the semantic system and the orthographic output lexicon. Again, this is not to deny that the phonological output lexicon does often play a role in the way in which familiar written word forms are retrieved from the orthographic output lexicon in normal subjects. What the case of PS shows is that access to the orthographic output lexicon can occur successfully even when phonological mediation does not appear to be taking place.

REFERENCES

Baddeley, A.D. (1992). Is working memory working? *Quarterly Journal of Experimental Psychology, 44A*, 1–31.
Barry, C. (1994). Spelling routes (or roots or rutes). In G.D.A. Brown & N.C. Ellis (Eds.), *Handbook of spelling* (pp. 320–335). Chichester: John Wiley.
Besner, D. (1987). Phonology, lexical access in reading, and articulatory suppression: A critical review. *Quarterly Journal of Experimental Psychology, 39A*, 467–478.
Bruce, V., & Young, A.W. (1986). Understanding face recognition. *British Journal of Psychology, 77*, 305–327.
Bub, D., & Kertesz, A. (1982a). Evidence for lexicographic processing in a patient with preserved written over oral single word naming. *Brain, 105*, 697–717.
Bub, D., & Kertesz, A. (1982b). Deep agraphia. *Brain and Language, 17*, 146–165.
Caplan, D., & Waters, G.S. (1995). On the nature of the phonological output planning processes involved in verbal rehearsal: Evidence from aphasia. *Brain and Language, 48*, 191–220.
Caramazza, A., Berndt, R.S., & Basili, A.G. (1983). The selective impairment of phonological processing: A case study. *Brain and Language, 18*, 128–174.
Coltheart, M., Curtis, B., Atkins, P., & Haller, M. (1993). Models of reading aloud: Dual-route and parallel-distributed processing approaches. *Psychological Review, 100*, 589–608.
Coltheart, V., Patterson, K., & Leahy, J. (1994). When a ROWS is a ROSE: Phonological effects in written word comprehension. *Quarterly Journal of Experimental Psychology, 47A*, 917–955.
Coltheart, M., Patterson, K., & Marshall, J. (1987). *Deep dyslexia*. London: Routledge & Kegan Paul.
de Haan, E.H.F., Young, A.W., & Newcombe, F. (1991). A dissociation between the sense of familiarity and access to semantic information concerning familiar people. *European Journal of Cognitive Psychology, 3*, 51–67.

Ehri, L.C. (1992). Reconceptualizing the development of sight word reading and its relationship to recoding. In P.B. Gough, L.C. Ehri, & R. Treiman (Eds.), *Reading acquisition* (pp. 107–143). Hillsdale, NJ: Lawrence Erlbaum Associates Inc.

Ellis, A.W. (1982). Spelling and writing (and reading and speaking). In A.W. Ellis (Ed.), *Normality and pathology in cognitive function*. London: Academic Press.

Ellis, A.W. (1984). *Reading, writing and dyslexia: A cognitive analysis*. London: Lawrence Erlbaum Associates Ltd.

Ellis, A.W., Miller, D., & Sin, G. (1983). Wernicke's aphasia and normal language processing: A case study in cognitive neuropsychology. *Cognition, 15*, 111–144.

Ellis, A.W., & Young, A.W. (1988). *Human cognitive neuropsychology*. London: Lawrence Erlbaum Associates Ltd.

Ellis, A.W., Young, A.W., & Critchley, E.M.R. (1989). Loss of memory for people following temporal lobe damage. *Brain, 112*, 1469–1483.

Feinberg, T.E., Rothi, L.J.G., & Heilman, K.M. (1986). "Inner speech" in conduction aphasia. *Archives of Neurology, 43*, 591–593.

Flude, B.M., Ellis, A.W., & Kay, J. (1989). Face processing and name retrieval in an anomic aphasic: Names are stored separately from semantic information about familiar people. *Brain and Cognition, 11*, 60–72.

Franklin, S., Howard, D., & Patterson, K. (1994). Abstract word meaning deafness. *Cognitive Neuropsychology, 11*, 1–34.

Friedman, R.B., & Kohn, S.E. (1990). Impaired activation of the phonological lexicon: Effects upon oral reading. *Brain and Language, 38*, 278–297.

Funnell, E. (1983). Phonological processes in reading. *British Journal of Psychology, 74*, 159–180.

Gough, P.B. (1972). One second of reading. In J. Kavanagh & I.G. Mattingly (Eds.), *Language by eye and by ear* (pp. 331–358). Cambridge, MA: MIT Press.

Hanley, J.R. (1995). Are names difficult to recall because they are unique? A case study of a patient with anomia. *Quarterly Journal of Experimental Psychology, 48A*, 487–506.

Hanley, J.R., Hastie, K., & Kay, J. (1992). Developmental surface dyslexia and dysgraphia: An orthographic processing deficit. *Quarterly Journal of Experimental Psychology, 44A*, 285–319.

Hanley, J.R., Young, A.W., & Pearson, N. (1989). Defective recognition of familiar people. *Cognitive Neuropsychology, 6*, 179–210.

Harris, D., & Kay, J. (1995). Selective impairment of the retrieval of people's names: A case of category specificity. *Cortex, 31*, 575–582.

Hillis, A., & Caramazza, A. (1989). The graphemic buffer and attentional mechanisms. *Brain and Language, 36*, 208–235.

Howard, D. (1989). Letter-by-letter readers: Evidence for parallel processing. In D. Besner & G.W. Humphreys (Eds.), *Basic processes in reading: Visual recognition*. Hillsdale, NJ: Lawrence Erlbaum Associates Inc.

Howard, D., & Franklin, S. (1988). *Missing the meaning*. Cambridge, MA: MIT Press.

Howard, D., & Patterson, K. (1992). *The Pyramids and Palm Trees Test*. Bury St Edmunds, UK: Thames Valley Test Company.

Humphreys, G.W., & Evett, L. (1985). Are there independent lexical and nonlexical routes in word processing? An evaluation of the dual-route theory of reading. *The Behavioral and Brain Sciences, 8*, 689–740.

Jared, D., & Seidenberg, M.S. (1991). Does word identification proceed from spelling to sound to meaning? *Journal of Experimental Psychology General, 120*, 358–394.

Kay, J., Lesser, R., & Coltheart, M. (1992). *Psycholinguistic assessment of language processing in aphasia*. Hove, UK: Lawrence Erlbaum Associates Ltd.

Kreiner, D.S., & Gough, P.B. (1990). Two ideas about spelling: Rules and word specific memory. *Journal of Memory and Language, 29*, 103–118.

Kucera, H., & Francis, W.N. (1967). *Computational analysis of present-day American-English.* Providence, RI: Brown University Press.
Levine, D.N., Calvanio, R., & Popovics, A. (1982). Language in the absence of inner speech. *Neuropsychologia, 20,* 391–409.
McKenna, P., & Warrington, E.K. (1983). *The graded naming test.* Windsor, UK: NFER Publishing Company.
Nickels, L. (1995). Getting it right? Using aphasic naming errors to evaluate theoretical models of spoken word recognition. *Language and Cognitive Processes, 10,* 13–45.
Parkin, A.J., McMullen, M., & Graystone, D. (1986). Spelling to sound regularity affects pronunciation latency but not lexical decision. *Psychological Research, 48,* 87–92.
Patterson, K.E. (1982). The relation between reading and phonological coding: Further neuropsychological observations. In A.W. Ellis (Ed.), *Normality and pathology in cognitive function.* London: Academic Press.
Patterson, K.E. (1992). Phonology in reading. *The Psychologist, 5,* 314.
Patterson, K.E., & Marcel, A. (1992). Phonological ALEXIA or PHONOLOGICAL alexia. In J. Alegria, D. Holender, J. Junca de Morais, & M. Radeau (Eds.), *Analytic approaches to human cognition.* Amsterdam: Elsevier Science Publishers.
Patterson, K.E., & Shewell, C. (1987). Speak and spell: Dissociations and word class effects. In M. Coltheart, G. Sartori, & R. Job (Eds.), *The cognitive neuropsychology of language.* Hillsdale, NJ: Lawrence Erlbaum Associates Inc.
Plaut, D., & Shallice, T. (1993). Deep dyslexia: A case study of connectionist neuropsychology. *Cognitive Neuropsychology, 10,* 377–500.
Rubenstein, H., Lewis, S.S., & Rubenstein, M.A. (1971). Evidence for phonemic recoding in visual word recognition. *Journal of Verbal Learning and Verbal Behavior, 10,* 645–657.
Seidenberg, M.S., & McClelland, J. (1990). A distributed, developmental model of word recognition and naming. *Psychological Review, 15,* 169–179.
Shallice, T. (1981). Phonological agraphia and the lexical route in writing. *Brain, 104,* 413–429.
Swinney, D.A. (1979). Lexical access during sentence comprehension: (Re)consideration of context effects. *Journal of Verbal Learning and Verbal Behavior, 18,* 645–659.
Van Orden, G.C. (1987). A ROWS is a ROSE: Spelling, sound and reading. *Memory and Cognition, 15,* 181–198.
Van Orden, G.C., Johnston, J.C., & Hale, B.L. (1988). Word identification in reading proceeds from spelling to sound to meaning. *Journal of Experimental Psychology: Learning, Memory and Cognition, 14,* 371–386.
Wydell, T.N., Patterson, K.E., & Humphreys, G.W. (1993). Phonologically mediated access to meaning for Kanji: Is a *rows* still a *rose* in Japanese Kanji. *Journal of Experimental Psychology: Learning, Memory and Cognition, 19,* 491–514.

APPENDIX 1

The Reading Responses that PS Made When Asked to Read the Names of the Famous People from the Lancaster/Radcliffe Set

	1st Name	2nd Name		1st Name	2nd Name
High Familiarity					
Princess Anne	Prince	+	Michael Foot	+	+
					(Continued)

PHONOLOGICAL MEDIATION 31

	1st Name	2nd Name		1st Name	2nd Name
John Wayne	+	+	Enoch Powell	/ɛn/	Power
Queen Mother	+	+	Jeremy Thorpe	/jɛrɛli/	+
Margaret Thatcher	Marry	/čæčʌs/	Henry Cooper	Entry	+
Denis Healey	/dɛnis/	+	Nikita Krushchev	Nicky	/krUskras/
Alan Whicker	/ælə/	/wIki/	Jimmy Savile	+	+
Prince Charles	/prIs/	+	Golda Meir	Goalie	Male
Harold Macmillan	Arrows	Macmiddles	James Callaghan	/jʌn/	+
Marilyn Monroe	/mærIlo/	/maroz/	General Smuts	NR	+
Diana Dors	/dæri/	Door	Harold Wilson	/ærIlo/	/wInsan/

Lower Familiarity

Max Bygraves	+	/braygrevz/	John McEnroe	+	/mækrʌno/
Patrick Moore	Mac	+	Esther Rantzen	/ɛsi/	/rænsʌn/
Alex Higgins	/ælis/	+	David Bellamy	Davey	Bellabelly
Marlene Dietrich	/mɑlik/	/daytriz/	Bjorn Borg	Born	Jaw
Lucille Ball	/luli/	—	David Dimbleby	Davey	Dimble..by
Charles De Gaulle	/čɑl/	/dI / /gal	Jack Nicklaus	+	/nIklz/
Geoff Boycott	/jɛp/	/bəkat/	Dirk Bogarde	+	/brogɑz/
Dora Bryan	Roadie	Brighton	James Hunt	/jem/	Hunt
David Attenborough	Davey	Hashburrows	Anna Ford	Annie	Fort
Lulu	+	+	Douglas Fairbanks	/dʌgli/	Fairfan

Unfamiliar

Lester Pearson	Settle	Person	Barry Ingham	Marry	Inham
Errol Winters	Ever	Windows	John Lawrenson	John	Wallson
June Ellis	+	/ɛsʌl/	Derek Beard	Derry	Burr
Judy Mackenzie	Julie	/MʌkɛK/	Joseph South	Joe	/θ/æws/
Denys Palmer	Denny	/pavɑs/	Bernard Woof	Don	Wood
Linda Coles	/lIntʌ/	+	Jackie Piper	+	+
Pat Bispham	+	+	Ann Greenland	+	Green..land
Richard Long	Nicky	John	Gary Warren	+	Ward
Frank Pemberton	+	Pendberton	Gareth Forwood	Gary	+
Simon Scott	+	+	John Carson	+	Car.Car.Son

APPENDIX 2

The Spelling Errors Made by PS

Neologistic Spelling Errors (N = 76)

Transpositions (N = 9)
ability → abitily, brigade → bridage, calendar → calander, chapel → chaple, develop → devolpe, exposure → exopsure, miracle → micrale, rescue → resuce, virtue → virute.

Insertions (N = 12)
assail → assailt, beneath → benearth, camera → carmera, giraffe → girrafe, lemon → lemmon, mustard → mustmard, purpose → purspose, robin → robbin, tenure → tenture, tobacco → tobbaco, tobacco → tobbaco, tragic → trategic.

Substitutions (N = 14)
ability → abitity, aeroplane → aeroplone, appear → appeer, century → certury, chute → shute, dark → derk, effort → effert, library → libery, margin → mergin, murmur → murmer, perjury → pergury, span → spay, tractor → tracter, welfare → welfere.

Deletions (N = 12)
ancient → anient, alcohol → achol, acholic, audience → audiene, buffoon → buffon, compliment → complint, essence → esence, genesis → gensis, literature → literte, opinion → opinon, rupture → rupur, rupure, rupute, upward → upard.

Transpositions & Deletions (N = 9)
absolute → aboluts, average → avarge, citizen → citzin, heredity → hederti, hospital → hosptil, insomnia → imsonia, pilgrim → prilm, priglim, pneumonia → pnomi, polaroid → polaird.

Transpositions & Substitutions (N = 4)
allegory → alorogy, anchor → anocher, generous → genouros, ignore → igerne.

Combinations of Reversals, Insertions, Substitutions, & Deletions (N = 16)
apathy → athamy, carnival → canaral, career → correer, colonel → concol, elephant → elanphant, episode → esponde, ignore → igrome, melancholy → melonchonlty, potato → pototoe, prodigy → progoy, purpose → pruspose,

pyjamas → pjympa, salute → slatutle, scissors → scirros, sublime → sumbline, virtue → virusty.

Paralexic Spelling Errors (N = 42)

Morphemic Errors (N = 23)
actual → actually, anybody → anyone, banana → bananas, grandad → grandfather, hear → heard, idea → ideal, image → imagine, justify → justice, knee → kneel, maybe → be, meet → met, misery → miserable, none → nor, nowhere → no one, onto → upto, outset → out, persona → person, potato → potatoes, sand → sands, sweep → swept, therefore → there, upward → upper, whom → who.

Visual Errors (N = 14)
analogy → allergy, candid → candidate, candy, candid, character → Chester, concept → constant, debut → deputy, insect → inspect, maybe → method, penetrate → pent, racial → radical, racial, satire → satin, severe → service, sop → sup, textile → testicle, whence → west.

Semantic Errors (N = 5)
anyone → else, ballot → electer, beneath → behind, enough → again, yourself → one else.

Other Spelling Errors (N = 29)

Incomplete (N = 15)
analogy → a, attitude → att, demented → den, despite → des, epitome → esp, hence → he, maximal → max, meanwhile → be, molecule → mol, nobody → noab, oriole → o, ought → o, ought → h, turmoil → tr, whence → wh.

No Response (N = 6)
acrobat → —, ancient → —, anyone → —, folly → —, maybe → —, somehow → —.

Miscellaneous Errors (N = 8)
antler → altas (crossed out), dogma → dogis, edible → edilate, inquiry → enquirey, meanwhile → bewhile, onto → usto, parachute → per?inng, valour → valluy.

The Independence of Phonological and Orthographic Lexical Forms: Evidence from Aphasia

G. Miceli

Istituto di Psicologie CNR, Università Cattolica del Sacro Cuore, and IRCCS S. Lucia, Roma, Italy

B. Benvegnù

IRCCS S. Lucia, Roma, Italy

R. Capasso

Università Cattolica del Sacro Cuore and IRCCS S. Lucia, Roma, Italy

A. Caramazza

Harvard University, Cambridge, USA

WMA suffers from damage to the semantic component of the lexical semantic system and from damage to sublexical phonology–orthography and orthography–phonology conversion procedures. His performance on picture naming tasks that require two consecutive responses was used to explore issues concerning the relations between the phonological and orthographic components of the lexical system. Responses to tasks requiring responses in different modalities (one oral and one written) often resulted in lexically "inconsistent" responses. For example, to a picture representing pliers, WMA said "pincers," but wrote *saw*; and, to a picture representing peppers, he wrote *tomato* but said "artichoke." By contrast, inconsistent responses never occurred in tasks that required two consecutive responses in the same modality (oral or written). In these tasks, WMA always produced the same (correct or incorrect) word twice. These results rule out the hypothesis that phonological mediation is necessary for writing, and suggest instead that orthographic word forms are autonomous from

---

Requests for reprints should be addressed to Gabriele Miceli, Neurologia, Università Cattolica del Sacro Cuore, Largo A. Gemelli, 8, 00168 Roma—Italia (fax: 06-35501909; e-mail:mc0354@mclink.it) or to Alfonso Caramazza, Cognitive Neuropsychology Laboratory, Department of Psychology, Harvard University, 33 Kirkland Street, Cambridge, MA 02138, USA (fax: 617-496-6262; e-mail: caram@wjh.harvard.edu).

The research reported here was supported in part by NIH grant NS22201 to Alfonso Caramazza, and by grants from the Ministero della Sanità and from the MURST. The authors wish to thank WMA for his cheerful cooperation throughout the study.

phonological forms, and that they are activated directly from lexical semantic information. However, the results do not allow us to distinguish between a weak version of the orthographic autonomy hypothesis—that there are direct connections between phonological and orthographic forms, which are impaired in WMA—and a strong version of the same hypothesis—that phonological and orthographic word forms are completely autonomous but that the selection of a word form for output in a given modality can be constrained by sublexical conversion mechanisms, which are impaired in WMA.

INTRODUCTION

There is widespread agreement in the psycholinguistic and cognitive neuropsychological literatures on some of the major aspects of the structure of the lexical system. Most models of lexical processing assume some type of network structure and distinguish between two main levels of processing—the lexical semantic (or lemma) and lexical form (or lexeme) levels (e.g. Bock & Levelt, 1994; Caramazza & Hillis, 1990; Dell & O'Seaghdha, 1992; Garrett, 1980; Kempen & Huijbers, 1983; Levelt, 1989; but see Seidenberg & McClelland, 1989, for a proposal in which lexical entries are not discretely represented). The lemma level is the level at which lexical-semantic and grammatical information is specified (but see following); the lexeme level is where the phonological and orthographic forms of a word are specified. Also, most models assume some type of parallel activation mechanism for lexical access (Caramazza, 1988; Dell, 1986; Jescheniak & Levelt, 1994; Morton, 1969; Roelofs, 1992; but see Forster, 1994, for a defence of search models).

Within the boundaries of these assumptions about the architecture of the lexical system, there are several hotly debated questions. One set of issues concerns what is represented at each of the hypothesised levels of processing; for example, is lexical-semantic information represented at the lemma level or are lemmas abstract nodes whose only function is to link semantic, grammatical, and lexical form information? Another set of issues concerns the nature of the mechanisms of access to lexical forms; for example, are lexical forms activated in parallel or is each form discretely activated? Yet another set of issues concerns the relations among the various components implicated in lexical processing; for example, does the activation of lexical-orthographic forms (orthographic lexemes) depend on the prior activation of lexical-phonological forms (phonological lexemes)? These issues are obviously interrelated: the type of answer one gives to any one of these questions has implications for the others. And, as might be expected, there is no agreement on most of these crucial aspects of the organisation and processing structure of the lexical system. In this paper we address some of these issues through the analysis of the lexical processing performance of an aphasic patient with damage at the level of lexical-semantic knowledge. The principal focus will be the relations among lexical components.

Virtually all the research on lexical access for word production has been concerned with speech production. Much of the research has exploited the production of slips of the tongue (Dell & Reich, 1981; Fromkin, 1971; Garrett, 1975, 1980; Shattuck-Hufnagel, 1979, 1986; Stemberger, 1985) and malapropisms (e.g. Fay & Cutler, 1977; see review in Levelt, 1989). However, there are also data from the tip-of-the-tongue phenomenon (Brown & McNeil, 1966; see A. Brown, 1991, for review), reaction time experiments (e.g. Jescheniak & Levelt, 1994; Levelt et al., 1991), and speech production disorders (e.g. Caramazza & Hillis, 1990; Martin, Dell, Saffran, & Schwartz, 1994; Martin, Weisberg, & Saffran, 1989; see Garrett, 1992, for review). By contrast, there is almost no research on the mechanisms of orthographic word production, and the little that there is has mostly been ignored in discussions of the organisation and processing structure of the lexical system. This is unfortunate, because there are a number of unresolved issues about the lexical system that can be illuminated by considering spelling performance in relation to speech production. Especially informative in this regard is the differential performance in spelling and speaking in subjects with lexical processing disorders. The contrasting patterns of performance in speaking and spelling can be used to identify the locus of functional damage within the lexical system and, in turn, the pattern of errors in each form of output can then be used to constrain claims about the types of representation and processing structure at specific levels of the system.

Consider in this context the issue of how lexical orthographic forms are accessed. If one were to assume that access of orthographic lexemes depended on the prior activation of their phonological counterpart, we would expect that an impairment in retrieving phonological forms should result in a corresponding deficit in retrieving orthographic forms. However, there is a large literature showing that the ability to spell is not infrequently spared in the face of severe impairment in phonological production (e.g. Alajouanine & Lhermitte, 1960; Assal & Buttet, 1981; Basso, Taborelli, & Vignolo, 1978; Caramazza, Berndt, & Basili, 1983; Ellis, Miller, & Sin, 1983; Hier & Mohr, 1977; Lecours & Rouillon, 1976; Lhermitte & Dérouesné, 1974; Patterson & Shewell, 1987). This dissociation has been interpreted as indicating that orthographic lexemes can be activated directly from lexical-semantics, bypassing the phonological lexicon (e.g. Allport & Funnell, 1981). However, this conclusion is not warranted unless it could be shown that the deficit in speech production is the result of direct damage to the phonological lexicon and not the result of damage to the post-lexical phonological processes. This reservation renders the mere observation of superior spelling performance relative to oral production theoretically uninformative for the purpose of determining whether orthographic production depends on some form of phonological mediation. However, there are a number of observations that cannot be so readily dismissed. For example, Caramazza and Hillis (1990) reported the performance of two brain-damaged subjects who made semantic errors in oral naming but not in written naming.

The fact that the subjects made semantic errors in the oral naming task restricts the locus of deficit to a lexical component of the system; the fact that they were able to retrieve the correct lexical form in spelling demonstrates that access of these lexical forms is not mediated by prior access of phonological lexemes. In other words, phonological and orthographic lexemes can be activated independently by lexical-semantic information (see Rapp & Caramazza, in press, for discussion of other relevant evidence).

Having argued for the autonomy of orthography in lexical access, we may now ask whether we can use the brain-damaged subjects' differential patterns of errors in producing written and spoken language to help decide finer-grained questions about the structure of the lexical system. Two issues will be considered: the relation of orthography to phonology and the relation between lexical-semantics and lexemes.

The evidence against the phonological mediation hypothesis of lexical orthographic access merely establishes that phonological mediation is not *necessary* for successful access of orthographic lexemes; it does not exclude other possible relations between phonological and orthographic forms, including direct activation between the two lexical components (as proposed, for example, by Allport & Funnell, 1981, and Patterson & Shewell, 1987). Another way in which phonological and orthographic outputs may constrain each other is through activation from sublexical transcoding mechanisms. That is, it is possible that the activated phonological and orthographic lexical forms are converted sublexically into orthographic and phonological representations, respectively. These nonlexical phonological and orthographic strings, in turn, activate the phonological and orthographic lexicons (as proposed by the summation hypothesis advanced by Hillis & Caramazza, 1991, and Patterson & Hodges, 1992). Thus, although the available evidence does not require that spelling is necessarily mediated by phonology, it does not exclude the possibility that phonology plays a highly constraining role in normal spelling.

Another issue that may be illuminated by considering the contrast in performance between spelling and speaking concerns the relation between lexical semantics and lexical forms. For example, as already noted, the occurrence of semantic errors only in speaking or only in writing in some brain-damaged subjects allows us to infer a locus of damage in lexical production at a point past the semantic component and before post-lexical processes. If this inference were correct, we would also be able to conclude that the normal semantic system (which, by hypothesis, is intact in these subjects) activates multiple, semantically related entries in the phonological and orthographic lexicons, creating the basis for semantic errors in the activation of lexemes (Caramazza & Hillis, 1990). This conclusion, in its most general form, is consistent with current models of lexical access in production (Bock & Levelt, 1994; Dell, 1990). However, there are two ways (at least) in which a semantic error may result from damage in accessing lexical forms from an intact semantic component: Either because there are multiple entries active at the lexical-semantic level (and each entry activates its corresponding lexeme in the phonological and orthographic lexicons) and damage in accessing lexical forms results in the selection of a semantically related lexeme, or because a single, correct lexical-semantic representation activates multiple, semantically related lexemes and damage to the access process results in the selection of an incorrect lexeme from the set of activated entries. Which of these two hypotheses is most consistent with available evidence depends in part on how we articulate the relation between lexical semantics and lexical forms. We return to this issue in the Discussion. For now, we simply want to point out that the analysis of contrasting performance in spelling and speaking may contribute to our understanding of the mechanisms of lexical access.

The preceding discussion has shown that one way to address the issue of the relation between lexical components is to investigate the performance of brain-damaged subjects who make semantic errors in speaking and/or writing. As already noted, the presence of this type of error in lexical production is especially valuable because it can only result from damage to lexical components of the system. That is, unlike neologisms and other phonological or orthographic errors, which can have both lexical and nonlexical causes, by their very nature semantic errors can only result from damage to lexical components of the system. Thus, we can take the presence of semantic errors as indicating a deficit to one or another component of the lexical system; since their cause is lexical in origin, the analysis of the pattern of these errors in spelling and speaking can be used to constrain claims about the organisation and access of lexical knowledge. In this report we analyse the performance of a brain-damaged subject whose semantic errors in speaking and spelling could be shown to result from damage to the lexical-semantic component. The investigation focuses on a peculiar aspect of the subject's performance: It was observed during clinical testing that he would sometimes orally produce a word different from the one he was writing. Thus, for example, he was noticed to be uttering "piano" while writing *organ*. If confirmed experimentally, this type of error implies a complete independence of orthographic and phonological lexemes.

CASE HISTORY

Patient WMA is a right-handed farm owner, with a high-school education. He suffered from an intracerebral haemorrhage on August 28, 1990. The resulting haematoma was surgically removed 10 days later. The patient was first seen 4 years post onset, and was tested between June and October, 1994.

The neurological examination revealed a dense right hemiplegia. On double simultaneous stimulation, frequent extinction phenomena on the right were demonstrated in all modalities (tactile, visual, and auditory). An MRI performed at the time of the present study revealed an extensive hypodensity in the deep anterior and central structures of the left hemisphere, corresponding to the site of the old haemorrhage; a marked atrophy of the frontal, temporal, and parietal cortices; and a conspicuous enlargement of the left lateral ventricle. Representative slices of the MRI are reported in Fig. 1.

NEUROPSYCHOLOGICAL EVALUATION

WMA scored within normal limits on Raven's Coloured Progressive Matrices, as well as on tasks of visual memory and constructional abilities. Limb praxis was mildly-to-moderately impaired. A severe buccofacial apraxia was present. Tasks requiring visual-spatial analysis demonstrated a mild, but clear, right-sided neglect. Because of the severe language disorder, verbal memory tasks requiring spoken output could not be administered. In memory probe tasks that require the ability to decide whether or not a word spoken by the examiner is included in a list presented a few seconds earlier, WMA performed relatively well but clearly worse than normal controls: in trials with 4, 6, and 8 words, he produced 20/24, 19/24, and 19/24 correct responses, respectively. In a similar task that used bisyllabic nonwords as stimuli, WMA also scored below normal (19/24 correct responses to series of 4 stimuli, and 16/24 to series of 6 stimuli). In both tasks, misses were more frequent than false alarms on short series; the reverse error distribution was observed on long series.

LANGUAGE EVALUATION

WMA's language abilities were tested by means of the BADA (Miceli, Laudanna, Burani, & Capasso, 1994). Performance on the battery demonstrated a very severe language deficit that involved multiple levels of language organisation.

Tasks Exploring Sublexical Orthography and Phonology

WMA was mildly impaired on a phoneme discrimination task with simple CV syllables. Although he produced a normal number of correct responses (57/60, or 95%) on this task, on 12 occasions he arrived at the correct response only after a second presentation of the stimulus.

Our subject was at chance level on a task that requires the ability to match an auditorially and a visually presented CV syllable (35/60 correct responses, 58.3%).

Nonword transcoding tasks were severely impaired. WMA produced 4/36 correct responses in repetition (11.1%), 6/45 in reading aloud (13.1%), and 0/25 in writing to dictation. All correct responses in repetition and in reading aloud were produced to monosyllabic stimuli; he failed to reproduce correctly any

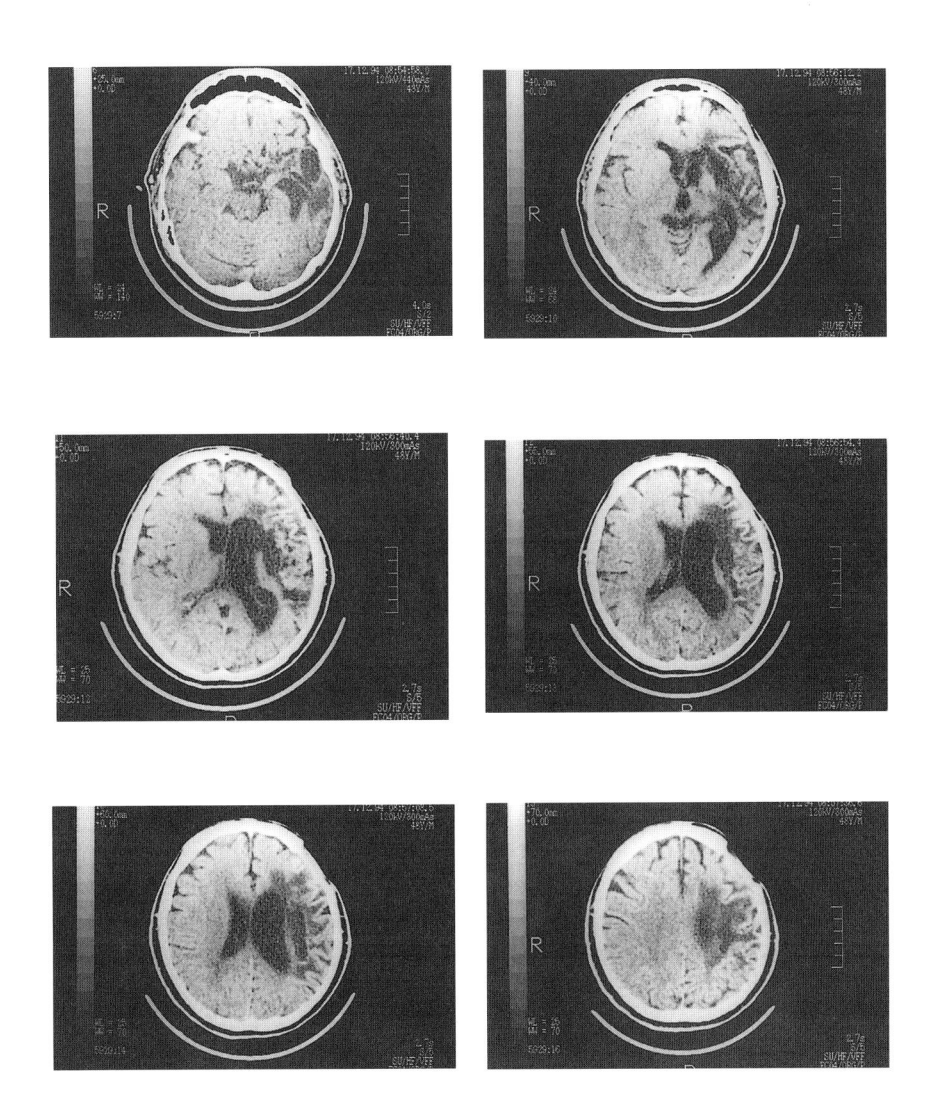

FIG. 1. Representative cuts of the CT scan, performed approximately 4 years post onset. Pictures show a massive, deep lesion of the left hemisphere, involving the globus pallidus, the putamen, the head of the caudate nucleus, possibly the thalamus, the internal and external capsule, as well as the white matter of the frontal, temporal, and parietal lobe. The lesion extends almost to the convexity of the hemisphere, and is associated with atrophy of the adjacent gyri, and with a marked dilation of the left ventricle.

bisyllabic or trisyllabic stimulus. A qualitative error analysis demonstrated that performance in repetition differed substantially from performance on the other tasks. In repetition, incorrect responses bore a phonological relationship to the stimulus (WMA repeated /ga'live/ as /ga'line/, and /ra'kone/ as /pa'lore[1]/); in reading and spelling, incorrect responses were often unrelated to the stimulus (WMA read *tena* as /ta'lante/, and wrote /kos'pivo/ as *nefa*). In reading aloud, WMA produced 39 incorrect responses (out of 45 stimuli, 86.9%), of which 16 (35.6% of total responses) resulted in words. Some of these were visually related to the stimulus (*volidia* → "volare," to fly), whereas others could be construed as the result of the activation of a word visually similar to the stimulus nonword, followed by a semantic substitution. For example, WMA read *ru* as "uccello," bird, presumably as the result of access to the visual representation *gru* (crane), followed by a semantic substitution. A similar error is *noste* → (*notte*, night) → "letto," bed. In writing to dictation, all incorrect responses were nonwords, and there was a very mild tendency to perseveration. Accuracy of responses to pseudowords was also measured on the basis of the percentage of letters reproduced correctly in each task. Only polysyllabic stimuli were included in this analysis. WMA reproduced correctly 50/79 (63.3%) letters in repeating 16 pseudowords; 56/165 (33.9%) letters in reading aloud 30 pseudowords; and 5/60 (8.3%) letters in writing 10 pseudowords to dictation. Since performance on tasks that required a spoken response was also affected by a moderate dysarthria, the figures reported for repetition and reading aloud must be taken only as the best possible approximation, but not as a precise measure. Even with these limitations, however, it is clear that WMA performed much more accurately on repetition than on reading aloud and writing to dictation.

Tasks Exploring the Lexical-semantic Level

Auditory lexical decision was marginally impaired (74/80 correct responses, 92.5%); WMA made the correct decision on 36/40 words (90%) and on 38/40 nonwords (95%). Performance on a visual lexical decision task was severely impaired (54/80 correct responses, 67.5%); WMA responded correctly to 23/40 words (57.5%) and to 31/40 nonwords (75.5%).

Word transcoding tasks were severely impaired. WMA produced 4/45 correct responses in repetition (8.9%), 10/92 in reading aloud (10.9%), and 5/46 in writing to dictation (10.8%). In all tasks a length effect was observed. However, this effect did not reach significance, because performance on all

---

[1] Throughout the present paper the following notations are used: stimuli presented visually and written responses are italicised; auditory stimuli and spoken responses are reported in quotation marks if they are words, and in phonetic transcription if they are nonwords; names of pictures presented for oral and written naming are neither italicised nor in quotes.

tasks was almost at floor. As with nonwords, performance in repetition differed qualitatively from that in reading aloud and in writing to dictation. In repetition, all incorrect responses were phonemically related to the target ("campanelli," little bells→/tampa'pElli/). In reading aloud, some incorrect responses were related visually/phonemically to the stimulus (*motore*, engine → /po'tore/, nonword). In many cases, however, WMA either failed to respond altogether to the stimulus (especially to long, low-frequency words), or produced a semantic paralexia (*poltrona*, armchair → "divano," sofa; *monumenti*, monuments → "antico," ancient). Some incorrect responses resulted from a failure to process correctly the right half of the stimulus (consider *bersaglio*, target → "borsa," purse; *gioia*, joy → "gioielli," jewels; *però*, but → "pera," pear). A fair number of incorrect responses resulted in morphological errors of the derivational type (*fucilati*, executed by firing squad → "fucile," rifle) and, more frequently, of the inflectional type (*frecce*, arrows → "freccia," arrow). The origin of these errors is unclear, as they might result from a deficit in morphological processing or from right-sided neglect. In writing to dictation, failures to respond and unrelated responses ("quindi," thus → *allacia*, nonword) accounted for most of the errors. In some cases, WMA produced semantic paragraphias, as in "intanto," meanwhile → *circa*, almost. Several incorrect responses resulted in spelling errors that frequently affected the right side of words (e.g. "volpe," fox → *volpa*, nonword), and occasionally took the form of inflectional errors ("vigne," vineyards → *vigna*, vineyard).

On a task requiring the ability to match an auditorially or visually presented word to one of two pictures (the correct response and a semantic or a visual/phonemic foil), WMA showed a mild but definite impairment. He produced 36/40 correct responses in the auditory task (90%), and 37/40 in the visual task (92.5%). In the auditory task, he chose 3/20 semantic foils and 1/20 phonemic foils incorrectly; in the visual task he selected 2/20 semantic foils and 1/20 visual foils incorrectly.

In picture naming tasks, WMA performed very poorly. He produced orally 8/30 correct responses to objects (26.7%), and 4/28 to actions (14.2%); in written naming, he responded correctly to 1/22 objects (4.5%), and to 1/22 actions (4.5%). The overall number of segmentally correct responses on these tasks was so low as to prevent a reliable assessment of WMA's difficulty in selecting the appropriate lexical form. To obtain such an estimate, phonetically and/or phonemically deviant, but clearly recognisable responses in oral naming (e.g. "sigaretta," cigarette → /si'retta'/; "morde," he bites → /'vorde/), graphemic errors in written naming (e.g. *telefono*, telephone → *telefone*; *zucca*, pumpkin → *zacca*) and inflectional errors (two in oral naming and five in written naming—e.g. 'foglia,' leaf → "foglie," leaves; *albero*, tree → *alberi*, trees) were scored as correct; responses that unequivocally indicated failure to select the appropriate word form (semantic substitutions, circumlocutions, failures to respond) were scored as incorrect; and neologistic responses were not counted (a response was considered to be neologistic when it contained less than 50% of the letters of the expected target, in the expected sequence—e.g. fiocco, ribbon → /ko'teto/; maniglia, door handle → *chechi*). With this scoring procedure, WMA produced correct oral responses to 14/30 objects (46.7%) and to 8/28 actions (29.6%), and correct written responses to 11/20 objects (55%) and to 3/19 actions (15.8%). Overall, he produced a comparable number of correct responses in oral and in written naming (22/58, or 37.9%, vs. 14/39, 35.9%), but responded much more accurately to objects than to actions (25/50 correct responses, 50%, vs. 11/47, 23.4%; $\chi^2 = 6.291$; $P < .02$). In object naming, WMA produced many semantic errors (window → "door"; cradle → *baby*); in action naming, most failures to select the correct target resulted in the production of a semantically related noun (lick → "ice cream"; sew → *needle*).

Tasks Exploring Sentence Processing

WMA performed poorly on grammaticality judgement tasks when the stimulus was presented auditorially (33/48 correct responses, 68.7%) and even worse when the stimulus was presented visually (8/24 correct responses, 33.3%).

When asked to repeat or to read aloud sentences, WMA failed to produce any correct response. All errors resulted in fragmented responses, in which free-standing grammatical morphemes (and frequently also major-class lexical items) were omitted and bound grammatical morphemes were substituted by other morphemes.

WMA also performed poorly in a sentence comprehension task requiring the ability to match a simple declarative sentence presented in the active or in the passive voice to one of two pictures, one representing the correct response, and the other representing the reversal of thematic roles, a morphological alternative, or a lexical-semantic alternative. He only produced 42/60 correct responses (70%) with auditorially presented sentences and 26/45 correct responses (57.8%) with visually presented sentences. He inappropriately chose 9/20 thematic foils (45%), 6/20 morphological foils (30%), and 3/20 lexical-semantic foils (15%) in the auditory task; 10/15 thematic foils (66.7%), 7/15 morphological foils (46.7%), and 2/15 lexical-semantic foils (13.3%) in the visual task. Across presentation modality, he was equally accurate with active (32/53 correct responses, 60.4%) and with passive sentences (36/52 correct responses, 69.2%).

Oral production tasks proved extremely difficult for WMA, whose speech was dysarthric, effortful, slow, and hypophonic. Very few (if any) correct grammatical structures could be identified in the transcripts of his picture description performance; he tended to produce one-word utterances or sequences of isolated words (usually nouns), devoid of free-standing grammatical morphemes and without a clearly recoverable syntactic structure. For example, presented with the picture of a car hitting a motorbike, he said: "Botta . . . auto

... motoretta ... botta," which roughly translates as "Crash (noun) ... auto ... motorbike ... crash (noun)." Connected written production was impossible.

Summary of the Language Screening Tasks

WMA made semantic errors in word–picture matching tasks and in picture naming tasks. He also made many semantic errors in reading aloud and in writing to dictation, but not in repetition. His abilities to convert print to sound and sound to print were severely impaired, whereas repetition was relatively spared. WMA's performance on the screening battery reveals a complex cognitive impairment, involving damage to sublexical conversion procedures (albeit to different extents) and the lexical-semantic system[2].

MORE DETAILED INVESTIGATION OF WMA'S DEFICIT(S)

In order to specify more precisely the nature of WMA's lexical processing deficit, he was asked to perform several tasks with the same set of 130 picturable nouns. The nouns belonged to 11 semantic categories (body parts, clothing, professions, animals, food, fruits and vegetables, furniture, tools, kitchen tools, transportation, musical instruments). Twenty nouns (body parts = 5; professions = 5; food = 4; clothing = 3; animals = 3) were in the high-frequency range (160–40/million); the remaining 110 ($N = 10$ in each category) were in the low-frequency range (15–1/million).

The 130 nouns were used in the following tasks: auditory and visual word–picture matching, oral and written picture naming, reading aloud, repetition, writing to dictation, and delayed copy. No more than one task was administered in each testing session. Because we were interested in identifying the source of semantic errors, only responses that clearly resulted from failure to retrieve a lexical form were considered to be incorrect. Hence, phonetic and phonemic deviations (in tasks that required spoken output) and minor spelling errors (in tasks that required written output) were scored as correct responses. WMA's few inflectional errors (five in reading aloud, six in writing to dictation, eight in written naming, and four in oral naming) were also scored as correct for present purposes. No derivational errors were observed in these tasks. Separate counts were made of semantic substitutions (foot → *elbow*), omissions, and neologisms (kangaroo → *scormano*, correct response *canguro*). WMA also produced incomplete responses (*autobus* → /au/ ...) or short words that bore no obvious phonemic or semantic relationship to the stimulus. These

---

[2] WMA also suffers from a visual input processing disorder that results in consistently poorer performance on tasks requiring the ability to process written input than on tasks requiring the ability to process auditory input. Because this deficit is not the focus of the present paper, it will not be discussed in detail.

responses were classified as unscorable. Performance on these tasks is shown in Table 1.

Auditory and Visual Word–Picture Matching

The examiner presented WMA with a picture while at the same time pronouncing a word (in the auditory task) or showing a written word (in the visual task). WMA was asked to say whether or not the word and the picture matched. Each picture was paired (on separate sessions) with the target word, with a semantically related word, or with an unrelated word. Thus, for example, the picture of a pear was paired with the word pear, or with the word orange, or with the word telephone. The order of presentation of the various word–picture pairs and the stimuli were varied randomly. In each session, the entire set of experimental words was administered, and approximately the same number of correct words, semantic foils, and unrelated foils was presented. The three sessions needed to complete each task were spaced at least one week apart. An item was scored as not having been comprehended correctly when the patient produced one or more incorrect responses to the three administrations of that item.

WMA was clearly impaired in the auditory (102/130, or 78.5%) and the visual task (103/130, or 79.2%). With one exception (in the auditory task), he never made more than one error on the same item and never accepted an unrelated word as the correct label for the stimulus picture. Errors resulted either from rejecting the correct word (3 times in the auditory task, 4 times in the visual task), or from incorrectly accepting a semantically related word as the correct label for the presented picture (26 times in the auditory task, 23 times in the visual task)[3].

---

[3] WMA performed much less accurately on these tasks than in the word comprehension tasks administered in the screening procedure. This discrepancy can be accounted for by the different demands of the two types of tasks. In the screening task, WMA was presented with a word, and had to select the response by pointing to one of two pictures. In order to respond correctly on this task, he had to compare the semantic information provided by the word with that provided by the two pictures. This procedure may have resulted in correct responses even in the presence of damaged semantic information. For example, presented with "dog" and with the pictures of a dog and of a cat, WMA may have responded correctly because, even though he did not activate sufficient semantic information to select the picture of a dog, he knew that "dog" is not appropriate for the picture of a cat. In the task reported here, he was required to say whether a picture and a word matched. In this case, in order to respond correctly, WMA had to compare the semantic information activated by the picture with that activated by the word, and to evaluate whether they constituted a reasonable match. This paradigm offers greater opportunity for incorrect responses. For example, failure to activate the semantic representation of dog may have resulted both in an incorrect rejection of "dog," and in an incorrect acceptance of "cat" as the correct match.

TABLE 1
Performance Obtained by WMA in Processing the Same 130 Words in the Context of Various Tasks. Incorrect Responses Resulting in Phonetically/Phonemically Related Errors, Spelling Errors, or Inflectional Errors Were Scored as Correct (Percentages Are in Parentheses)

	Correct	Semantic	Omissions	Neologisms	Unscorable
Word–Picture matching					
Auditory	102(78.5)	28(21.5)	–	N/A	–
Visual	103(79.2)	27(20.8)	–	N/A	–
Oral naming	78(60.5)	39(30.0)	10(7.7)	2 (1.6)	1(0.8)
Written naming	57(43.8)	35(27.0)	7(5.6)	27(20.8)	4(3.1)
Reading aloud	101(77.7)	21(16.2)	4(3.1)	4 (3.1)	–
Writing to dictation	71(54.6)	33(25.4)	1(0.8)	22(17.0)	3(2.3)
Repetition	126(96.9)	3 (2.3)	1(0.8)	–	–
Delayed copy	122(93.8)	5 (3.8)	–	3 (2.3)	–

Oral and Written Picture Naming

WMA produced 78/130 (60.5%) correct responses in oral naming, and 57/130 (43.8%) in written naming. Roughly the same numbers of semantic substitutions (39 and 35, respectively, or 30% and 27% of total responses) and of omissions (10 and 7, respectively, or 7.7% and 5.6% of total responses) were observed in the two tasks. The major difference between the oral and the written task resulted from neologistic responses being produced often in written naming (27, or 20.8% of total responses), but very infrequently in oral naming (2, or 1.6% of total responses).

Transcoding Tasks

Results obtained in the screening battery pointed to an impairment of the lexical-semantic system, and of orthography–phonology and phonology–orthography sublexical conversion procedures, with spared phoneme(input)–phoneme(output) conversion procedures. Consistent with the view that semantic errors in reading, spelling, and repetition only occur when both lexical and sublexical conversion procedures are damaged, WMA produced semantic errors in reading aloud and in writing to dictation, but not in repetition (nor in delayed copy). The performance observed with the 130 words used for this task is consistent with that observed in the screening procedure.

Reading aloud resulted in 101 correct responses (77.7), 21 semantic substitutions (16.2% of total responses), 4 omissions (3.1%), and 4 unscorable responses (3.1%). Writing to dictation was severely impaired. WMA responded correctly to 71 words (54.6%), made semantic errors to 33 (25.4%), and produced 22 neologistic responses (17%). He also produced five unscorable responses (3.8%) and one omission (0.8%).

Performance on repetition was markedly different from reading aloud and writing to dictation. WMA repeated correctly 126 words (96.9%). He produced three semantic substitutions (2.3%) and failed to respond to one stimulus (0.8%). However, errors scored as semantic were also phonologically related to the target. "Autobus" was reproduced as the short (but commonly used) form "auto"; "cinta" (belt) as the synonym "cinghia" (belt); to "baffi" (moustache), WMA produced the sequence "/bakki/.../pappi/.../sbalbi/.../babbi/...sbarbi" (you shave)[4].

In all tasks except repetition (and delayed copy), WMA scored somewhat more accurately on high- than on low-frequency items. A significant effect of frequency was found when the tasks that yielded semantic errors (word–picture matching, picture naming, reading aloud and writing to dictation) were considered ($\chi^2 = 7.635$, $P < .01$), but not when each task was considered separately, nor when all tasks were lumped together ($\chi^2 = 0.007$, $P = $ n.s.).

Performance was also influenced to some extent by semantic category. Repetition and delayed copy were excluded from this analysis, due to the absence of unambiguous semantic errors. Foods and animals were relatively less impaired, and body parts relatively more impaired than professions, clothing, fruits and vegetables, kitchen tools, and musical instruments.

The following analyses were aimed at identifying the cognitive damage responsible for the occurrence of semantic errors. These errors may arise either from damage to the semantic component or from a deficit in accessing lexical forms (Caramazza & Hillis, 1990)[5]. In order to evaluate the two possibilities, item-specific effects were investigated, by contrasting the degree of consistency for each item across all tasks. Item-specific effects could arise from a single source or from multiple sources. In the first case, they would have to be construed as the result of semantic damage (the semantic component is the only component shared by all comprehension and production tasks); as a consequence, items that result in semantic errors in one task should result in semantic errors in all tasks (excluding those where relatively spared sublexical procedures would block such errors). In the second case, item-specific effects would result from the independent impairment of modality-specific components of

---

[4] A similar picture was observed in delayed copy. WMA was presented with a written word, and was allowed to look at it until he felt confident that he could reproduce it. He was then instructed to remove the stimulus, and to copy it after approximately 10 seconds. WMA reproduced correctly 122 words (92.3%). He produced five responses that were scored as semantic errors (3.8%) and three neologisms (2.3%). As in repetition, "semantic" errors were also visually similar to the target. For example, WMA copied *salame* (pepperoni) as *saluma* (a nonword string that is similar to both the target and to *salumi*—a term that refers to all types of salted pork meat). He never produced incorrect responses that were semantically related but graphemically unrelated to the target.

[5] The locution "deficit in accessing lexical forms" is intended agnostically to refer either to damage to access procedures or damage to lexical forms, making them inaccessible for output.

the lexical system; as a consequence, the same item may be difficult in one (or more than one) task, but is less likely to be difficult in all tasks.

In order to establish whether semantic errors resulted from a single source in the case of WMA, his performance on the tasks that resulted in semantic errors was used to test for the presence of interdependence among tasks. On the assumption of a single cause for all the semantic errors, we would expect interdependence among tasks. As a first step in this analysis, the distributions of various error types in each of the six tasks under consideration were examined. These distributions were used to calculate the expected incidence of a given number of incorrect responses to the same item, based on the hypothesis of no interdependence across tasks (Coltheart & Funnell, 1987; Hillis, Rapp, Romani, & Caramazza, 1990). Separate estimates were made of the occurrence of semantic substitutions only, of semantic substitutions and omissions, of semantic substitutions, omissions, and neologisms, and of all errors. These estimated values were compared with the actual incidence of errors in WMA's performance. For example, the expected incidence of exactly 0, 1, 2, 3, 4, 5, or 6 semantic substitutions to the same item across the six tasks was compared to the observed incidence of 0, 1, 2, 3, 4, 5, or 6 semantic substitutions[6]. Results of these analyses are shown in Table 2. Independent of the error types used in the analysis (semantic substitutions only; semantic substitutions and omissions; semantic substitutions, omissions, and neologisms; all error types), observed and expected occurrence are significantly different (P always $\leq .001$), rejecting the hypothesis of no interdependence. That is, this result does not support the hypothesis that damage to independent mechanisms determines WMA's performance, and favours the alternative account, that damage to just one component, involved in all the tasks included in the analysis, is responsible for the observed distribution of errors. Since the semantic component is the only component shared by the six tasks considered for this analysis, the results invite the conclusion that semantic damage is responsible for the errors produced by WMA (see Hillis et al., 1990, for more detailed discussion of this argument).

To conclude, then, the observed pattern of performance—very poor performance in reading nonwords aloud and in writing nonwords to dictation; semantic errors in word–picture matching tasks, in naming tasks, in reading words aloud and in writing words to dictation—results from damage to the semantic component of the lexical system, and from damage to sublexical phonology–orthography and orthography–phonology conversion mechanisms.

---

[6] For example, the expected probability of two semantic errors to the same item was calculated by summing all permutations that would result in two errors on that item: ($P1 \times P2 \times Q3 \times Q4 \times Q5 \times Q6$) + ($P1 \times Q2 \times P3 \times Q4 \times Q5 \times Q6$) + ($P1 \times Q2 \times Q3 \times P4 \times Q5 \times Q6$) + ($P1 \times Q2 \times Q3 \times Q4 \times P5 \times Q6$) + ($P1 \times Q2 \times Q3 \times Q4 \times Q5 \times P6$) + (…) × 130. In this formula, P corresponds to the probability that WMA would make a semantic error in a given task, and Q to the probability that he would not make a semantic error in a given task, and the numbers 1 to 6 correspond to the six tasks under consideration.

TABLE 2
Observed and Expected Incidence of a Given Number of Incorrect Responses Produced to the Same Item in the Course of Six Experimental Tasks (Percentages Are in Parentheses)

Types of Errors

No. of Errors	Semantic		Semantic+Omissions		Sem.+Om.+Neologisms		All Errors	
	Expected	Observed	Expected	Observed	Expected	Observed	Expected	Observed
0/6	22(16.9)	47(36.1)	18(13.8)	41(31.5)	8 (6.1)	26(20.0)	7 (5.4)	24(18.5)
1/6	43(33.1)	23(17.7)	39(30.0)	25(19.2)	28(21.5)	27(20.8)	27(20.8)	29(22.3)
2/6	32(24.6)	31(23.8)	34(26.1)	31(23.8)	37(28.5)	27(20.8)	37(24.5)	20(15.4)
3/6	31(23.8)	19(14.6)	34(26.1)	17(13.1)	47(36.1)	31(23.8)	48(36.9)	33(25.4)
4/6	2 (1.5)	9 (6.9)	4 (3.1)	14(10.8)	8 (6.1)	12 (9.2)	9 (6.9)	16(12.3)
5/6	—	1 (0.8)	1 (0.8)	2 (1.5)	2 (1.5)	6 (4.6)	2 (1.5)	7 (5.4)
6/6	—	—	—	—	—	1 (0.8)	—	1 (0.8)
χ^2	21.502		23.722		18.247		22.980	
P	<.001		<.001		<.001		<.001	

EXPERIMENTAL STUDY

A subject with the pattern of cognitive/linguistic impairments reported for WMA (semantic damage in the presence of abolished orthography–phonology and phonology–orthography conversion procedures) provides a unique opportunity to test whether writing requires phonological mediation or whether orthographic and phonological lexical representations are activated independently. The two hypotheses make different predictions concerning the types of errors that should occur when the subject is asked to produce two consecutive responses (one spoken, one written) to the same picture. Under the phonological mediation account, semantic damage will result at times in the activation of a semantically incorrect phonological lexical representation. Since under this hypothesis the activation of orthographic representations is driven by phonological information, the incorrectly activated phonological representation will activate the corresponding orthographic representation. Hence, written output should always be "lexically consistent" with spoken output. By "lexically consistent" it is meant that the subject either should respond correctly in both modalities, or, when in error, should produce the same incorrect word in both modalities. For example, given the picture of a tiger, he might fail to respond in both output modalities, or might produce two semantic substitutions resulting in the same word (lion → "tiger" → *tiger*). The hypothesis also predicts that errors resulting in lexically "inconsistent" responses should not occur. For example, a correct spoken response should never be followed by a semantic substitution (lion → "lion" → *tiger*) or by a failure to respond (lion → "lion" → …); a semantic substitution or an omitted response should never be followed by the correct response (lion → "tiger" → *lion*; lion → " … " → *lion*), and, in the case of two semantic substitutions, responses should never result in different words (lion → "tiger" → *leopard*). The hypothesis of orthographic autonomy, by contrast, predicts that both lexically consistent and lexically inconsistent errors should occur in the event of semantic damage. On this account, impoverished semantic information will activate sets of conceptually related lexical representations independently in the phonological and in the orthographic lexicon. If the same entry (or no entry) reaches threshold in both output systems, lexically consistent responses will occur. If, on the other hand, the lexical representation most active in the phonological component differs from that most active in the orthographic component (or, if an entry reaches threshold in an output system, whereas none of the activated representations reach threshold in the other), lexically inconsistent responses will be produced.

Anecdotal observations of WMA's behaviour during the administration of the screening battery are consistent with the orthographic autonomy account. WMA sometimes produced an unsolicited response in one modality before responding in the required modality. On some occasions, the two responses resulted in different words. For example, in writing to dictation "scarpe," shoes, WMA kept repeating to himself "scarpe" while at the same time writing *calze*, socks; in written naming, to the picture of pincers, he kept saying "pinze," pliers, while writing *sega*, saw; and, in oral naming, to the picture of an organ, he said "suona," plays, while tracing with a finger the word *piano*. These errors are, at face value, problematic for the hypothesis that writing requires phonological mediation. Later we explore in detail the relation between spoken and written responses.

In order to contrast the phonological mediation and the orthographic autonomy hypotheses, the ideal experiment would require the subject to produce spoken and written responses simultaneously to each stimulus. Such a task would provide information on the lexical representations available in the phonological and in the orthographic output lexicons at a given moment. However, this task could not be administered since WMA wrote very slowly (he used his left hand because of right hemiplegia) and spoke very slowly, due to a severe dysarthria. Thus, tasks that required two consecutive responses to the same stimulus, one spoken and one written, were administered.

Performance on Immediate, Across-modality Picture Naming Tasks

Two tasks were administered. In the first task, WMA was asked to say, then write, the name of a picture; in the second task, the response order was reversed. In both tasks, the stimulus remained in view until both responses had been produced. The patient was given no feedback as to the correctness of his responses. Whenever he attempted to produce more than one response, only the last attempt was scored. The 130 pictures used in the tasks described in the previous section were used in this and the following tasks.

Overall performance on the two tasks is shown in Table 3. The number of correct responses and of semantic and unscorable errors is comparable in the two tasks. Neologisms are much more frequent in spelling than in speaking (12.3% vs. 2.3% in the oral-then-written task; 13.1% vs. 1.5% in the written-then-oral task), whereas failures to respond are more frequent in speaking than in spelling (10% vs. 1.5% in the oral-then-written task; 8.5% vs. 0.8% in the written-then-oral task)[7]. Further analyses considered performance across modalities of output.

---

[7] The different distribution of neologisms and of omissions as a function of response modality might reflect different constraints on the minimal amount of information required to support output in the oral as opposed to the written modality. Extremely reduced phonological information may not suffice to allow spoken output—for example, the phoneme sequence /b[-]t[-]lm[-]a/ may be blocked either because it is too distant from the intended target, or because it is unpronounceable. By contrast, the same amount of information might still allow a written response, as there are no motoric constraints preventing the output of BTMA.

TABLE 3
Overall Performance in the Two Across-modality Picture
Naming Task (Percentages Are in Parentheses)

	Oral-then-Written		Written-then-Oral	
	Oral	Written	Written	Oral
Correct	77(59.2)	69(53.1)	69(53.1)	83(63.8)
Semantic	36(27.7)	40(30.8)	39(30.0)	34(26.2)
Neologism	3 (2.3)	16(12.3)	17(13.1)	2 (1.5)
No response	13(10.0)	2 (1.5)	1 (0.8)	11 (8.5)
Unscorable	1 (0.8)	3 (2.3)	4 (3.1)	–

On both tasks, WMA produced many lexically inconsistent responses. Examples of sequences resulting in a correct response and in an incorrect response are presented in Table 4. The first quantitative analysis considered the number of stimuli to which WMA produced either two correct responses or two incorrect responses, and the number of stimuli to which he produced a correct-then-incorrect response, or an incorrect-then-correct response (Table 5). He produced consistently correct, or consistently incorrect responses to 90 (69.2%) items in the oral-then-written picture naming (resulting from 53 pairs of correct responses and from 37 pairs of incorrect responses, corresponding to 40.8% and to 28.5% of total responses, respectively), and to 86 (66.2%) items in the written-then-oral picture naming (resulting from 54 pairs of correct responses and from 32 pairs of incorrect responses, corresponding to 41.6% and to 24.6% of total responses, respectively). The inconsistent responses in oral-then-written picture naming (30.8%) resulted from 24 correct spoken responses followed by incorrect written responses and from 16 incorrect spoken responses followed by correct written responses; in written-then-oral naming the inconsistent responses (33.8%) resulted from 15 correct written responses followed by incorrect spoken responses and from 29 incorrect written responses followed by correct spoken responses. A breakdown of these sequences by error type is reported in Table 6. In the oral-then-written naming task, the correct-then-incorrect sequences resulted from correct responses being followed by 14 semantic substitutions, by 1 failure to respond, by 7 neologisms, or by 2 unscorable responses; the incorrect-then-correct sequences resulted from the correct response being preceded by a semantic substitution ($N = 8$), by a failure to respond ($N = 5$), or by a neologism ($N = 3$). In the 44 lexically inconsistent responses observed in the written-then-oral naming task, correct responses were followed by a semantic error ($N = 10$), by a failure to respond ($N = 4$), or by a neologism ($N = 1$), and were preceded by a semantic substitution ($N = 15$), by a failure to respond ($N = 1$), by a neologism ($N = 12$) or by an unscorable response ($N = 1$).

TABLE 4
Across-modality Picture Naming Tasks: Examples of Response Sequences Resulting in One Correct, One Incorrect Response

	Oral-then-Written Naming	
Picture	*Oral Response*	*Written Response*
tromba (trumpet)	"orchestra" (orchestra)	+
baffi (moustache)	+	*barba* (beard)
vino (wine)	No response	+
pasta (pasta)	+	No response
piedi (feet)	/djommike/ (neol)	+
gomito (elbow)	+	*smeggio* (neol)

	Written-then-Oral Naming	
Picture	*Written Response*	*Oral Response*
scarpa (shoe)	*calza* (socks)	+
farfalla (butterfly)	+	"libellula" (dragonfly)
suora (nun)	No response	+
pera (pear)	+	No response
stivali (boots)	*gimeto* (neol)	+
mantello (cape)	+	/ven'tado/ (neol)

TABLE 5
Incidence of Various Response Sequences in the Two Across-modality Picture Naming Tasks (Percentages Are in Parentheses)

1st Response	*2nd Response*	*Oral-then-Written*	*Written-then-Oral*
Correct	Correct	53(40.8)	54(41.6)
Correct	Incorrect	24(18.5)	15(11.5)
Incorrect	Correct	16(12.3)	29(22.3)
Incorrect	Incorrect	37(28.4)	32(24.6)

TABLE 6
Immediate, Across-modality Naming Tasks: Breakdown of Sequences Resulting in a Correct Response Followed by an Incorrect Response, or in an Incorrect Response Followed by a Correct Response

	Oral-then-Written	Written-then-Oral
Correct response *followed by*		
Semantic substitution	14	10
Failure to respond	1	4
Neologism	7	1
Unscorable response	2	–
Correct response *preceded by*		
Semantic substitution	8	15
Failure to respond	5	1
Neologism	3	12
Unscorable response	–	1

This pattern of results is problematic for the phonological mediation hypothesis. Production of the correct phonological word form should always result in the activation of the corresponding orthographic word form and, barring damage directly to the orthographic lexicon or more peripheral processes, in the correct written response. The production of a semantic error in writing after the production of the correct spoken response cannot easily be explained by the phonological mediation hypothesis[8]. Even more damaging for this hypothesis are the 15 correct written responses followed by a lexically incorrect oral response (11.5% of total responses). These cases simply cannot be explained by the phonological mediation hypothesis, as that assumes that the activation of an orthographic representation is driven by the prior activation of its associated phonological word form, and thus a correct written response presupposes the activation of the correct phonological form.

---

[8] A correct spoken response followed by a semantic error in the presence of semantic damage may still be accounted for under phonological mediation, if a complex set of assumptions is made. Impoverished semantic information activates multiple phonological representations, and by chance the correct response is produced. At the same time, all the phonological forms activated by impoverished semantic information (and not just the form that has just reached threshold) pass activation on to the corresponding orthographic forms, one of which (different from the one that has just reached threshold in the phonological output system) is produced. Of course, the last step is only possible if an entry that does not reach threshold in the phonological system can activate the corresponding orthographic entry above threshold. This would be possible if the phonological and orthographic lexemes corresponding to the same lemma are associated with very different levels of activation. But, since under phonological mediation an orthographic form can *only* be activated by its corresponding phonological form, it is difficult to see how the activation level of phonological and orthographic lexemes can be so different.

Analysis of the actual responses produced by WMA in those trials in which he failed to produce either the correct spoken response or the correct written response to the same stimulus (Table 5) provides further support for the orthographic autonomy hypothesis. In the oral-then-written and in the written-then-oral picture naming tasks there were 18/37 (48.7%) and 10/32 (31.2%) instances, respectively, in which WMA produced different types of incorrect responses to the same stimulus. For example, in oral-then-written naming, he produced no spoken response to doctor, but wrote *drugs*; in another instance, he responded "scodella" (soup dish) to spoon, and immediately thereafter wrote the uninterpretable response *mendrona*. Similarly, in written-then-oral naming, he correctly wrote *chin* to the corresponding picture, but then said "elbow"; and, presented with a picture of scissors, wrote *tailor* but was unable to produce any written response. When sequences resulting in two semantic substitutions were considered, 6/19 (31.6%) and 7/22 (31.8%), in the oral-then-written naming and in the written-then-oral naming task, respectively, responses were inconsistent. Examples are shown in Table 7.

Overall, in the oral-then-written naming task, only 66/130 sequences (50.8%) resulted either in the same word (correct or semantically incorrect), or in the same type of incorrect response (two neologisms, or two failures to respond). The remaining 64/130 sequences (49.2%) resulted in lexically inconsistent responses (a correct and an incorrect word, two semantically incorrect words, or a failure to respond followed or preceded by a correct word, an incorrect word, or a neologism). In the written-then-oral naming task, compa-

TABLE 7
Across-modality Picture Naming Tasks: Examples of Incorrect Responses Resulting in Two Different Semantic Substitution Errors

	Oral-then-Written Naming	
Picture	Oral Response	Written Response
cuoco (cook)	"pietanza" (food)	*forchette* (forks)
pollice (thumb)	"mignolo" (little finger)	*mani* (hands)
tenaglia (pliers)	"pinza" (pincers)	*sega* (saw)

	Written-then-Oral Naming	
Picture	Written Response	Oral Response
caviglia (ankle)	*piede* (foot)	"gamba" (leg)
fisarmonica (accordion)	*zampogna* (pipes)	"grammofono" (gramophone)
peperoni (peppers)	*pomodoro* (tomato)	"carciofo" (artichoke)

rable results were obtained: WMA produced 69/130 (53.1%) lexically consistent responses and 61/130 (46.9%) lexically inconsistent responses.

At face value, the observations reported in the previous paragraphs cannot be accounted for by the phonological mediation hypothesis, and invite the conclusion that orthographic word forms are represented and activated autonomously from phonological word forms. However, an alternative explanation of the observed data that is consistent with the phonological mediation hypothesis must be ruled out before a firm conclusion is reached.

Lexically "inconsistent" responses may have occurred for reasons that have nothing to do with orthographic independence. Suppose that WMA suffered from a deficit characterised by the abnormally rapid decay of activated representations. If this were the case, the phonological mediation hypothesis could still account for inconsistent oral and written responses to the same item. Sequences like those reported in Tables 6 and 7 can be explained as follows. When producing the first response, the stimulus picture activates a semantic representation, which activates a phonological representation that is selected for output. When producing the second response, because of the abnormal decay of the previously activated representation, the just-activated semantic and lexical information is no longer available, and the process must start anew. The stimulus again activates semantic information, which activates a phonological output representation, which in turn activates the corresponding orthographic output representation. If the semantic representation or the phonological output representation differ from those activated in the first attempt at responding, two different responses may be produced. Thus, within the framework of the phonological mediation hypothesis, the assumption of an abnormally rapid decay of activated representations can account for the observed response sequences.

This hypothesis, however, relies on the assumption that the information activated in producing the first response has no effect on the production of the second response, independent of whether the two responses are produced in the same or in different modalities. This allows an obvious prediction: Consistency of responses to the same item in within-modality naming tasks should be comparable to that observed in across-modality naming tasks. In fact, abnormally fast decay of activated representations should affect performance on both types of tasks similarly—i.e. by lowering response consistency to the same extent, irrespective of whether the two responses must be produced in the same or in different modalities.

The orthographic autonomy hypothesis, by contrast, can easily accommodate the association of across-modality inconsistency and within-modality consistency. In the presence of semantic damage, the independent activation of phonological and orthographic word forms results in lexically inconsistent responses. By contrast, when two responses in the same modality are required, the semantic and the lexical information activated during the first attempt will still be above their resting state when the second response has to be produced; as a consequence, the lexical form produced during the first attempt is more likely to be produced than any other form.

Performance Obtained by WMA on Picture Naming Tasks that Require the Production of Two Consecutive Responses in the Same Modality

In order to verify the predictions based on the hypothesis of abnormal decay of activated representations, two tasks were administered. The first task required two consecutive spoken responses; the second task required two consecutive written responses. The 130 pictures used for the previous tasks served as stimuli.

For the oral-then-oral picture naming task, WMA was asked to name the picture. After he had produced his response, the picture was withdrawn and the subject was asked to count aloud backwards from five to zero. Subsequently, the picture was shown again and WMA was asked to name it a second time. This procedure was intended to prevent him from responding by simply repeating the first response, and to ensure that the two responses resulted from separate attempts at naming the stimulus. For the written-then-written naming task, the stimulus picture and WMA's written production were removed as soon as WMA completed his first response. Five seconds later, the picture was shown again, and WMA was asked to produce the second response. It was assumed that the second response was unlikely to result simply from the reiteration of a motoric sequence, given WMA's laborious writing.

The overall results obtained by WMA on these tasks are shown in Table 8. An almost perfect level of consistency is observed (Table 9). In 129/130 (99.2%) trials, WMA produced either two correct responses (86 in the oral task, 66.2%; 81 in the written task, 62.3%) or two incorrect responses (43 in the oral task, 33.1%; 48 in the written task, 36.9%). Incorrect responses always resulted in errors of the same type (two failures to respond, two semantic substitutions, two neologisms, etc.). Furthermore, almost all semantic errors resulted in the same incorrect response being produced twice. Only one exception each was observed in the oral–oral and written–written conditions: In the oral task, WMA made the semantic error shoes → "para" (rubber sole) followed by the correct response "scarpe"; in the written task, his first response to organ was the neologistic sequence *anede*, followed by the neologism *obano* (correct response: *organo*), which was scored as correct. The occurrence of lexically consistent vs. inconsistent responses on the two within-modality picture naming tasks is significantly different ($\chi^2 = 91.4$, $P \leq .001$) from the occurrence of the same response types on the two across-modality picture naming tasks.

The virtually perfect consistency of responses in the within-modality condition rules out the possibility that the inconsistent responses on the across-

TABLE 8
Overall Performance in the Two Within-modality Picture Naming Tasks (Percentage Are in Parentheses)

	Oral		Written	
	Oral 1	Oral 2	Written 1	Written 2
Correct	86(66.2)	87(66.9)	81(62.3)	82(63.1)
Semantic	40(30.8)	39(30.0)	32(24.6)	32(24.6)
No response	3 (2.3)	3 (2.3)	–	–
Neologism	1 (0.8)	1 (0.8)	11 (8.5)	10 (7.7)
Unscorable	–	–	6 (4.6)	6 (4.6)

TABLE 9
Incidence of Various Response Sequences in the Two Within-modality Picture Naming Tasks (Percentages Are in Parentheses)

1st Response	2nd Response	Oral	Written
Correct	Correct	86(66.2)	81(62.3)
Correct	Incorrect	1 (0.8)	1 (0.8)
Incorrect	Correct	–	–
Incorrect	Incorrect	43(33.1)	48(36.9)

modality tasks reported earlier resulted from an abnormally rapid decay of activated representations. This leaves, as the main candidate explanation for the inconsistent responses in speaking and spelling, the hypothesis that orthographic and phonological lexemes are activated independently by the damaged lexical semantic component. But, if this were the case, we would also expect that inconsistency of responses should be observed not only across modalities of output but also within the same modality on different occasions. In the within-modality naming task reported earlier, the two responses were produced too closely together in time for us to observe inconsistencies between responses. In such tasks, the form selected as the first response is still very likely to be the most active a few seconds later, when the second response must be produced. A different outcome is expected when the two responses are spaced by a long interval (i.e. days or weeks). In this case, whatever changes were induced in the pattern of semantic-lexical activation during the first naming trial will have subsided; thus, during the second trial the form produced on the first attempt should be no more likely to be selected than other, semantically related forms. To evaluate properly whether different responses would be produced within a modality on different occasions, we could consider naming responses produced in different testing sessions. To this purpose, we reanalysed WMA's performance on the various administrations of the oral and of the written picture naming tasks.

TABLE 10
Summary of Overall Performance on the Administration of the Picture Naming Task in the Same Modality Used to Assess Delayed, Within-modality Response Consistency
(Percentage Are in Parentheses)

	Oral Naming			Written Naming		
	Session a	Session b	Session c	Session a	Session b	Session c
Correct	78(60.0)	77(59.2)	86(66.2)	57(43.8)	69(53.1)	81(62.3)
Semantic	39(30.0)	36(27.7)	40(30.8)	35(26.9)	39(30.0)	32(24.6)
Neologism	2 (1.5)	3 (2.3)	2 (1.5)	27(20.8)	17(13.1)	12 (9.2)
Omission	10 (7.7)	13(10.0)	2 (1.5)	7 (5.4)	1 (0.8)	–
Unscorable	1 (0.8)	1 (0.8)	–	4 (3.1)	4 (3.0)	5 (3.9)

Session a: "canonical" task; Session b: first response to the immediate, across-modality task; Session c: first response to the immediate, within-modality task.

Performance on Delayed, Across-modality Picture Naming Tasks

The data used in this analysis were those obtained in the various naming tasks already reported (e.g. the first response produced in the immediate, within-modality task and the first response in the oral–written naming task). The three oral and the three written tasks—sessions a, b, and c—had been administered at approximately one-month intervals.

Performance on the various test sessions, as reported in Tables 1, 3, and 9, are summarised in Table 10. Consistency of overall performance is high. More correct responses are produced in the later-administered tasks, probably due to extensive practice with the experimental set[9]. However, the incidence of semantic substitutions is stable across sessions of the same task, and is comparable across tasks (it ranges between 27.7% and 30.8% in oral naming, and between 24.6% and 30% in written naming).

In order to measure performance consistency, responses produced in sessions a and b, and responses produced in sessions b and c, were paired. Because there were no marked differences in performance across test sessions, analyses were carried out on the 260 pairs resulting from collapsing sessions a–b and sessions b–c for the oral task, and on the 260 pairs resulting from collapsing sessions a–b and sessions b–c for the written task.

---

[9] It should be stressed that not all the tasks administered to WMA are reported here. The 130 word list was used also in the context of transcoding tasks requiring dual (reading aloud–writing; repetition–writing; writing to dictation–repetition) and triple responses (repetition–writing–repetition; writing to dictation–repetition–writing; reading aloud–writing–repetition; delayed copy–repetition–writing). Thus, each word was spoken and spelled several times by WMA.

For each task, the number of items to which WMA produced two correct responses, two incorrect responses, or a correct response and an incorrect response, is reported (Table 11). To facilitate comparison, Table 11 also reports the same data for the immediate, within-modality tasks (see also Table 9), and for the immediate, across-modality tasks (see also Table 4). Analysis of the 260 response pairs in the oral naming task yielded 196/270 (75.4%) pairs of consistent responses, resulting from 126 (48.5%) pairs of correct responses and 70 (26.9%) pairs of incorrect responses, and 64/260 (24.6%) pairs of inconsistent responses, resulting from 27 correct-then-incorrect sequences (10.4%) and from 37 incorrect-then-correct sequences (14.2%). The same analysis for written naming showed very similar results: 188/260 (72.3%) pairs of consistent responses, resulting from 103 (39.6%) pairs of correct responses and 85 (32.7%) pairs of incorrect responses, and 72/26 (27.7%) pairs of inconsistent responses, resulting from 24 correct-then-incorrect sequences (9.2%) and 48 incorrect-then-correct sequences (18.5%).

There are two aspects of the results in Table 11 that are relevant for our present purposes. First, the observation that 64/260 (24.6%) pairs in the delayed, oral naming task and 72/260 (27.7%) pairs in the delayed, written naming task yielded inconsistent responses stands in stark contrast with the virtual absence of inconsistent responses in the immediate, within-modality oral (1/130, 0.8%) and written naming tasks (1/130, 0.8%)—see Table 9. The statistical comparison of immediate vs. delayed, within-modality naming is highly significant, both for the oral task ($\chi^2 = 42.5; P \leq .001$) and for the written task ($\chi^2 = 48.7; P \leq .001$). Second, the number of inconsistent responses observed in delayed, within-modality naming is very similar to that observed in the immediate, across-modality naming tasks (oral-then-written: 37/130, or 28.4%; written-then-oral: 32/130, or 24.6%)—see Table 4. And in fact, non-significant differences are obtained when comparing delayed, oral naming with immediate, oral-then-written naming ($\chi^2 = 0.038; P =$ n.s.), or delayed, written naming with immediate, written-then-oral naming ($\chi^2 = 0.036; P =$ n.s.)[10].

The consecutive semantic substitutions produced by WMA in the delayed, within-modality tasks were also analysed (Table 12—this table also shows the corresponding data for the other two tasks, to facilitate comparison). WMA produced consecutive semantic substitutions to 38 stimuli in the oral task, and to 37 stimuli in the written task. Of these, 19/38 in the oral task (50%) and 12/37 in the written task (32.8%) resulted in different words. These values are significantly different from those observed in the immediate, within-modality tasks, in which consecutive semantic substitutions resulted in the same word

---

[10] Note that item consistency in the delayed, within-modality condition was also comparable across tasks (oral vs. written naming: $\chi^2 = 0.442; P =$ n.s.). This observation further supports the notion that the cognitive lesion in WMA damages a component that affects performance equally in oral and written naming—the semantic component.

TABLE 11
Delayed, Within-modality Picture Naming Task: Incidence of Various Response Sequences Observed in the Oral and the Written Task (Percentages are in Parentheses)

1st Resp	2nd Resp	Delayed, Within-modality		Immediate, Within-modality		Immediate, Across-modality	
		Oral	Written	Oral	Written	Oral, then Written	Written, then Oral
Correct	Correct	126(48.5)	103(39.6)	86(66.2)	81(62.3)	53(40.8)	54(41.6)
Correct	Incorrect	27(10.4)	24 (9.2)	1 (0.8)	1 (0.8)	24(18.5)	15(11.5)
Incorrect	Correct	37(14.2)	48(18.5)	–	–	16(12.3)	29(22.3)
Incorrect	Incorrect	70(26.9)	85(32.7)	43(33.1)	48(36.9)	37(28.4)	32(24.6)

Results of the same analysis for the immediate, within-modality (from Table 9) and for the immediate, across-modality (from Table 4) task are also reported.

TABLE 12
Response Consistency on the Same Items in the Delayed, Within-modality Picture Naming Task (Percentages are in Parentheses)

	Delayed, Within-modality		Immediate, Within-modality		Immediate, Across-modality	
	Oral	Written	Oral	Written	Oral, then Written	Written, then Oral
Same word	19(50.0)	25(67.6)	39(100)	32(100)	12(66.7)	14(63.6)
Different words	19(50.0)	12(32.8)	–	–	6(33.3)	8(36.4)
Total	38 (100)	37 (100)	39(100)	32(100)	18 (100)	22 (100)

The cases in which WMA produced two semantic substitutions in response to the same picture are analysed, and the number of responses resulting in the same semantically incorrect word and in two different semantically incorrect words is reported. The figure of the same analysis conducted on immediate, within- and across-modality tasks is also reported for comparison.

almost without exception (oral naming: $\chi^2 = 20.6$; $P \leq .001$; written naming: $\chi^2 = 11.08$; $P < .001$). By contrast, response consistency for consecutive semantic substitutions was comparable in the delayed, within-modality tasks and in the immediate, across-modality tasks (delayed oral naming vs. immediate, oral-then-written naming: $\chi^2 = 1.004$; $P = $ n.s.; delayed written naming vs. immediate, written-then-oral naming: $\chi^2 = 0.001$; $P = $ n.s.). Thus, the results demonstrate that similar forms of inconsistent responses are obtained in the delayed, within-modality and the immediate, across-modality naming conditions.

DISCUSSION

The results we have reported for WMA can be summarised succinctly: (1) He makes semantic errors in all word comprehension and production tasks as well as in those transcoding tasks where sublexical conversion procedures are severely damaged; and (2) he frequently produces inconsistent written and oral responses in the same naming trial. The facts in (1)—that WMA makes semantic errors in all comprehension and production tasks—imply that he has a deficit to the lexical-semantic component (see Hillis et al., 1990, for a similar case); the fact that he produces different oral and written responses in the same naming trial disconfirms the phonological mediation hypothesis of written production, and supports the hypothesis that phonological and orthographic lexemes are independently activated by lexical semantic information (for a different case and similar arguments see Rapp, Benzing, & Caramazza, this issue).

The hypothesis of phonological mediation in spelling predicts that there should be a close correspondence between the orthographic and phonological lexemes produced in the same trial in a naming task. More specifically, the prediction is that the same *lexical* response must be produced in spelling and speaking[11]. This expectation was clearly disconfirmed in WMA. He frequently produced inconsistent lexical responses in spelling and speaking, including cases where an incorrect phonological lexeme was followed by a correct orthographic lexeme, and cases where a semantic error in speaking was followed by a different semantic error in spelling. These two types of errors cannot be accommodated in any straightforward manner within the phonological mediation hypothesis. However, the occurrence of inconsistent lexical errors in oral and written naming tasks receives a ready explanation within the orthographic autonomy hypothesis.

In the normal, unimpaired system, a lexical-semantic representation will normally maximally activate the correct phonological and orthographic lexical forms. That is, the semantic representation for CAT will correctly activate the phonological form /kæt/ and the orthographic form <cat>. Why, then, should damage to the semantic system lead to inconsistent responses in the two modalities of output? Why should it not lead to the same response in the two modalities, albeit an incorrect one, as it does in the case of correct responses? The answer to this question is tied to a more basic question: Why do subjects with damage to the semantic component make semantic errors at all? Our answer to the latter question is based on the following assumptions about the structure of the semantic component and its relation to lexical forms (see Caramazza & Hillis, 1990).

We have assumed that the meaning of a word is represented by a set of semantic features (or a set of nodes corresponding to meaning primitives). The semantic features activate all lexical forms whose meanings contain those features. Thus, for example, the semantic properties [has legs] and [living] will activate all lexical forms referring to living things and those referring to objects with legs, including such diverse things as dog, boy, hippopotamus, chair, and table[12]. Under normal circumstances the lexical form that receives maximal activation is the correct one because it is the one with the largest number of connections to the activated meaning. On this view, the semantic representation of CAT will maximally activate the phonological and orthographic forms of

---

[11] The hypothesis allows responses to be different at the segmental level if post-lexical phonological or orthographic deficits are present. For example, the responses/kæt/ and /kæg/'*cag* or *cta* to a picture of a cat or to a picture of a dog (hence representing a semantic error) would be consistent with the phonological mediation hypothesis, as the spelling errors could be attributed to a post-lexical deficit.

[12] For illustrative purposes we have made the assumption that there is a single semantic property [has legs] that is shared by animate and inanimate objects. This assumption may be false—perhaps chairs and boys do not share the semantic property [has legs] because there are two distinct properties [has legs]: one referring to a property used for motion and the other referring to a property used for holding up surfaces.

"cat," but will also activate, though to a lesser degree, the lexical forms for "dog" and "lion," still less "hippopotamus" and "eagle," and lesser still "chair." However, if damage to semantic representations were to result either in the destruction of some of the semantic features or some type of generalised "noisiness" in the semantic network, one consequence would be that the active semantic representation would no longer maximally activate the correct lexical form but might activate a roughly equal number of semantically related forms. In this situation, the selection of a response could well depend on the momentary fluctuations of activation levels of the activated cohort of lexical forms (for cat these might include cat, dog, lion, pet, meow, ...). In other words, there will not be a systematic relationship between a stimulus and a response: Any one of several responses could be produced for a stimulus on any one occasion. If orthographic and phonological lexemes were activated independently by semantic representations, we would then expect that on some occasions the orthographic and phonological responses would be the same—both correct or both incorrect—and on other occasions one response would be correct and the other incorrect; and when both responses are incorrect, on some occasions the same incorrect response would be produced whereas on other occasions different incorrect responses would be produced. This is precisely the pattern of performance we have reported for WMA, which thus unequivocally supports the hypothesis that phonological and orthographic forms are autonomously represented and activated by semantic information.

We have presented compelling evidence in favour of the orthographic autonomy hypothesis. But if the orthographic and phonological lexicons were to be truly independent, as argued here, why is it that anomic disorders so often seem to involve both written and spoken forms? Why is it that the pattern of inconsistent semantic errors reported for WMA is not reported more frequently? A consideration of these issues requires a discussion of the relations among lexical components and those between lexical forms and sublexical phonology–orthography and orthography–phonology conversion processes.

There is a weak and a strong version of the orthographic autonomy hypothesis. The weak version holds that orthographic and phonological lexemes are directly and independently activated by lexical semantic representations, and that phonological and orthographic lexemes are directly connected to each other (e.g. as hypothesised by Allport & Funnell, 1981; and by Patterson & Shewell, 1987). The strong version holds only the first part of the conjunction; on this version of the orthographic autonomy hypothesis there are no direct connections between phonological and orthographic forms. The weak version of the hypothesis provides a ready account for the observation that there are brain-damaged subjects who produce inconsistent semantic errors in oral and written naming as well as for the observation that these cases may be rather rare. Because of the hypothesised connection between lexical forms, the activation of one lexical form—either phonological or orthographic—will lead to the activation of its corresponding lexeme in the other modality. On this view, the selection of a lexeme in one modality involves both the direct activation from the semantic component and the indirect activation from its corresponding lexeme in the other modality. This type of lexical architecture guarantees that the same word is activated in the phonological and orthographic lexicons. An implication of this view is that selective damage to the semantic system would result in a deficit in oral and written naming, but because of the interaction between lexical forms the same lexical response is expected in the two modalities of output. In order to account for the production of inconsistent responses in oral and written naming, we would have to assume not only a deficit in the semantic component but also damage to the connections between lexical forms. Thus, by making different assumptions about the form of damage to the lexical system, the weak orthographic autonomy hypothesis can account both for cases such as WMA and for those cases where the same lexical errors are consistently produced in oral and written naming.

The strong version of the orthographic autonomy hypothesis could also account for consistent and inconsistent error patterns in oral and written naming tasks if we were to assume the summation hypothesis of lexical activation (Hillis & Caramazza, 1991; Miceli, Giustolisi, & Caramazza, 1991; Patterson & Hodges, 1992); that is, the hypothesis that phonological and orthographic lexical forms receive input both from the semantic component and from sublexical orthography–phonology and phonology–orthography conversion procedures, respectively. On this view, the interaction between orthographic and phonological lexical forms is mediated by sublexical conversion procedures. Thus, for example, the successful activation of /kæt/ makes available to the orthographic lexicon, through the sublexical phonology–orthography conversion process, candidate spellings that further constrain the selection of the orthographic lexeme <cat> activated from the semantic component. This type of lexical architecture also guarantees that the same word is selected in the phonological and orthographic lexicons. Thus, damage to the semantic component would result in consistent errors in oral and written naming, because the selection of a lexeme in the phonological or orthographic lexicon will *indirectly* affect the selection of the same word in the other lexicon. In order to account for the pattern of inconsistent errors in oral and written naming we must also assume severe damage to the sublexical orthography–phonology and phonology–orthography conversion processes. This latter damage would have the effect of completely isolating the orthographic and phonological lexicons from each other, with the consequence that damage to the semantic component would often result in the activation of different lexemes in the two production lexicons. Thus, just like the weak version of the orthographic autonomy hypothesis, the strong version of the hypothesis is also able to account for both consistent and inconsistent patterns of naming errors but does so by having to postulate multiple loci of damage to the lexical system and sublexical conversion processes.

The two hypotheses of the functional architecture of the lexical processing system embodied in the strong and weak versions of the orthographic autonomy hypotheses can be distinguished empirically. The strong version of the hypothesis predicts that inconsistent naming errors should only be produced by brain-damaged subjects who are severely impaired in sublexical conversion processing, as is the case in WMA. Further anecdotal information that would seem to favour the strong version of the orthographic autonomy hypothesis is provided by those cases who seem to be unable to name an object orally until they have produced some of the letters in the word, and also by those cases who seem to be unable to write the word until they have articulated the beginning of the word. Of course, these observations are only anecdotal but they are consistent with the performance profile we have reported for WMA. The strong version of the orthographic autonomy hypothesis would be disconfirmed if a subject with damage to the semantic component and spared sublexical conversion procedures were to produce inconsistent errors, or if a subject with damage to the semantic component and damaged sublexical procedures were to produce only consistent naming errors. Either pattern would demonstrate that sublexical conversion mechanisms play no (or a very minimal) role in allowing an interaction between phonological and orthographic lexemes. These observations would provide indirect support to the possibility that this interaction is subsumed by direct lexical links, as suggested by the weak version of orthographic autonomy. Further detailed investigations of other cases are needed to distinguish between the two versions of the orthographic autonomy hypotheses.

In conclusion, the results we have reported have implications for two aspects of lexical processing: the functional architecture of the lexical system and the dynamics of lexeme activation. With respect to the functional architecture of the lexical system, WMA's inconsistent semantic errors in oral and written naming provide compelling evidence against the phonological mediation hypothesis of lexical-orthographic access and suggest, instead, that orthographic lexemes are activated directly by lexical-semantic information. The data do not allow an unambiguous choice between the strong and weak versions of the orthographic autonomy hypotheses but they are consistent with the strong version. The results are also relevant to correct discussions about the dynamics of activation of lexical forms. The fact that WMA made different semantic errors in the same naming trial suggests that semantic representations activate multiple lexical forms in each lexical form component.

REFERENCES

Alajouanine, T., & Lhermitte, F. (1960). Les troubles des activités expressives du langage dans l'aphasie. Leurs relations avec les apraxies. *Revue Neurologique, 102*, 604–629.

Allport, D.A., & Funnell, E. (1981). Components of the mental lexicon. *Philosophical Transactions of the Royal Society of London, B295*, 397–410.

Assal, G., & Buttet, J. (1981). Dissociations in aphasia: A case report. *Brain and Language, 13*, 223–240.
Basso, A., Taborelli, A., & Vignolo, L.A. (1978). Dissociated disorders of speaking and writing in aphasia. *Journal of Neurology, Neurosurgery and Psychiatry, 41*, 556–563.
Bock, J.K., & Levelt, W.J.M. (1994). Language production: Grammatical encoding. In M.A. Gernsbacher (Ed.), *Handbook of psycholinguistics*. San Diego, CA: Academic Press.
Brown, A.S. (1991). A review of the tip-of-the-tongue experience. *Psychological Bulletin, 109*, 204–223.
Brown, R., & McNeill, D. (1966). The "tip-of-the-tongue" phenomenon. *Journal of Verbal Learning and Verbal Behavior, 5*, 325–337.
Caramazza, A. (1988). Some aspects of language processing revealed through the analysis of acquired aphasia: The lexical system. *Annual Review of Neuroscience, 11*, 395–421.
Caramazza, A., Berndt, R., & Basili, A. (1983). The selective impairment of phonological processing: A case study. *Brain and Language, 18*, 128–174.
Caramazza, A., & Hillis, A. (1990). Where do semantic errors come from? *Cortex, 26*, 95–122.
Caramazza, A., & Hillis, A. (1991). Lexical organization of nouns and verbs in the brain. *Nature, 349*, 788–790.
Coltheart, M., & Funnell, E. (1987). Reading and writing: One lexicon or two? In A. Allport, D.G. MacKay, W. Prinz, & E. Scheerer (Eds.), *Language perception and production: Relationships between speaking, reading and writing*. London: Lawrence Erlbaum Associates Ltd.
Dell, G.S. (1986). A spreading activation model of retrieval in sentence production. *Psychological Review, 93*, 283–321.
Dell, G.S. (1990). Effects of frequency and vocabulary type on phonological speech errors. *Language and Cognitive Processes, 5*, 313–349.
Dell, G.S., & O'Seaghdha, P.G. (1992). Stages of lexical access in language production. *Cognition, 42*, 287–314.
Dell, G.S., & Reich, P.A. (1981). Stages in sentence production: An analysis of speech error data. *Journal of Verbal Learning and Verbal Behavior, 20*, 611–629.
Ellis, A., Miller, D., & Sin, G. (1983). Wernicke's aphasia and normal language processing: A case study in cognitive neuropsychology. *Cognition, 15*, 111–144.
Fay, D., & Cutler, A. (1977). Malapropisms and the structure of the mental lexicon. *Linguistic Inquiry, 8*, 505–520.
Forster, K.I. (1994). Computational modeling and elementary process analysis in visual word recognition. Special section: Modelling visual word recognition. *Journal of Experimental Psychology: Human Perception and Performance, 20*, 1292–1310.
Fromkin, V.A. (1973). *Speech errors as linguistic evidence*. The Hague: Mouton.
Garrett, M.F. (1975). The analysis of sentence production. In G. Bower (Ed.), *Psychology of learning and motivation: Vol. 9* (pp. 133–177). San Diego, CA: Academic Press.
Garrett, M.F. (1980). Levels of processing in sentence production. In B. Butterworth (Ed.), *Language production: Vol. 1: Speech and talk*. London: Academic Press.
Garrett, M. (1992). Disorders of lexical selection. *Cognition, 42*, 143–180.
Hier, D.B., & Mohr, J.P. (1977). Incongruous oral and written naming. *Brain and Language, 4*, 115–126.
Hillis, A.E., & Caramazza, A. (1991). Mechanisms for accessing lexical representations for output: Evidence from a category-specific semantic deficit. *Brain and Language, 40*, 106–144.
Hillis, A.E., Rapp, B.C., Romani, C., & Caramazza, A. (1990). Selective impairment of semantics in lexical processing. *Cognitive Neuropsychology, 7*, 191–244.
Jescheniak, J.D., & Levelt, W.J.M. (1994). Word frequency effects in speech production: Retrieval of syntactic information and of phonological form. *Journal of Experimental Psychology: Learning, Memory, and Cognition, 20*, 824–843.
Kempen, G., & Huijbers, P. (1983). The lexicalisation process in sentence production and naming: Indirect selection of words. *Cognition, 14*, 185–209.

Lecours, A.R., & Rouillon, F. (1976). Neurolinguistic analysis of jargonaphasia and jargonagraphia. In H. Whitaker & H. Whitaker (Eds.), *Studies in neurolinguistics, Vol. 2*. New York: Academic Press.

Levelt, W.J.M. (1989). *Speaking*. Cambridge, MA: MIT Press.

Levelt, W.J.M., Schriefers, H., Vorberg, D., Meyer, A.S., Pechmann, T., & Havinga, J. (1991). The time course of lexical access in speech production: A study of picture naming. *Psychological Review, 98*, 122–142.

Lhermitte, F., & Dérouesné, J. (1974). Paraphasies et jargonaphasie dans le langage oral avec conservation du langage écrit. *Revue Neurologique, 130*, 21–38.

Martin, N., Dell, G.S., Saffran, E.M., & Schwartz, M.F. (1994). Origins of paraphasias in deep dysphasia: Testing the consequences of decay impairment to an interactive spreading of activation model of lexical retrieval. *Brain and Language, 47*, 609–660.

Martin, N., Weisberg, R.W., & Saffran, E.M. (1989). Variables influencing the occurrence of naming errors: Implications for models of lexical retrieval. *Journal of Memory and Language, 28*, 462–485.

Miceli, G., Giustolisi, L., & Caramazza, A. (1991). The interaction of lexical and nonlexical processing mechanisms: Evidence from anomia. *Cortex, 27*, 57–80.

Miceli, G., Laudanna, A., Burani, C., & Capasso, R. (1994). *Batteria per l'Analisi dei Deficit Afasici*. Rome: CEPSAG.

Morton, J. (1969). The interaction of information in word recognition. *Psychological Review, 76*, 165–178.

Patterson, K., & Hodges, J.R. (1992). Deterioration of word meaning: Implications for reading. *Neuropsychologia, 30*, 1025–1040.

Patterson, K., & Shewell, C. (1987). Speak and spell: Dissociations and word-class effects. In M. Coltheart, G. Sartori, & R. Job (Eds.), *The cognitive neuropsychology of language*. London: Lawrence Erlbaum Associates Ltd.

Rapp, B., & Caramazza, A. (in press). The modality-specific organization of grammatical categories: Evidence from impaired spoken and written sentence production. *Brain and Language*.

Roelofs, A. (1992). A spreading-activation theory of lemma retrieval in speaking. *Cognition, 42*, 107–142.

Seidenberg, M.S., & McClelland, J.L. (1989). A distributed, developmental model of word recognition and naming. *Psychological Review, 96*, 523–568.

Shattuck-Hufnagel, S. (1979). Speech errors as evidence for a serial-ordering mechanism in sentence production. In W.E. Cooper & E.C.T. Walker (Eds.), *Sentence processing: Psycholinguistic studies presented to Merrill Garrett*. Hillsdale, NJ: Lawrence Erlbaum Associates Inc.

Shattuck-Hufnagel, S. (1986). The role of word-onset consonants in speech production planning: New evidence from speech error patterns. In E. Keller & M. Gopnik (Eds.), *Motor and sensory processes of language*. Hillsdale, NJ: Lawrence Erlbaum Associates Inc.

Stemberger, J.P. (1985). An interactive activation model of language production. In A.W. Ellis (Ed.), *Progress in the psychology of language, Vol. 1*. London: Lawrence Erlbaum Associates Ltd.

The Autonomy of Lexical Orthography

Brenda Rapp and Lisa Benzing
Johns Hopkins University, Baltimore, USA

Alfonso Caramazza
Harvard University, Cambridge, USA

Do we need to access the spoken form of a word in order to retrieve the word's spelling or in order to understand the meaning of its written form? In this paper we focus on the relationship between lexical phonology and orthography *specifically in production* and we present the case of a neurologically impaired individual who is often unable to provide the correct spoken name of an object although he may be able to write its name correctly. We argue that this evidence is seriously problematic for the hypothesis of obligatory phonological mediation and conclude that orthographic lexical forms can indeed be independently accessed for production without the mediating role of phonology.

INTRODUCTION

Do we need to access the spoken form of a word in order to retrieve the word's spelling or in order to understand the meaning of its written form? This question concerns the extent to which orthographic and phonological lexical forms can be represented and processed *independently* and is central to our understanding of the fundamental relations amongst the various aspects of our word knowledge—orthographic-phonological-semantic-syntactic. Traditionally it has been assumed that written language skills and knowledge are entirely dependent upon spoken language knowledge and processes. This assumption is found both in work with individuals with acquired neurological deficits (Brown, 1972; Geschwind, 1969; Grashey, 1885; Head, 1926; Hecaen & Angelergues, 1965; Lichtheim, 1885; Luria, 1966; Wernicke, 1886) as well as in the study

---

Requests for reprints should be addressed to Brenda Rapp, Dept. of Cognitive Science, Johns Hopkins University, Baltimore, MD 21218, USA (e-mail: brenda@cog.jhu.edu).

Research reported here was supported by NIH grant NS22201 to Alfonso Caramazza. We are grateful to Michael McCloskey, Marie-Josephe Tainturier, Gabriele Miceli, and Jennifer Shelton for their many helpful suggestions on earlier versions of this paper. We are especially appreciative of the time and effort that PW has given to this project.

of normal subjects (in the context of writing see Frith, 1979; Hotopf, 1980; and for discussions of the issue with respect to reading see Perfetti & Bell, 1991; Van Orden, Johnston, & Hale, 1988). However, there are a number of lines of evidence from impaired performance indicating that phonological mediation is not required either in written comprehension or in written production (Ellis, 1982; Lhermitte & Dérouesné, 1974; Patterson & Marcel, 1977).

Here we will focus on the relationship between lexical phonology and orthography *specifically in production* and we will present the case of a neurologically impaired individual who is often able to write the name of a pictured object correctly in the face of a persistent inability to provide the correct spoken name of the object. For example, in response to a picture of a pear:

Examiner:	Can you write the name?
PW:	(writes) P-E-A-R
Examiner:	Can you say it?
PW:	Fruit . . . damn that's wrong. Piece of fruit that I love . . . uh, uh, uh . . . damn it . . .
Examiner:	Can you come up with the name?
PW:	I can sit here and spell it for you all day long . . .

This pattern of performance would seem to be problematic for a functional architecture in which access to phonology is a necessary prerequisite for access to orthographic lexical forms.

We will first review the various patterns of impaired performance that have been put forward in support of the autonomy of orthography and we will then consider objections that can, or have been, raised regarding each of them. Finally we will indicate how, with the case at hand, we will be able to address certain of these objections.

The Relationship between Lexical Orthography and Phonology

According to the obligatory *phonological mediation hypothesis*, written language is entirely parasitic upon spoken language. As a consequence, in reading one must go from a written stimulus to a phonological representation before one can gain access to the meaning of a word. Similarly, in writing one must retrieve the spoken form of a word in order to gain access to the graphemic form (see Fig. 1a). This hypothesis (sometimes referred to in reading as phonological recoding) is consistent with our introspective experiences of inner speech as well as with the fact that the development of written language has followed that of spoken language both in the species and the individual. Nonetheless these observations do not preclude the possibility that the adult processing system is organised so that knowledge of the written and spoken forms of the language can be accessed independently. According to this alternative view, which we will call the *orthographic autonomy hypothesis* (Fig. 1b), orthographic knowledge can make contact with the more abstract aspects of lexical knowledge (such as meaning and syntax) *directly*, without phonological mediation. It is important to note that we are considering the issue of whether or not lexical (or sublexical) phonology is *required* for written language processing. Thus, evidence in support of a direct relationship between meaning and orthography does not rule out the possibility of *optional* phonological mediation either by means of lexical connections between orthography and phonology (Fig. 1c) or via sublexical processes (Fig. 1d). Questions concerning whether or not such optional processes exist and when, and to what extent, they are used are important and interesting issues, but distinct from the possibility of orthographic autonomy that we will explore here. We will return to this issue in the Discussion.

As would be predicted by the phonological mediation hypothesis, a large proportion of those individuals who exhibit impairments in spoken language also exhibit impairments of comparable or greater magnitude in written language production (Alajouanine & Lhermitte, 1960; Basso, Taborelli, & Vignolo, 1978; Head, 1926; Hecaen & Angelergues, 1965; Luria, 1966). Although consistent with phonological mediation, the finding of associated deficits can also be accounted for under the hypothesis of orthographic autonomy if we assume that the errors in the two output modalities are either the result of a deficit to shared levels of representation (such as to the lexical semantic store) or the consequence of two independent deficits affecting each of the written and spoken lexical stores. Thus, given that the association of deficits in written and spoken naming can be accounted for under either hypothesis, the truly informative finding would be that of spared knowledge of orthographic forms in the context of an impairment affecting phonological lexical forms. This pattern would be problematic for obligatory phonological mediation yet predicted by orthographic autonomy.

Establishing the Locus of Impairment: Lexical vs. Post-lexical

Clearly, however, not all observations of superior written vs. oral responding are relevant. For example, cases in which difficulties in oral responding result from motor difficulties affecting the articulators would be irrelevant. A number of cases exhibiting superior written vs. spoken naming with intact articulatory abilities have, in fact, been reported across a number of languages (Assal, Buttet, & Jolivet, 1981; Basso et al., 1978; Bub & Kertesz, 1982; Caramazza, Berndt, & Basili, 1983; Caramazza & Hillis, 1990; Coslett, Gonzalez-Rothi, & Heilman, 1984; Ellis, Miller, & Sin, 1983; Friederici, Schoenle, & Goodglass,

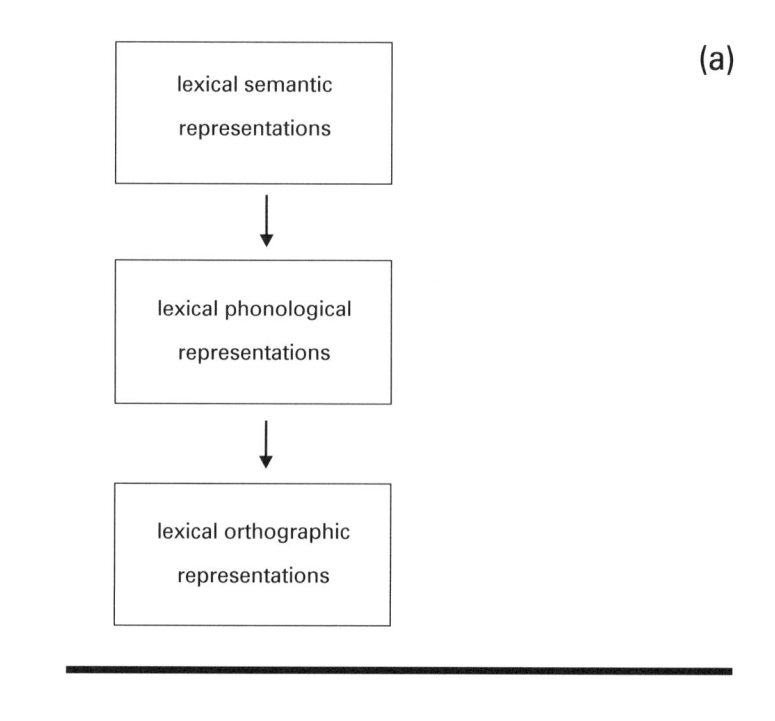

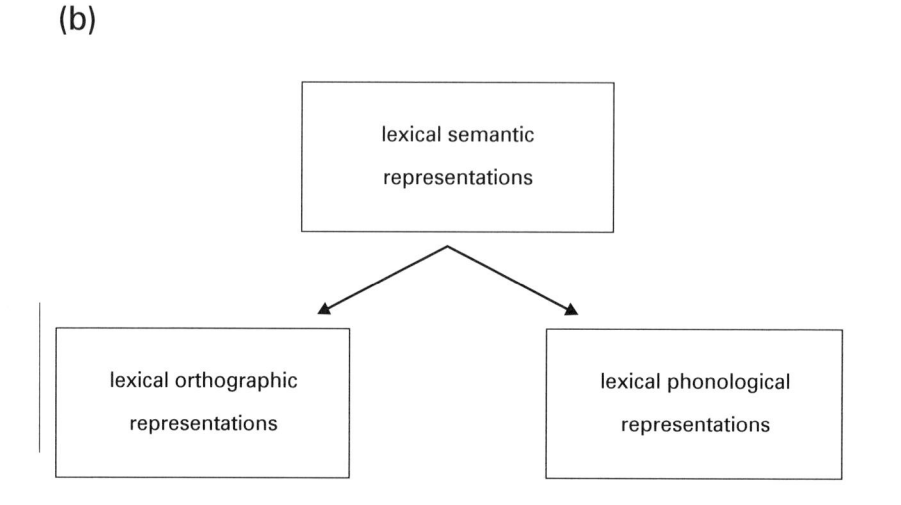

FIG. 1. Schematic representation of various possible relationships between lexical orthography and phonology: (a) obligatory phonological mediation; (b) orthographic autonomy.

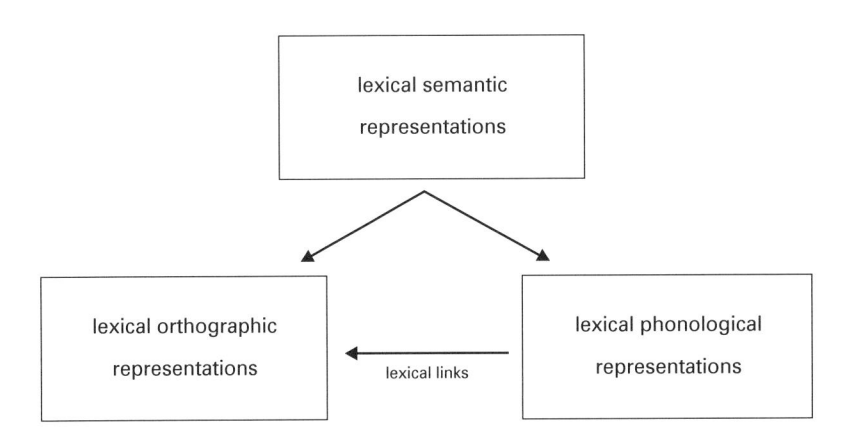

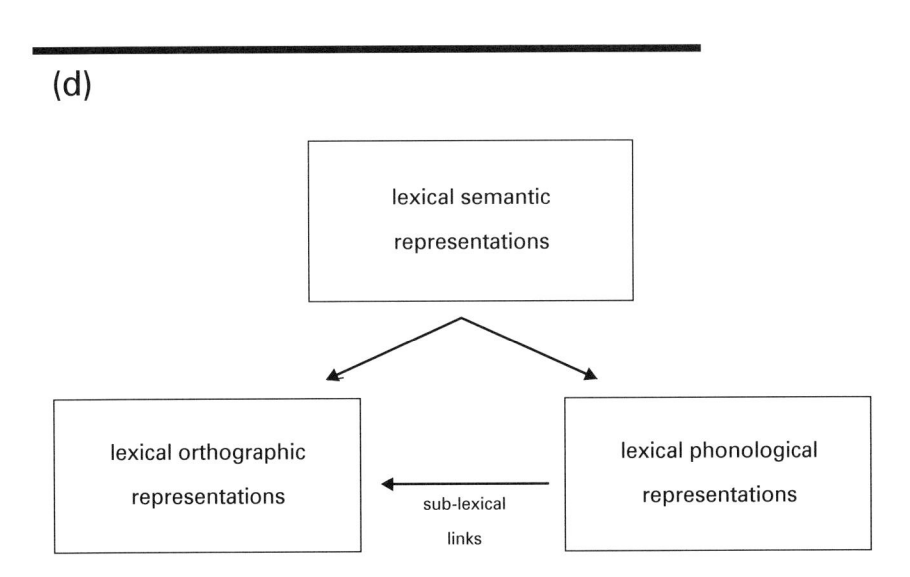

FIG. 1. Schematic representation of various possible relationships between lexical orthography and phonology: (c) orthographic autonomy + optional phonological mediation via lexical links; (d) orthographic autonomy+optional phonological mediation via sublexical links.

1981; Grashey, 1885; Hier & Mohr, 1977; Lecours & Rouillon, 1976; Leischner, 1969; Levine, Calvanio, & Popovics, 1982; Lhermitte & Dérouesné, 1974; Lichtheim, 1885; Mohr, Sidman, Stoddart, Leicester, & Morton, 1980; Mohr, Pessin, Finkelstein, Funkenstein, Duncan, & Davis, 1978; Nickels, 1992; Patterson & Shewell, 1987; Rapp & Caramazza, 1997; Semenza, Cipolotti, & Denes, 1992). However, although it is obviously necessary to rule out a peripheral articulatory source of the spoken errors, the finding of intact articulation is also insufficient. What is critical in determining if a pattern of superior written vs. spoken responding is problematic for the hypothesis of obligatory phonological mediation is that the spoken deficit be located at the level of phonological *lexical form*. Thus it is essential to establish that the source of spoken errors is lexical rather than post-lexical. In order to evaluate the relevance of any case of superior written vs. spoken responding with intact articulation, we must first determine if a lexical locus for the spoken errors can be established.

In reviewing the potentially relevant performance patterns that have been reported we will differentiate the patterns of superior written vs. spoken production according to the primary error type produced in spoken output: (1) phonemic/neologistic errors, (2) no responses, and (c) semantic paraphasias. To be clear: We make these distinctions because the different error types are subject to somewhat different objections regarding their evidential role in the phonological mediation/orthographic autonomy debate; they are not meant to imply specific claims regarding common or distinct functional etiology[1].

Phonemic Errors and Spoken Neologisms + Relatively Good Written Responding

There are a number of individuals who exhibit fluent, well-articulated speech characterised by neologisms and phonemic errors in the context of relatively spared written performance (Assal et al., 1981; Caramazza et al., 1983; Coslett et al., 1984; Ellis et al., 1983; Lhermitte & Dérouesné, 1974; Patterson & Shewell, 1987; Rapp & Caramazza, in press; Semenza et al., 1992). For example, one of the individuals described by Lhermitte and Dérouesné (1974) was 74% correct in written production but only 8% correct in oral production. Likewise, the Italian patient described by Semenza et al. (1992) was only 3% correct in oral naming of pictures and objects, but 85% in written naming. Another individual, PBS (Rapp & Caramazza, 1977), orally named the picture of a castle, which we will refer to as p(castle), as /krɛstIt/ but spelled the name

---

[1] For example, given our incomplete understanding of their origins within a functional architecture, it is possible that neologistic responses, phonemic errors, and no responses correspond to different points in a continuum of errors resulting from a common locus. Alternatively, it may turn out that these various error types have clearly distinct functional origins.

correctly; p(taxi) yielded /waz/ and T-A-X-I. Cases such as these are apparently problematic for the phonological mediation claim since it is difficult to argue that spoken neologistic responses form the basis for the retrieval of correct written responses; thus, it is hard to imagine how the phonological representations that support incorrect spoken responses (such as /waz/) also allow access to correct orthographic representations (such as T-A-X-I).

However, the considerable uncertainty regarding the functional origin of these nonarticulatory spoken errors (see Buckingham & Kertesz, 1976; Butterworth, 1992; Ellis et al., 1983) makes it difficult to establish unambiguously a specifically lexical locus of impairment in these cases. Thus, one could argue that in spite of the typically intact articulatory abilities of these individuals, their spoken errors arise from a deficit before the level at which the articulators are engaged and yet beyond the stage at which lexical phonological representations are retrieved. If such were the case then it still could be maintained that intact phonological representations serve as the basis for the retrieval of the correct orthographic forms and that it is a subsequent deficit, specific to the phonological output system, that is responsible for the spoken error. Such an account would render these cases irrelevant to the issue of phonological mediation.

Ruling out a post-lexical impairment is not easy because accounts of post-lexical yet pre-articulatory mechanisms have not been formulated so as to allow for clear predictions regarding the range and characteristics of errors that should result from damage at these levels of processing. Generally speaking, post-lexical/pre-articulatory stages include: (1) those processes/structures responsible for maintaining lexical phonological material in memory (Caramazza et al., 1983) during the course of (2) the application of procedures dedicated to developing the appropriate phonetic representations. These latter processes are assumed by some to involve the proper assignment of both segmental and prosodic material to specific positions within a syllabically organised word frame (Butterworth, 1979; Dell, 1989; Levelt, 1989; Shaffer, 1976; Shattuck-Hufnagel, 1987) as well as whatever elaboration may be required to generate appropriate allophones or (depending on one's theory) to flesh out underspecified lexical phonological forms (Archangeli, 1985; Kiparsky, 1982). Although it is unclear which specific performance features should result from disruption to these processes, Butterworth (1992) has suggested that post-lexical/pre-articulatory deficits might be expected to create particular difficulties with longer words and with specific phonemes and, additionally, that performance should be relatively unaffected by lexical frequency[2].

In spite of these interpretive difficulties, one could nonetheless argue for a lexical locus of impairment in at least some cases of phonemic errors/spoken

---

[2] Additionally, Butterworth has argued that lexical vs. post-lexical deficits could be distinguished by the consistency vs. inconsistency of responding. Elsewhere we have indicated some difficulties involved in the use of a consistency criterion (Rapp & Caramazza, 1993).

neologisms + good written responding on the basis of the observation that certain of these individuals exhibit little or no trouble in oral reading (Miceli & Caramazza, 1993) or repetition (Semenza et al., 1992). This observation would seem to make it difficult to claim that their phonological difficulties arise at a post-lexical stage. It would seem to indicate, instead, that the difficulty lies specifically in the retrieval of the lexical phonological forms themselves, as has more generally been argued (Butterworth, 1979). However, the counter-objection could be raised that improved performance in reading and repetition results from the fact that these tasks, unlike naming, allow for the contribution of nonlexical processing. That is, it could be argued that better performance is possible in reading and repetition because in these tasks phonological information generated by nonlexical processes dedicated to grapheme–phoneme conversion (in reading) and acoustic–phonology conversion (in repetition) can be used alone, or in combination with partial lexically derived material.

In sum, there are a number of cases involving phonemic and neologistic errors in the context of relatively intact written production that seemingly create difficulties for the phonological mediation hypothesis. The primary difficulty with these cases lies in convincingly ruling out a pre-articulatory, yet post-lexical, locus of the spoken production deficit.

No Response + Relatively Good Written Responding

There are also a number of individuals who typically produce no spoken response although they are able to write the names of a target either correctly or with sufficient accuracy that the written name is recognisable (e.g. Bub & Kertesz, 1982; Grashey, 1885; Hier & Mohr, 1977; Levine et al., 1982). For example, MH, whose performance was described by Bub and Kertesz (1982), was able to write the name of 15/20 objects correctly although she was able to name only 1/20 orally. Some of the written errors were clearly identifiable as the target word: p(salt) → S-A-L-K, p(pillow) → P-E-L-L-O-W. In addition to her inability to arrive at a spoken response, MH was also unable to make rhyme judgements about pictures whose names she couldn't produce (this was also observed in Hier & Mohr, 1977; and Levine et al., 1982). These cases have been interpreted as involving deficits affecting the retrieval of lexical phonological forms and have been considered to be problematic for the hypothesis of obligatory phonological mediation. Thus, it is argued that it seems unlikely that phonology could be required to access orthography when an individual, unable to come up with a spoken response or experience the sound of an intended target subjectively, is nonetheless able to write the name of the word correctly.

However, as in the cases involving neologisms and phonemic errors, a post-lexical locus of impairment might be entertained. One might argue that "don't know" responses result when phonemic distortions are generated and either the patients are adept at self-monitoring and refrain from any production at all or the distortions are so severe that they cannot be articulated. In response, one could point out that under this scenario we would certainly expect to observe at least *some* evidence of phonemic distortion. Contrary to this expectation, the cases described by Bub and Kertesz (1982) and Grashey (1885) involved individuals who, although unable to name most open-class items orally, were otherwise able to speak without phonemic errors.

Although the absence of overt phonemic distortions in the speech produced by these subjects perhaps renders a post-lexical locus unlikely, the difficulties involved in unambiguously establishing a lexical origin of the spoken "don't know" responses remains a primary concern with this line of evidence.

Spoken Semantic Paraphasias + Good Written Responding

Although phonological errors and "don't know" responses may be ambiguous with respect to their lexical or post-lexical origin, semantic errors are typically not thought to be. It has been proposed that semantic errors in production may arise from either a semantic or lexical form level of damage (Caramazza & Hillis, 1990). Furthermore, in contrast to the difficulties involved in adjudicating between a lexical and a post-lexical locus for phonemic errors and "don't know" responses, the locus of semantic errors can often clearly be established by assessing the integrity of the subject's comprehension of misnamed items. For example, a subject who names a picture of a lion as "tiger" and describes it as a "cat with stripes" is quite different from one who produces the same naming error but describes it as "a big, blond cat, referred to as the king of the jungle." The former presumably has a semantic impairment, whereas the latter may have difficulties in retrieving the appropriate lexical phonological form. In neither would a post-lexical locus seem to be implicated. As a consequence, a pattern of performance in which semantic errors are produced exclusively or primarily in spoken but not written output is one line of evidence that cannot readily be dismissed by proposing a post-lexical locus of the spoken errors. Given this, the reports of semantic errors in the spoken modality with largely correct or recognisable responses in the written modality constitute some of the strongest pieces of evidence to date in support of the autonomy of orthography in language production.

Few cases exhibiting this pattern have been well documented. One of them, RGB (Caramazza & Hillis, 1990), made frequent (25–30%) semantic errors in reading and in oral naming of pictures: p(kangaroo) → "giraffe," p(mittens) → "glove," p(thumb) → "wrist" (see also Basso et al., 1978; subject JSR in Hillis & Caramazza, 1995; and Nickels, 1992). However, RGB made no semantic errors in written naming or in writing to dictation, where errors consisted only of recognisable misspellings of the target word [p(celery) →

C-E-L-E-Y; p(kangaroo) → K-A-G-O-O]. In addition, he gave clear evidence of intact semantic knowledge of the misnamed items. Thus, although RGB orally named a p(leopard) as a "rhinoceros" he described it as "a kind of cat with spots." The intact comprehension of misnamed terms indicates that the locus of impairment must be post-semantic. The fact that semantic errors (rather than phonemically based errors) were produced makes a post-lexical locus of impairment unlikely. In fact, in order to entertain a post-lexical locus for the semantic errors one would have to argue something like the following: Although phonemic distortions are generated, the responses are aborted and subsequent attempts result in the production of correct or semantically related forms. However, the total absence of phonemic errors in RGB's performance in any task and the absence of an account for why semantic errors in particular should be produced (e.g. as opposed to "don't know" responses or phonologically similar word errors) render this line of reasoning vacuous. Consequently, the deficit responsible for the semantic errors in RGB's case has been attributed to the level at which lexical phonological representations are activated for output. Specifically, Caramazza and Hillis proposed that a semantic representation (e.g. [hairy-barking-domestic-young-animal]) serves as the basis for the activation of a set of lexical form representations to varying degrees depending upon the extent to which they match the semantic features of the target (e.g. "puppy," "dog," "cat," "fox," "seal"). The most active representation, normally the correct word, is then made available for output. However, if the target name is not available then the most highly activated member of the set will be produced, and a semantic error will result (e.g. PUPPY → cat).

Orthographic Access via Multiple Attempts at Phonological Retrieval

Although the evidence provided by cases such as RGB crucially avoids the concern about a post-lexical locus of impairment, it is, nonetheless, subject to a different type of objection. While granting that the semantic errors produced in speech result from difficulties encountered in the retrieval of lexical phonological forms[3], one might nonetheless be concerned that the absence of semantic errors in writing results simply from the opportunity afforded by the writing task to attempt to gain access to a phonological form repeatedly before producing a written response. According to this hypothesis of "phonological mediation + multiple retrieval attempts," semantic errors are not present in writing because the subject produces a written response only *when* the correct

---

[3] We make no claims that the deficit is one specifically affecting retrieval processes vs. stored forms. As indicated in Rapp and Caramazza (1993), this is not a straightforward distinction to make.

response becomes available phonologically (whether it is overtly produced or not). This objection gains further plausibility if we consider that in the reported cases written and spoken naming were apparently assessed on different occasions. It is possible that when subjects are in a writing task they may be more likely to make repeated attempts at phonological retrieval before producing a written response.

Given this concern, the hypothesis of phonological mediation should, ideally, be tested by having a subject concurrently say and write the names of objects. However, given the obvious problems with this procedure, we can approximate it by having an appropriate subject systematically produce the written and the spoken name of each item in close temporal proximity on each naming trial. If success in writing is necessarily mediated by successful phonological retrieval, then the subject should typically follow a correct written response with a correct spoken one, and an incorrect written response with an incorrect spoken one.

In sum, one critical type of evidence in the phonological mediation/orthographic autonomy debate would consist of: (1) a spoken deficit that can be localised to a level of lexical phonological representation and (2) correct written vs. incorrect spoken responses assessed *for the same items on the same trial*. The performance of the subject of this report, PW, fulfils both of these criteria.

PW was an individual with largely intact comprehension who produced semantic errors and "don't know" responses in both written and spoken naming. Critically, however, when tested on the same trial in both output modalities, PW was often consistently able to produce correct written responses in the face of persistent difficulties with spoken responding. In the Case Study section we establish a lexical locus of the spoken naming errors; in the Experimental Studies section we document the critical performance pattern. Additionally, we take up (and reject) the possibility that this pattern can be attributed to: (1) phonological instability or (2) partial activation of phonological representations.

CASE STUDY

In this section we first present a description of the subject and the results of background testing; we then go on to report results of production and comprehension tasks that allow us to establish the functional loci of his deficits in spoken and written production.

PW was a right-handed male who had completed one semester of college and was employed as a manager of a meat department when he suffered a left-hemisphere stroke (following oral surgery) at the age of 51 (2/1990). CT scanning revealed an ischaemic infarction of the left parietal and posterior frontal areas (see Fig. 2). The CVA resulted in language difficulties as well as right-sided hemiplegia. Although PW was forced to write with his left hand, he

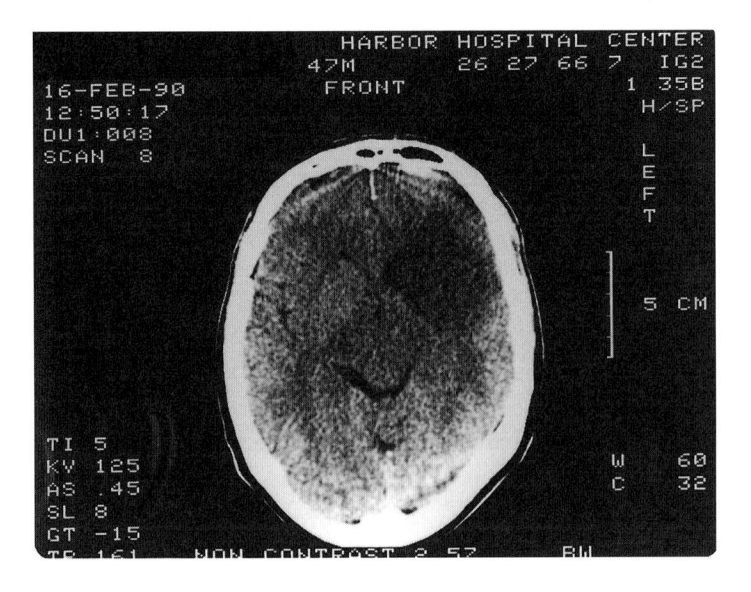

FIG. 2. CT scan for PW indicating left parietal and posterior frontal damage.

wrote quite easily and legibly. PW's visual fields were full and there was no sign of neglect. This investigation was carried out between 24 and 48 months after the CVA. PW's naming performance improved somewhat over this time period, although his pattern of errors remained virtually unchanged.

In our preliminary examination we noted that PW's speech was grammatically correct and that he exhibited no signs of phonemic or articulatory disturbance. In spontaneous speech we observed frequent hesitations due to word-finding difficulties, numerous circumlocutions, and semantic errors. In addition, he was able to generate only six animal names in 90sec. In contrast, he was able accurately to repeat words (90%), nonwords (100%), and sentences containing 5–8 words (100%). His ability to complete aurally presented sentences was also intact (100%). In terms of auditory sentence comprehension he was able to make sentence–picture matching judgements involving reversible sentences with 88% accuracy and grammaticality judgements with 80% accuracy.

In an assessment of his sublexical processing abilities, PW was given a set of 50 three- and five-letter nonwords for reading, repetition, and writing to dictation. PW repeated 92% of the nonwords correctly, with the occasional errors consisting of the production of phonologically similar words (/higl/ → "eagle"). In reading and writing to dictation, however, none of the nonwords were produced correctly. However, if instead of considering whole-stimulus accuracy we evaluate his nonword performance by considering the accuracy of each letter (in writing) and each phoneme (in reading), his accuracy was 35% in writing and 61% in reading. Errors in writing nonwords consisted predominantly of similar nonwords (e.g. /fum/ → F-O-M or /dItl/ → D-I-X) that typically included correct first or second letters. In reading, errors consisted predominantly of similar word responses (e.g. BOT → "bottle"; TASIN → "tasty"), although other nonword errors were also produced (e.g. DOX → /dræk/).

Single Word Production

In order better to understand the locus of his difficulties in spoken and written word production, we asked PW to carry out the following tasks with 258 items of the Snodgrass and Vanderwort (1979) picture set: spoken picture naming, written picture naming, reading, writing to dictation, repetition, and written name copying.

The results are presented in Table 1. Considering first the tasks involving spoken output, the results indicate that PW's spoken picture naming was marked by numerous semantic errors (19%), which were often accompanied by a verbal indication that he knew he had not produced the correct word [e.g. p(zebra) → "horse, not really (...) a horse in the jungle"]. Similarly, PW's "don't know" responses (6%) were also often accompanied by a description indicating that he was familiar with the item but could not come up with its name [e.g. p(thimble) → "I don't know the name, you put it over your finger and you sew"]. His overall spoken naming accuracy of 72% correct reveals a marked impairment with respect to that of elderly control subjects, for whom accuracy ranged from 91–100%.

TABLE 1
Percentage of Response Types on Various Tasks with the Same Stimuli (N = 258)

	Oral Pix Naming	Reading	Repetition	Written Pix Naming	Writing to Dictation	Copying
Correct	72.1	89.2	99.6	45.8	43.8	94.2
Semantic	19.0	2.3	0.0	12.4	8.1	0.0
Don't know	5.8	0.0	0.0	16.3	15.1	0.0
Similar nonword	0.0	0.8	0.0	10.9	9.7	5.8
Other nonword	0.0	0.8	0.0	5.8	9.3	0.0
Similar word	0.0	4.2	0.4	3.1	4.2	0.0
Other word	2.3	1.2	0.0	4.7	7.0	0.0
Other	0.8	1.6	0.0	1.2	2.7	0.0

In contrast to spoken naming, in reading PW produced only very few semantic errors (e.g. FISH → "horse") and he never produced a "don't know" response. PW's reading included a number of "similar word" responses (4%), which were responses sharing at least 50% of the target letters in the same relative order (e.g. SLED → "shed"), as well as various "other word" responses that did not meet this 50% similarity criterion (e.g. TOP → "tie"). The observed reduction in semantic error rate between picture naming and reading as well as the presence of mixed semantic/similar word errors [4/6 of the semantic errors produced in reading also met the criterion of similar word errors: p(cigar) → "cigarette"; p(shirt) → "shirt"] is consistent with the notion that, in reading, the opportunity exists for combining (inadequate) information generated by the lexical route with (inadequate) information from the sublexical orthography-to-phonology route. This summation of lexical and sublexical phonological information allows for a decrement in semantic error rates in reading vs. spoken naming (for further discussion of this summation hypothesis see Hillis & Caramazza, 1991, 1995). Because of this summation possibility, subsequent analyses directed at establishing the locus of the spoken and written naming deficits use only spoken and written naming data and do not include data from reading and writing to dictation.

As we had observed in our preliminary testing, Table 1 indicates that PW's repetition of words was practically flawless.

PW's performance was quite comparable in written naming and writing to dictation. In both we observe, as in spoken naming, a considerable proportion of semantic errors and "don't know" responses[4]. However, written production contrasts markedly with spoken naming in terms of the presence of a large number of similar word [e.g. p(stove) → S-T-O-R-K] and other word errors [e.g. p(stool) → S-O-C-K] as well as similar nonword [e.g. p(sandwich) → S-A-N-D-I-S-H] and other nonword errors [e.g. p(skunk) → S-Q-U-A-M]. The large number of similar nonword responses is an indication of post-lexical difficulties involving the graphemic buffer and/or letter form selection. We will return to this point later.

Finally, 6% errors were observed when PW was asked to copy written words directly. The errors were typically one-letter substitutions or deletions (e.g. HAND → H-A-N-b; PENCIL → p-e-N-I-L)). These errors may be indicative of a post-lexical deficit involving letter form selection; alternatively they may simply represent trials in which PW did not actually copy the stimuli but simply read them and then proceeded to retrieve the lexical orthographic forms as he would in a written naming task.

---

[4] The reduction in semantic errors in writing to dictation (as compared to written naming) was accompanied by an increase in other word and nonword responses. Again, this pattern of semantic error reduction is consistent with the possibility of combining lexical and sublexical information in the task of writing to dictation.

Single Word Comprehension

The fact that PW often provided correct definitions of items he could not name or which resulted in a semantic error indicates that the primary source of semantic errors in written and spoken naming was not at the level of the lexical semantic system. However, in order to examine the possibility of semantic deficit more directly we used the same set of 258 Snodgrass and Vanderwort items in two comprehension tasks: (1) drawing items named by the examiner and (2) auditory yes/no word-picture verification.

In drawing, PW produced two errors (0.8% error rate) ("lamp" → picture of a rug; "key" → picture of a lamp). One of these can be classified as a semantic error. This error rate, although perhaps indicative of a slight semantic deficit, is certainly not comparable to the semantic error rates observed in spoken or written naming.

In the word–picture verification task, PW was shown each of the 258 pictures in the set on three different occasions accompanied either by the correct name, a semantically related word, or a phonologically related word. He was asked to indicate (yes/no) if picture and word matched. His accuracy on this task was 95%. The majority of his errors involved accepting a semantically related foil (e.g. chain for lock, grasshopper for beetle). This accuracy level was just slightly below the low end of the rates exhibited by normal elderly control subjects, whose accuracy ranged from 96% to 100%.

The Localisation of the Spoken Production Deficit/s

In order to consider the possible contribution of a post-lexical deficit to PW's spoken naming errors, we evaluated whether phonological length, phonemic complexity, and/or word frequency played a role in PW's spoken picture naming accuracy. As indicated earlier, it has been argued (e.g. Butterworth, 1992) that deficits affecting post-lexical processes involved in the buffering or elaboration of abstract phonological material may be especially sensitive to length and complexity and relatively insensitive to lexical frequency. Lexical deficits should show the reverse effects.

Phonological Length and Lexical Frequency

We submitted the results of PW's spoken picture naming to an analysis of variance to examine the relationship between accuracy, length, and lexical frequency[5]. Lexical frequencies were assigned to low, medium, or high categories according to the following frequency ranges from Carroll et al. (1971): lo = <5, mid = 5–60, hi = >60. The results for spoken naming were comparable

---

[5] Compound word stimuli were excluded from this and subsequent analyses of written naming errors due to obvious ambiguities in assigning length and frequency values.

TABLE 2
Results in Spoken Naming by Phoneme Length and Frequency
(6+ Phomemes Includes Words from 6–10 Phonemes)

	Low Freq.	Mid Freq.	High Freq.	Totals
2+3 phonemes	75%	82%	93%	86% (N=70)
4+5 phonemes	50%	73%	87%	70% (N=108)
6+ phonemes	57%	78%	–	70% (N=33)
Totals	55% (N=38)	76% (N=129)	91% (N=44)	

whether length was assessed in terms of number of syllables or phonemes, so we report results obtained with number of phonemes (see Table 2). The analyses indicate a significant effect of lexical frequency [$F(2,190) = 5.28, P < .006$], no significant effect of length [$F(8,190) = 1.21, P < .29$], and no interaction between the two [$F(10,190) = 0.55, P < .85$]

Relationship between Spoken Targets and Errors

Additionally, we considered whether the items that induced semantic errors were either longer or more complex than the semantic error responses that were produced. One might expect that if post-lexical phonological factors played any role in the PW's spoken errors, error responses might be phonologically simpler than targets. We found no evidence for this. Target words had, on average, 4.4 phonemes and .4 clusters while responses had an average of 4.5 phonemes and .4 clusters [$F(7,77) = 1.23, P<.31; F(2,77) = 1.25, P<.30$].

As indicated in the Introduction, it is crucial to establish a specifically lexical phonological locus for the spoken naming impairment if superior written vs. spoken naming is to be used as a strong argument against obligatory phonological mediation. In the case of PW we have quite effectively been able to rule out significant deficits to post-lexical components or the lexical semantic system and thus we conclude that the spoken deficit originates specifically at the level of phonological lexical form in production. To recapitulate, this conclusion is based on the following reasons: (1) good comprehension of misnamed items makes a primary lexical semantic deficit unlikely; (2) excellent repetition performance rules out a peripheral articulatory contribution; (3) the presence of semantic errors and "don't know" responses in the context of a complete absence of phonological errors in naming make a pre-articulatory/post lexical locus highly unlikely; (4) the absence of significant effects of factors such as phonological length and complexity further diminish the likelihood of pre-articulatory/post-lexical difficulties, and (5) the presence of a significant effect of lexical frequency is specifically predicted by a lexical level deficit.

The Localisation of the Written Production Deficit/s

Given PW's relatively intact comprehension, the primary source of written semantic errors presumably lies with difficulties in retrieving lexical orthographic forms. However, the numerous nonword errors and misspellings suggest an additional post-lexical deficit affecting the graphemic buffer. To provide confirmation of this characterisation of the writing deficits we examined the influence of word frequency and length on PW's written naming. As before, we submitted the results of PW's written naming to analyses of variance to examine the relationship between accuracy, length, and lexical frequency (see Table 3).

In contrast to the pattern observed for spoken naming, PW's written accuracy was significantly influenced both by number of letters [$F(9,188) = 4.74$, $P<.0001$] and (marginally) by lexical frequency [$F(2,188) = 2.93$, $P<.06$]; the interaction between the two was not significant [$F(11,188) = 0.35$, $P<.97$]. The frequency and length effects are predicted by lexical and graphemic buffer deficits respectively. On this basis we assume that both lexical level and post-lexical deficits affect written output.

EXPERIMENTAL STUDY

Predictions for Phonological Mediation/Orthographic Autonomy

To summarise, PW's performance on a number of lexical processing tasks reveals the following: (1) difficulties in spoken production that can be localised to the lexical level; (2) difficulties in written production that can also be localised to the lexical level; (3) an additional post-lexical disturbance affecting written production only; and (4) a possible slight semantic deficit. This case is

TABLE 3
Percent Correct in Written Naming by Letter Length and Frequency (7+ Letters Includes Words from 7–12 Letters in Length)

	Low Freq.	Mid Freq.	High Freq.	Totals
3+4 letters	71%	59%	82%	68% ($N=80$)
5+6 letters	33%	42%	69%	46% ($N=88$)
7+ letters	11%	24%	–	16% ($N=43$)
Totals	29% ($N=38$)	45% ($N=129$)	72% ($N=44$)	

different from a number of the others reviewed in the Introduction in that both spoken and written production were significantly affected. However, the fact that semantic errors and "don't know" responses were observed in *both* written and spoken naming can be interpreted in one of two ways: (1) under obligatory phonological mediation, the written errors must (at least in part) reflect the inadequacy of mediating phonological representations; (2) under orthographic autonomy the written errors represent an independent deficit to the orthographic output lexicon. One might expect that a case such as this one—involving deficits to both orthographic and phonological lexical representations—would not be ideal for observing correct written responses on the same trial as incorrect spoken responses. However, one should keep in mind that the presence of phonological and orthographic lexical deficits should simply reduce rather than eliminate the probability of observing this pattern. In fact, a situation in which both of the modality-specific lexical stores are affected provides a unique opportunity to evaluate additional predictions that follow specifically from the hypothesis of orthographic autonomy.

If access to orthographic and phonological lexical forms can occur independently, then when *both* modality-specific lexicons are damaged (as appears to be the case for PW) and when spoken and written naming are evaluated on the same trial, we would expect to observe the following: (1) the previously described critical pattern of correct responding in written picture naming and incorrect responding in spoken picture naming on at least some trials [p(pig) → "cow, no, cow, P-I-G, cow?, no!]; and *additionally*, (2) if we assume (as indicated in the Introduction) that a semantic representation activates a set of lexical form representations to varying degrees depending on the extent to which they match the semantic features of the target then, when the correct lexical form is unavailable in both of the modalities, we should expect to see different semantic errors in spoken vs. written output on the very same trial [p(knife) → S-P-O-O-N, "fork"]; (3) based on similar reasoning we should expect different "correct," roughly synonymous responses in the two output modalities [p(pig/hog) → P-I-G, "hog"]; and (4) when the phonological lexical form is available but the orthographic form is not, we should see the pattern of semantic errors in writing accompanied by correct spoken responses [p(lips) → N-A-I-L, "lips"].

We administered four tasks in order to determine if these response patterns could be observed when written and spoken naming were examined on the very same trial. As indicated earlier, multi-modality responding on the same trial should allow us to address the primary reservation regarding cases where semantic errors have been observed exclusively or primarily in the spoken modality. Specifically we should be able to address the concern that the absence of semantic errors in the writing of these individuals may have been due to the possibility that written responses were produced only after multiple (and eventually successful) phonological retrieval attempts.

Task 1: Written/Spoken naming

We asked PW to first write and then say the name of 256 black-and-white drawings of objects. PW was asked to look away as he wrote the object's name in order to eliminate the possibility that he would read his written response. This procedure was maintained throughout all of the subsequent tasks that we administered. On the few occasions when multiple responses were produced we scored the final written response and the first spoken one in order to examine the temporally most proximal responses. We first present overall response types for written and spoken naming (Table 4). We then go on to focus on the specific patterns of responding that are relevant to the orthographic autonomy/phonological mediation debate (Table 5).

In spoken naming PW produced 74% correct lexical choices; no phonemic errors were observed. In written naming 62% of PW's responses were correct lexical choices that were either spelled correctly or incorrectly. *Misspelled correct responses* were those nonword responses that contained more than 50% of the target letters in the correct relative order [e.g. p(church) → C-H-U-R-S-H; p(guitar) → G-U-A-R-T-I-A]. Similar rates of semantic errors were observed in both written and spoken naming (17% and 18% respectively). "Don't know" responses were produced at a rate of 13% in written naming and 7% in spoken naming. Additionally, neologisms and other word responses were observed almost exclusively in written naming. *Neologisms* were nonword responses sharing 50% or less of the target letters [p(rocket) → R-O-T-O-H]. *Other word* responses include all incorrect responses that are actual words of the language, regardless of their degree of overlap with the target [p(razor) → R-A-Y-O-N].

Critical Error Patterns

According to the hypothesis that written naming is based on phonological mediation + multiple retrieval attempts, the accuracy of the written response

TABLE 4
Distribution of Response Types for Task 1:
Written and then Spoken Picture Naming on
Each Trial (*N*=256 Trials)

Response Type	Written	Spoken
Correct/misspelled	159 (62%)	190 (74%)
Semantic/misspelled	43 (17%)	46 (18%)
No response	33 (13%)	19 (7%)
Neologism	10 (4%)	0
Other word	11 (4%)	1 (0.4%)
Total errors	97 (38%)	66 (26%)

signals the integrity of the phonological form that eventually mediated the written response. Thus we expect that correct spoken responses should typically be preceded on the same trial by correct written responses and, more importantly, that incorrect phonological responses should be preceded on the same trial by incorrect written responses. Critically we *do not* expect to find semantic errors and/or don't know responses in the spoken modality to be *preceded* by correct written responses.

This task should also allow us to observe the presence of those additional patterns of written and spoken naming that are clearly predicted by orthographic autonomy: different semantic errors in the two modalities, roughly synonymic responses in the two modalities, and correct spoken responses following semantic errors in writing.

Table 5 indicates that on 12 occasions PW's incorrect spoken responses were preceded by a correct [e.g. p(brush) → B-R-U-S-H + "comb"] or a recognisable written name [e.g. p(raccoon) → R-A-C-O-O-N-A + "sheep"]. In fact this critical pattern occurred on 12 of the 66 trials (Table 4) on which PW produced a spoken error. Additionally, as would be expected under orthographic autonomy, on 10 occasions PW produced different semantic errors in immediate succession in the 2 modalities [p(knife) → S-P-O-O-N + "fork"] as well as different "correct" responses in the 2 modalities (M-O-N-E-Y-S + "coins"; S-H-E-E-P + "lamb"). PW also produced 12 semantic errors in writing that were followed by a correct spoken response [p(lips) → N-A-I-L, "lips"].

TABLE 5
Number of Occurrences of the Critical Error Patterns for Task 1:
Written and Then Spoken Picture Naming

Examples	Write		Say	No.
p(brush)→	CORRECT/MISSPELL B-R-U-S-H	+	SEMANTIC "comb"	12
	CORRECT/MISSPELL		NO RESPONSE	0
p(thread)→	SEMANTIC 1 I-R-O-N	+	SEMANTIC 2 "thread"	10
p(sheep/lamb)→	CORRECT 1 S-H-E-E-P	+	CORRECT 2 "lamb"	2
p(lips)→	SEMANTIC/MISSPELL N-A-I-L	+	CORRECT "lips"	12

Actual examples are included (*correct/misspell* refers to responses that were the correct lexical choice; they may or may not have been spelled correctly; *semantic/misspell* refers to responses that were semantic errors; they may or may not have been spelled correctly).

In an architecture involving obligatory phonological mediation, an individual with a lexical level phonological deficit should not be able to write correctly a name that he/she cannot say, yet this pattern of responding was apparently attested on 18% of the trials on which PW produced a spoken error. In addition, all other patterns specifically predicted under orthographic autonomy were observed. On the basis of these results it appears that correct written responding cannot be explained away simply as the result of the opportunity for increased attempts at phonological retrieval afforded by a writing task. These results are problematic for obligatory phonological mediation and yet are entirely consistent with orthographic autonomy.

Phonological Mediation + Instability

One might argue, however, that superior written vs. spoken naming results by chance from instability in the availability of phonological forms. Under such a phonological mediation + instability account, the trials in which superior orthographic vs. phonological responding is exhibited simply represent occasions on which the correct phonological representation is unavailable at the time of the overt spoken response, but happens to become accessible at a point in time when a (covert) phonological form is being used as the basis for generating a correct written response. Such an account would save the phonological mediation claim by arguing that the differences in spoken and written responding simply reflect changes in the availability of the appropriate lexical *phonological* representations: At one point in time a correct phonological representation is accessed and serves as the basis for the appropriate written response; at another point in time the representation is no longer available and a semantic error or "don't know" response is produced in spoken naming.

In order to examine if the discrepancies between PW's spoken and written responses were stable, we administered three additional tasks that required PW to produce multiple written and spoken responses on each trial. In Task 2 PW was asked to Write/Say/Write each item name, in Task 3 he was asked to Say/Write/Say the name of each item and, finally, Task 4 required PW to Say/Write/Say/Write/Say/Write the name of each picture. We first present results from these three tasks that relate to the critical response types. We then go on to present an analysis carried out specifically to assess the reliability of superior written vs. spoken responding.

Task 2: Written/Spoken/Written Naming

We presented PW with 33 pictures and asked him to write, say, and then again write the name of each picture.

The results presented in Table 6 indicate that PW did not produce the correct spoken form on 11 trials. Additionally, the results reveal a highly similar overall distribution of responses for first and second written responses. However, we

TABLE 6
Distribution of Response Types for Task 2: Written,
Spoken, Written Picture Naming (N = 44 Trials)

Response Type	$Write_1$	Say_1	$Write_2$
Correct/misspelled	26 (59%)	33 (75%)	27 (61%)
Semantic	13 (30%)	6 (14%)	13 (30%)
No response	2 (5%)	5 (11%)	1 (2%)
Neologism	1 (2%)	0	1 (2%)
Other word	2 (5%)	0	2 (5%)
Total errors	18 (41%)	11 (25%)	17 (39%)

TABLE 7
Number of Occurrences of the Critical Error Patterns for Task 2: Written then Spoken
then Written Picture Naming on Each Trial

Examples	$Write_1$		Say_1		$Write_2$	No.
p(onion)→	CORRECT/MSP O-N-I-O-N	+	SEMANTIC "banana"	+	CORRECT/MSP O-N-I-O-N	1
p(pumpkin)→	CORRECT/MSP P-U-W-P-I-N	+	NO RESPONSE "don't know"	+	CORRECT/MSP P-U-M-P-I-N	3
p(table)→	SEMANTIC 1 D-E-N	+	SEMANTIC 2 "table"	+	SEMANTIC 1 D-E-N	1
	CORRECT 1		CORRECT 2		CORRECT 1	0
p(tongue)→	SEMANTIC T-E-E-T-H	+	CORRECT "tongue"	+	SEMANTIC T-E-E-T-H	7

Msp = misspell.

were specifically interested in determining if incorrect spoken responses could be preceded and followed by appropriate written responses. It was also important to determine if the three other patterns of responding predicted under orthographic autonomy would be reliably observed.

Table 7 indicates that there were four trials involving consistently superior written vs. spoken responding [e.g. p(onion) → O-N-I-O-N + "banana" + O-N-I-O-N]; three of these involved "don't know" responses in spoken naming and one involved a spoken semantic error. Thus, PW was consistently able to produce a correct written response on 4 of the 11 trials (36%) on which he produced a spoken error. With respect to the additional error types expected under orthographic autonomy: On one occasion a different semantic error was produced in the two modalities and on seven occasions semantic errors in writing were followed by correct spoken responses and again by the same

TABLE 8
Distribution of Response Types for Task 3: Spoken,
Written, Spoken Picture Naming (N = 368 Trials)

Response Type	Say_1	$Write_1$	Say_2
Correct/misspelled	292(79%)	239(65%)	298(81%)
Semantic	27 (7%)	51(14%)	25 (7%)
No response	49(13%)	40(11%)	45(12%)
Neologism	0	21 (6%)	0
Other word	0	17 (5%)	0
Total errors	76(21%)	129(35%)	70(19%)

TABLE 9
Number of Occurrences of the Critical Error Patterns for Task 3: Spoken then Written
then Spoken Picture Naming on Each Trial

Examples	Say_1		$Write_1$		$Say2$	No.
p(tiger)→	SEMANTIC "lion"	+	CORRECT/MSP T-I-G-E-R	+	SEMANTIC "lion"	2
p(bagel)→	NO RESPONSE "don't know"	+	CORRECT/MSP B-A-G-E-L	+	NO RESPONSE "don't know"	11
p(barrel)→	SEMANTIC 1 "bucket"	+	SEMANTIC 2 H-A-M-M-E-R	+	SEMANTIC 1 "bucket"	4
p(octopus/squid)→	CORRECT 1 "octopus"	+	CORRECT 2 S-Q-U-I-D	+	CORRECT 1 "octopus"	3
p(elbow)→	CORRECT "elbow"	+	SEMANTIC K-N-E-E	+	CORRECT "elbow"	20

Msp = misspell.

semantic error in writing [e.g. p(tongue) → T-E-E-T-H + "tongue" + T-E-E-T-H].

Task 3: Spoken/Written/Spoken Naming

With Task 3 we attempted to assess the possibility of correct orthographic responding in the context of *persistent* difficulties in spoken production: –Say_1/ + $Write_1$/–Say^2. We presented PW with 368 picture trials and asked him to say, write, and then again attempt to say, the name of each picture.

The distribution of overall response types is quite similar for first and second spoken naming trials (Table 8). Spoken errors were observed on 76 of the initial spoken responses. Importantly, Table 9 indicates that the pattern of good written naming in the face of persistent difficulties in spoken naming was observed on 13 of these 76 trials [e.g. p(tiger) → "lion" + T-I-G-E-R + "lion"; p(bagel) → "don't know" + B-A-G-E-L + "don't know"]. Additionally, on four trials different semantic errors were produced in the two modalities [p(tweezers) → "pliers" + N-E-E-D-L-E + "pliers"] and on three occasions different correct responses were produced ["hog" + P-I-G + "hog"]. Finally, semantic errors in writing were preceded and followed by correct spoken responses on 20 trials [p(spool) → "spool" + N-E-E-D-L-E + "spool"]

Task 4: Spoken/Written/Spoken/Written/Spoken/Written Naming

In order to push yet further at the possibility of appropriate written naming in the face of persistent errors in spoken naming, on each trial we asked PW to attempt to: say, write, say, write, say, and then write the name of each of 300 pictures. Recall that in our testing procedure PW is not permitted to look at the written responses until the entire trial is completed.

The overall distribution of response types are reported in Table 10. There were 38 trials involving an initial spoken error. In Table 11 we report the number of occurrences of the critical error patterns. We can see that, of the 38 trials involving an initial spoken error, there were 7 trials (18%) where an incorrect spoken response alternated with an appropriate written response throughout the course of the entire trial ($-Say_1/ + Write_1/-Say_2/ + Write_2/ - Say_3/ + Write_3$) [e.g. p(owl) → "turtle" O-W-L "turtle" O-W-L turtle O-W-L]. That is, although PW was consistently able to write the name of a pictured object, he was then repeatedly unable to produce the correct spoken form. Instead he systematically produced either a spoken semantic error (5/7) or a "don't know" response (2/7).

In addition, the other response patterns predicted by orthographic autonomy were also observed. There were 4 trials in which different semantic errors were consistently produced within each modality [e.g. p(hanging) → "throwing" T-O-U-C-H "hanging" T-O-U-C-H, etc.], 1 trial in which different correct responses were produced and 22 trials on which a correct spoken response was consistently followed by a semantic error in writing [e.g. p(shower) → "shower" T-O-I-L-E-T, etc.].

TABLE 10
Distribution of Response Types for Task 4: Spoken, Written, Spoken, Written, Spoken, Written Picture Naming (N = 299 trials)

Response Type	Say_1	$Write_1$	Say_2	$Write_2$	Say_3	$Write_3$
Correct/Msp	256(86%)	206(69%)	256(86%)	207(69%)	257(86%)	207(69%)
Semantic	21 (7%)	37(12%)	20 (7%)	32(11%)	18 (6%)	32(11%)
No response	17 (6%)	20 (7%)	18 (6%)	23 (8%)	19 (6%)	24 (8%)
Neologism	0	10 (3%)	0	12 (4%)	0	11 (4%)
Other word	0	26 (9%)	0	26 (9%)	0	26 (9%)
Total errors	38(14%)	93(31%)	38(14%)	93(31%)	37(14%)	93(31%)

Msp = misspell.

TABLE 11
Number of Occurrences of the Critical Error Patterns for Task 4: Spoken, Written, Spoken, Written, Spoken, Written Picture Naming on Each Trial

Examples	Say_1	$Write_1$	Say_2	$Write_2$	Say_3	$Write_3$	No.
p(owl)→	SEMANTIC "turtle"	CORR/MSP O-W-L	SEMANTIC "turtle"	CORR/MSP O-W-L	SEMANTIC "turtle"	CORR/MSP O-W-L	5
p(grapes)→	NO RESP "don't know"	CORR/MSP G-R-A-P-E	NO RESP "don't know"	CORR/MSP G-R-A-P-E	NO RESP "don't know"	CORR/MSP G-R-A-P-E	2
p(blouse)→	SEM 1 "sweater"	SEM 2 S-T-I-R-K	SEM 1 "sweater"	SEM 2 S-T-I-R-K	SEM 1 "sweater"	SEM 2 S-T-I-R-K	4
p(pillow)→	CORRECT "pillow"	SEMANTIC B-E-D	CORRECT "pillow"	SEMANTIC B-E-D	CORRECT "pillow"	SEMANTIC B-E-D	21
p(diaper)→	CORR 1 "Pampers"	CORR 2 D-I-A-P-A-M	CORR 1 "Pampers"	CORR 2 D-I-A-P-A-M	CORR 1 "Pampers"	CORR 2 D-I-A-P-A-M	1

Corr = correct; Msp = misspell; Sem = semantic; Corr = correct.

Evaluation of the Phonological Mediation + Instability Hypothesis

The results of Tasks 2–4 indicate that PW often consistently produced the correct lexical item in writing in the face of persistent failure in producing its spoken form. Of course, under the phonological mediation + instability hypothesis some number of such trials might be expected by chance. In order to evaluate whether the observed consistency is greater than that expected by chance, we must also take into account how many *in*consistent sequences were produced.

Under the phonological mediation + instability hypothesis, if the accuracy of a written response depends on the availability of the appropriate phonological form and, furthermore, if this availability changes over time, then the observation of a correct written response should not be specifically predictive of the accuracy of subsequent written responses on that trial. That is, subsequent responses—written or spoken—on a given trial will be correct or incorrect depending on the stability of the *phonological* form; accuracy should not be systematically related to output modality. Specifically, the expectation for those critical trials initiated by an incorrect spoken response and correct written response ($-Say_1/+Write_1$) is that the accuracy of subsequent spoken and written responses should be comparable. Or, because of additional problems in the orthography, for subsequent within-trial responses *spoken accuracy should be superior to, but certainly no less than, written accuracy*. The hypothesis of orthographic autonomy makes a contrasting prediction: The pattern of superior written vs. spoken responding at the beginning of a trial is a reflection of the integrity of independent underlying phonological and orthographic forms and therefore under orthographic autonomy the prediction is that on $-Say_1/+Write_1$ trials, subsequent within-trial responses should *show consistently superior written vs. spoken responding*.

Written vs. Spoken Responding

In order to evaluate these contrasting predictions, we considered all of those trials in Tasks 2, 3, and 4 that began with the critical $-Say_1/+Write_1$ response pattern. If it is true that the observed superiority of written responding on these trials resulted from the chance availability of the correct (covert) phonological form, then on each trial subsequent spoken responses (Say_2 in Expt. 3; Say_2 and Say_3 in Expt. 4) should be correct no less often than the subsequent written ones ($Write_2$ in Expt. 2; $Write_2$ and $Write_3$ in Expt. 4).

In Task 2 there were a total of 4 trials starting with $+Write_1/-Say_1$; in Task 3 there were 16 trials beginning with $-Say_1 + Write_1$; in Task 4 there were a total of 9 trials initiated by correct written and incorrect spoken responding. Table 12 reports the accuracy of subsequent written and spoken responses on these critical trials. The results indicate that on trials initiated with a correct

TABLE 12
Accuracy of Subsequent Written and Spoken
Responses on Trials Initiated with a Correct Written
and Incorrect Spoken Response

	$-Say_1/+Write_1$ (N)	$+ Write_{2,3}$	$+ Say_{2,3}$
Task 2	4	100% (4/4)	–
Task 3	16	–	19%(3/16)
Task 4	9	100%(18/18)	22%(4/18)
Totals	29	100%(22/22)	21%(7/34)

written and an incorrect spoken sequence, 100% (22/22) of subsequent written responses were correct lexical choices, but only 21% (7/34) of the subsequent spoken responses were correct [$\chi^2(1,53) = 28.6$, $P<.001$). Yet, as indicated earlier, if superior written vs. spoken responses result simply from changes in the availability of phonological forms, then the initial responses should not predict that subsequent written (Write$_{2,3}$) should be any more accurate than subsequent spoken (Say$_{2,3}$) ones. These results reveal strong within-modality consistency and clearly render untenable the possibility that superior written vs. spoken responding may have resulted merely from phonological mediation via inconsistently available phonological forms.

Summary of Experimental Results

Across the four experimental tasks PW was administered 958 picture trials for written and spoken naming, involving a total of 3488 responses. Of these picture naming trials, 20% (191/958) involved initial spoken errors—nearly half of these were semantic errors and the rest were "don't know" responses. In terms of the issues that these tasks were designed to address, the results indicate that on 19% of trials involving spoken errors (36/191), PW consistently produced an appropriate written response. That is, in spite of considerable damage to the orthographic lexicon, PW was able to produce the appropriate lexical orthographic form on one out of five occasions on which he was unable to produce the appropriate spoken form. Furthermore, we have shown that this response pattern cannot be attributed to instability in the availability of correct phonological forms. In addition, all other error patterns expected under the orthographic autonomy hypothesis were observed: 19 of the 100 trials involving semantic errors in spoken naming involved the consistent production of a different semantic error in written production; on 6 trials, correct but different synonymic responses were produced in the two modalities, and 61 trials involved a correct spoken response accompanied by a semantic error in writing.

The evidence that is problematic for obligatory phonological mediation seems to be clear and overwhelming: Consistently appropriate written responses can be produced in the context of the persistent inability to produce the spoken form. We now make one further attempt to salvage the hypothesis of obligatory phonological mediation.

Phonological Mediation via Impoverished Phonological Material

An alternative interpretation of the data that would preserve an architecture of obligatory phonological mediation might be suggested by the fact that the subjects previously reported with a pattern of semantic errors restricted to the spoken modality typically produce written responses containing orthographic distortions: p(thumb) → T-__-M-B, p(envelope) → E-N-V-O-L-E-P-E, p(banana) → B-A-N-A-S-H-A (Caramazza & Hillis, 1990; Nickels, 1992). For example, RGB produced these written errors at a rate of 80% and approximately 90% of HW's written responses contained spelling errors (Caramazza & Hillis, 1990). This raises the possibility that *impoverished, partial* phonological representations of target items *are* retrieved and, in fact, serve as the basis for orthographic retrieval. According to this account, it is the inadequacy of the phonological representations that results in the orthographic distortions. The difference between phonological and orthographic response types (semantic errors vs. misspellings) is due to the fact that, although there are no restrictions on the production of orthographically distorted forms, phonological distortions may be such that they cannot be articulated. In those cases the subject may provide a circumlocution, a "don't know" response or, when another related and intact phonological representation is available, a semantic error[6]. In this way, this hypothesis would allow one to maintain phonological mediation, albeit via "inadequate" phonological material. Recall that under orthographic autonomy the misspellings arise from a post-lexical locus such as the graphemic buffer.

The possibility that distorted, partial lexical phonological forms underlie PW's appropriate written responses can be rejected for two reasons. First, this scenario is improbable in light of the absence of any evidence of phonological distortions in PW's spoken production as well as the finding that phonological variables (length, complexity) do not contribute to his spoken error rates. One would have to argue that the distortion of phonological lexical forms never manifests itself except through errors in writing. Clearly, this is not only ad hoc but also irrefutable. Second, we can examine spelling accuracy on +Write/–Say

---

[6] The orthographic responses need not be faithful reflections of the available phonological material. That is, it is not necessarily the case that the fact that D-O-K-E-Y is produced means that the mediating phonological material consisted of /douki/.

trials where, until now, we have grouped together both correctly spelled and misspelled correct lexical choices. When we do so, we find (across the four tasks) that written responses on the critical + Write/–Say trials were correctly spelled fully 61% of the time. Thus, it is simply not the case that the pattern of superior written vs. spoken responding occurs only in the context of misspellings. Both of these reasons make it difficult to sustain a hypothesis of obligatory phonological mediation via impoverished phonological material.

DISCUSSION

We have described the performance of an individual who is often unable to produce the correct spoken name of an item although he is able to produce its written name. We have shown that this individual demonstrates the two critical features that are necessary for such a performance pattern to be used as evidence against obligatory phonological mediation: (1) the deficit in spoken production can be characterised as one affecting the retrieval of lexical phonological forms and (2) a pattern of consistently superior written vs. spoken naming is observed for the same items on the very same trials. Given that under the obligatory phonological mediation hypothesis this conjunction of events should never occur, the hypothesis would seem to be invalidated. We have specifically considered and rejected the possibility that these results could be attributed either to the instability of phonological representations or to phonological mediation via impoverished phonological representations. We now consider the issue of optional phonological mediation (see Miceli, Benvegnù, Capasso, & Caramazza, this issue, for additional discussion).

As we indicated in the Introduction, our goal with this study was to examine the hypothesis of *obligatory* phonological mediation—the claim that orthographic lexical forms *cannot* be retrieved without prior access to their corresponding phonological lexical forms. With the earlier discussion we hope to have dealt with possible remaining concerns regarding the strength of the relevant evidence. We have argued that the findings presented here convincingly deal with the inadequacies in the previously existing results and that they demonstrate that orthographic lexical forms can indeed be retrieved without prior access to the corresponding lexical phonological representations. We can also ask if *optional* phonological mediation occurs in written language production.

The evidence that points to the possibility of optional phonological mediation in production is basically of two types. First, there is the strong subjective experience that most people report of "hearing" themselves while they are writing. Second, certain classes of written errors that normal, unimpaired subjects produce seem to have a phonological basis—writing HERE for HEAR, for example. We shall briefly consider each of these in turn.

The subjective experience of listening to oneself as one is writing can be interpreted in at least two ways. One possibility is that, indeed, in those situations we are engaging in phonologically mediated writing. The second is that the covert production of spoken forms plays no causal role in orthographic retrieval but is simply a *concomitant* process. That is, having generated a message to be communicated and having selected the corresponding lexical semantic items to be used in expressing the message, we then proceed—as a matter of course, albeit unnecessarily—to retrieve both written *and* spoken forms. A similar point can be made with respect to the subjective experience of hearing words as we read. It does not imply that we *must* retrieve the phonological form before we are able to understand the meaning of the printed stimulus; it may simply be that we *also* retrieve the phonological form in the course of processing the written item. Thus, although the subjective experience is compelling it certainly does not require that we posit phonological mediation. In this regard, it is interesting that the individual described by Levine et al. (1982) (see also Martin et al., 1995) was described as lacking the experience of inner speech, yet he was able to write coherent sentences and paragraphs.

A stronger case can be made for optional phonological mediation from evidence provided from normal writing errors—slips of the pen. The error type that most clearly points to the role of phonology in orthographic retrieval are homophone substitutions—writing HEAR for HERE, SEEN for SCENE, YOUR for YOU'RE—and, to a lesser extent, structurally similar word substitutions—SURGE for SEARCH, A NUMBER for ANOTHER, COULD for GOOD. Hotopf (1983) attempts to determine if the basis for these substitutions is phonemic or orthographic. He does so by calculating the extent to which the written homophone and similar word substitutions share phonemes and graphemes with the intended target words. He then compares this with the proportion of graphemes and phonemes shared between targets and errors in *spoken* slips. As Hotopf himself indicates, the results are not definitive. Although for spoken and written slips involving open-class items, target words and errors share, on average, a slightly greater number of phonemes than graphemes, the effect is reversed for closed-class items. Furthermore, a consideration of the individual errors in all categories indicates many instances in which targets and errors share greater numbers of graphemes than phonemes. The difficulty in using this type of analysis derives from the large degree of overlap between phonological and orthographic units—words that are phonologically similar will also be orthographically similar and vice versa.

However, even if the analysis of slips of the pen had clearly shown their phonological origin, the results would still be open to a number of interpretations. The first possibility, of course, is that these errors reflect optional phonological mediation. A second possibility is that the errors result from connections made between semantics and orthography in the course of learning. If, for example, in learning there was confusion in establishing HEAR vs.

HERE as the appropriate orthographic form for the meaning [listen] then, to the extent to which those associations remain in adulthood, they may serve as the source of occasional error. A third possibility is that the homophone and structurally similar word confusions are the consequence of concomitant phonological processes. This alternative depends on the following: (1) phonological forms are (often or even typically) retrieved in the course of writing and (2) when these phonological forms are subjectively "heard" they do, in fact, engage a number of the mechanisms dedicated to auditory comprehension. In that case, /hir/ may be retrieved when the semantics of /listen/ is activated in the course of preparing a written message. Given that auditory comprehension mechanisms use phonological information to access the phonological lexicon, we expect /hir/ to activate any identical, and, presumably, similar lexical entries. Thus, lexical entries for "hear" and "here" should both receive activation. The activation of these lexical entries may, in turn, result in the passing on of activation through semantics and on to the orthographic lexicon. When that occurs there may be occasions where both H-E-A-R and H-E-R-E are active when the time comes to retrieve the written form. Occasional confusions would not then be surprising. This scenario is especially plausible if we consider that written production processes are considerably slower than speech processes (Hotopf, 1980).

In sum, none of the available evidence requires that we adopt optional phonological mediation in written language production. However, the possibility of optional phonological mediation is an important one that merits, and presumably is amenable to, further empirical scrutiny. If it turns out that both autonomous orthographic retrieval and optional phonological mediation are possible, we need to consider the following questions: With what frequency and under what circumstances are these two options employed? Does optional phonological mediation occur via direct lexical–lexical connections (Fig. 1c) or via sublexical connections (Fig. 1d)?

This paper focuses specifically on the question of *obligatory* phonological mediation. In this context, we have been able to: (1) document a pattern of consistently correct written responding in the face of persistently incorrect spoken production; (2) we have considered and rejected a number of alternative interpretations of this pattern that would allow us to retain obligatory phonological mediation; and finally (3) we have reported the full range of error patterns expected under orthographic autonomy. On this basis we conclude that orthographic lexical forms can indeed be independently accessed for production without an obligatory mediating role for phonology.

REFERENCES

Alajouanine, T., & Lhermitte, F. (1960). Les troubles des activités expressives du langage dans l'aphasie. Leurs relations avec les apraxies. *Revue Neurologique, 102,* 604–629.

Archangeli, D.B. (1985). Yokuts harmony: Evidence for coplanar representation in nonlinear phonology. *Linguistic Inquiry, 16*, 335–372.
Assal, G., Buttet, J., & Jolivet, R. (1981). Dissociations in aphasia: A case report. *Brain and Language, 13*, 223–240.
Basso, A., Taborelli, A., & Vignolo, L.A. (1978). Dissociated disorders of speaking and writing in aphasia. *Journal of Neurology, Neurosurgery and Psychiatry, 41*, 556–563.
Brown, J.W. (1972). *Aphasia, apraxia and agnosia*. Springfield, IL: Charles C. Thomas.
Bub, D., & Kertesz, A. (1982). Evidence for lexicographic processing in a patient with preserved written over oral single word naming. *Brain, 105*, 697–717.
Buckingham, H., & Kertesz, A. (1976). *Neologistic jargon aphasia*. Amsterdam: Swets & Zeitlinger.
Butterworth, B. (1979). Hesitation and production of verbal paraphasias and neologisms in jargon aphasia. *Brain and Language, 8*, 133–161.
Butterworth, B. (1992). Disorders of phonological encoding. *Cognition, 42*, 261–286.
Caramazza, A., Berndt, R., & Basili, A. (1983). The selective impairment of phonological processing: A case study. *Brain and Language, 18*, 128–174.
Caramazza, A., & Hillis, A. (1990). Where do semantic errors come from? *Cortex, 26*, 95–122.
Carroll, J.B., Davies, P., & Richman, B. (1971). *Word frequency book*. NY: American Heritage.
Coslett, H.B., Gonzalez-Rothi, L.J., & Heilman, K.M. (1984). Reading: Selective sparing of closed-class words in Wernicke's aphasia. *Neurology, 34*, 1038–1045.
Dell, G. (1989). The retrieval of phonological forms in production: Tests of predictions from a connectionist model. In W. Marslen-Wilson (Ed.), *Lexical representation and process*. Cambridge, MA: MIT Press.
Ellis, A.E. (1982). Spelling and writing (and reading and speaking). In A. Ellis (Ed.), *Normality and pathology in cognitive functions*. NY: Academic Press.
Ellis, A., Miller, D., & Sin, G. (1983). Wernicke's aphasia and normal language processing: A case study in cognitive neuropsychology. *Cognition, 15*, 111–144.
Friederici, A.D., Schoenle, P.W., & Goodglass, H. (1981). Mechanisms underlying writing and speech in aphasia. *Brain and Language, 13*, 212–222.
Frith, U. (1979). Reading by eye and writing by ear. In P.A. Kolers, M. Wrolstad, & H. Bouma (Eds.), *Processing of visible language, 1*. New York: Plenum Press.
Geschwind, N. (1969). Problems in the anatomical understanding of aphasia. In A.L. Benton (Ed.), *Contributions of clinical neuropsychology*. Chicago, IL: University of Chicago Press.
Grashey, H. (1885). On aphasia and its relations to perception (Über Aphasie und ihre Beziehungen zur Wahrnehmung). *Archiv für Psychiatrie und Nervenkrankheiten, 16*, 654–688. (English version [1989]. *Cognitive Neuropsychology, 6*, 515–546.)
Head, H. (1926). *Aphasia and kindred disorders of speech*. London: Cambridge University Press.
Hecaen, H., & Angelergues, R. (1965). *Pathologie du language, Vol. 1*. Paris: Larousse.
Hier, D.B., & Mohr, J.P. (1977). Incongruous oral and written naming. *Brain and Language, 4*, 115–126.
Hillis, A.E., & Caramazza, A. (1991). Mechanisms for accessing lexical representations for output: Evidence from a category-specific semantic deficit. *Brain and Language, 40*, 106–144.
Hillis, A.E., & Caramazza, A. (1995). Converging evidence for the interaction of semantic and sublexical phonological information in accessing lexical representations for spoken output. *Cognitive Neuropsychology, 12*, 187–227.
Hotopf, N. (1980). Slips of the pen. In U. Frith (Ed.), *Cognitive processes in spelling*. London: Academic Press.
Hotopf, W.H.N. (1983). Lexical slips of the pen and tongue: What they tell us about language production. In B. Butterworth (Ed.), *Language Production, Vol. 2*. London: Academic Press.
Kiparsky, P. (1982). From cyclic phonology to lexical phonology. In H. van der Hulst & N. Smith (Eds.), *The structure of phonological representations: Part 1*. Dordrecht: Foris.

Lecours, A.R., & Rouillon, F. (1976). Neurolinguistic analysis of jargonaphasia and jargonagraphia. In H. Whitaker & H. Whitaker (Eds.), *Studies in neurolinguistics, Vol. 2*. New York: Academic Press.
Leischner, A. (1969). The agraphias. In P.G. Vinken & G.W. Bruyn (Eds.), *Handbook of clinical neurology, Vol. 4*. Amsterdam: North-Holland.
Levelt, W.J.M. (1989). *Speaking*. Cambridge, MA: MIT Press.
Levine, D.N., Calvanio, R., & Popovics, A. (1982). Language in the absence of inner speech. *Neuropsychologia, 4*, 391–409.
Lhermitte, F., & Dérouesné, J. (1974). Paraphasies et jargonaphasie dans le langage oral avec conservation du langage écrit. *Revue Neurologique, 130*, 21–38.
Lichtheim, L. (1885). On aphasia (Über Aphasie). *Deutsches Archiv für klinische Medizin, 36*, 204–268. (English version: *Brain, 7*, 433–485).
Luria, A.R. (1966). *Higher cortical functions in man*. New York: Basic Books.
Martin, R.C., Blossom-Stach, C., Yaffee, L.S., & Wetzel, W.F. (1995). Consequences of a motor programming deficit for rehearsal and written language comprehension. *Quarterly Journal of Experimental Psychology: Human Experimental Psychology, 48A*(3), 536–572.
Miceli, G., & Caramazza, A. (1993). The assignment of word stress in oral reading: Evidence from a case of acquired dyslexia. *Cognitive Neuropsychology, 10*, 273–295.
Mohr, J.P., Pessin, M.S., Finkelstein, S., Funkenstein, H., Duncan, G.W., & Davis, K.R. (1978). Broca's aphasia: Pathologic and clinical. *Neurology, 28*, 311–324.
Mohr, J.P., Sidman, M., Stoddart, L.T., Leicester, J., & Rosenberger, P.B. (1973). Evolution of the deficit in total aphasia. *Neurology, 23*, 311–324.
Nickels, L. (1992). The autocue? Self-generated phonemic cues in the treatment of a disorder of reading and naming. *Cognitive Neuropsychology, 9*, 155–182.
Patterson, K.E., & Marcel, A.J. (1977). Aphasia, dyslexia and the phonological coding of written words. *Quarterly Journal of Experimental Psychology, 29*, 307–317.
Patterson, K., & Shewell, C. (1987). Speak and spell: Dissociations and word-class effects. In M. Coltheart, G. Sartori, & R. Job (Eds.), *The cognitive neuropsychology of language*. London: Lawrence Erlbaum Associates Ltd.
Perfetti, D., & Bell, L. (1991). Phonemic activation during the first forty milliseconds of word identification: Evidence from backward masking and priming. *Journal of Memory and Language, 30*, 473–485.
Rapp, B., & Caramazza, A. (1993). On the distinction between deficits of access and deficits of storage: A question of theory. *Cognitive Neuropsychology, 10*, 113–141.
Rapp, B., & Caramazza, A. (1997). The modality specific organization of grammatical categories: Evidence from impaired spoken and written sentence production. *Brain and Language, 56*, 248–286.
Semenza, C., Cipolotti, L., & Denes, G. (1992). Reading aloud in jargonaphasia: An unusual dissociation in speech output. *Journal of Neurology, Neurosurgery and Psychiatry, 55*, 205–208.
Shaffer, L.H. (1976). Intention and performance. *Psychological Review, 83*, 375–393.
Shattuck-Hufnagel, S. (1987). The role of word-onset consonants in speech production planning: New evidence from speech error patterns. In E. Keller & M. Gopnik (Eds.), *Motor and sensory processes of language*. Hillsdale, NJ: Lawrence Erlbaum Associates Inc.
Snodgrass, J., & Vanderwort, M. (1980). A standardized set of 260 pictures: Norms for name agreement, image agreement, familiarity, and visual complexity. *Journal of Experimental Psychology: Human Learning and Memory, 6*(2), 174–215.
Van Orden, G.C., Johnston, J.C., & Hale, B.L. (1988). Word identification in reading proceeds from spelling to sound to meaning. *Journal of Experimental Psychology: Learning, Memory, and Cognition, 14*, 371–386.

Wernicke, C. (1816). Neurology: Recent contributions on aphasia (Nervenheilkunde. Die neueren Arbeiten über Aphasie). *Fortshcritte der Medizin, 4*, 463–482. (English version [1989]. *Cognitive Neuropsychology, 6*, 547–569.)

Further Evidence of a Dissociation between Output Phonological and Orthographic Lexicons: A Case Study

Jennifer R. Shelton and Michael Weinrich

University of Maryland School of Medicine, Baltimore, USA

We describe a patient who is significantly better at written picture naming than at spoken picture naming. His difficulty in oral production is argued to result from damage to lexical-phonological output processing, suggesting that activation of lexical-phonological output is not necessary to support writing. Nor can his writing be supported by phoneme-to-grapheme conversion rules, as evidenced by a complete inability to write nonwords to dictation. In addition, his reading comprehension appears to be independent of phonological mediation, due to severely impaired phoneme-to-grapheme conversion abilities and impaired understanding of aurally presented words when these words are presented without supporting context. It is argued that writing and reading comprehension do not *require* the generation of a phonological representation.

INTRODUCTION

Traditionally, neuropsychologists thought that the ability to write was dependent on the generation of phonology (e.g. Dejerine, 1914; Luria, 1970; cited in Ellis, 1988; Wernicke, 1908, cited in Bub & Chertkow, 1988). It was proposed that successful writing required a person to say the word to themselves, translate the internally generated sounds into a string of letters, and finally write those letters. This idea has been termed the "phonic mediation theory" of writing (e.g.

Requests for reprints should be addressed to Jennifer Shelton, who is now at Harvard University, William James Hall-Room 910, Dept. of Psychology, 33 Kirkland St., Cambridge, MA 02138 (email:jshelton@wjh.harvard.edu).

This research was supported by NIDCD Grant RO1–00856 to the University of Maryland Medical School. The authors would like to thank Dr. Rita Berndt for referring EA to us, making available various tests, and for comments on an early version of the manuscript. We also would like to thank Dr. Sarah Wayland, Denise McCall, Brenda Rapp, and Gabriele Miceli for their comments on earlier versions of the manuscript. Our sincere gratitude is extended to EA for his willing and steadfast participation in this study.

© 1997 Psychology Press, an imprint of Erlbaum (UK) Taylor & Francis Ltd

Ellis, 1988). Although once a quite popular theory, a number of neuropsychological reports concerning aphasic patients whose written output is superior to their spoken output have challenged this view (e.g. Assal, Buttet, & Jolivet, 1981; Bub & Kertesz, 1982; Caramazza, Berndt, & Basili, 1983; Ellis, Miller, & Sin, 1983; Hier & Mohr, 1977; Kremin, 1987; Levine, Calvanio, & Popovics, 1982; Patterson & Shewell, 1987). For example, Bub and Kertesz (1982) report that their patient, MH, could name very few pictures orally but wrote the picture names correctly. Further, she could not select objects whose names rhymed, indicating little knowledge of the phonology associated with the object names. MH's pattern of performance suggests that her writing was not supported by the inner generation of the sounds of words.

A case described by Shallice (1981) also provides evidence that writing is possible without phonetic knowledge. His patient, PR, was able to write words successfully but was unable to write nonwords (which he could repeat). Shallice interpreted PR's inability to write nonwords as evidence that he could not generate the letters corresponding to the sounds of the stimuli. Successful writing, in this case, could not have been supported by the mediation of sublexical phonological processing.

The notion that writing can occur without phonological support can be interpreted within an information processing model that describes specific components responsible for different aspects of cognitive processing. For example, consider the functional architecture presented in Fig. 1 (taken from Patterson & Shewell, 1987)[1]. In this model, the spoken and written language processing components are represented independently[2]. According to this model, writing is achieved by phoneme-to-grapheme conversion rules, by

---

[1] The model predicts differences in performance between input and output processing, as evidenced by a separation of input and output lexicons. The issue of separate or communal input and output representations for phonological and orthographic representations is debated (see, for example, Allport, 1984; Howard & Franklin, 1988; Monsell, 1987; Shallice, 1988). Due to the underspecified nature of the models, data that support separate input and output processors can usually be accommodated by a single lexicon by making new but not necessarily unreasonable assumptions. Until models are developed that make specific claims about representation and processing, the issue will remain unresolved. It is also important to note that we will consider the cognitive system and the semantic system to be the same thing. Although some researchers separate a cognitive system from a semantic system (e.g. Howard & Franklin, 1988), the issue is not relevant in this paper.

[2] We will be reporting results from a number of language processing tasks and will interpret our patient's pattern of performance using the model shown in Fig. 1. Thus, the components and/or processes represent a number of language comprehension and production abilities and not only written word production. Note that this particular model does not specify a component for visual analysis/object recognition. We assume that such a component exists to allow interpretation of pictures, and that there is a connection between visual analysis and the cognitive system.

direct activation of the orthographic output lexicon from semantics, and/or by direct activation of the orthographic output lexicon from the phonological output lexicon. That is, successful word writing can occur through the lexical system, via activation from semantics to the appropriate item in the orthographic output lexicon, and/or via activation from semantics to the appropriate item in the phonological output lexicon, which in turn activates the orthographic entry corresponding to that item. Successful writing can also occur sublexically, via implementation of phoneme-to-grapheme conversion rules that specify the appropriate orthographic representation by converting phonological word forms onto graphemic strings.

This model easily accommodates the reports of patients who show dissociations in performance between writing (words and nonwords) and speaking. For example, patients who cannot write nonwords but who can write regular and irregular words are assumed to have a breakdown in their ability to convert phonological information to graphemic information (e.g. Shallice, 1981). In this case, information stored in the orthographic output lexicon is used to write, and it is possible that lexical-phonological information activated from the phonological output lexicon could also support writing. On the other hand, the patient reported by Bub and Kertesz (1982) appears to activate information in the orthographic output lexicon directly from semantics, given the poor performance on rhyming tasks and nonword writing. This pattern of performance suggests that their patient was not using any phonological information to determine the accurate spelling of a word. However, the limited scope of their investigation makes it difficult to draw any strong conclusions concerning the role of lexical phonology in writing.

An impaired pattern of spelling performance that relies mainly on phonological information can also be accounted for by the model presented in Fig. 1. Patients who cannot write irregular words, make regularisation errors when attempting to write these words (e.g. yacht → yot), but write nonwords and regular words successfully, are assumed to have a breakdown in their ability to access and use information in the orthographic output lexicon (e.g. Coltheart & Funnell, 1987; Hatfield & Patterson, 1983). In this case, phoneme-to-grapheme conversion rules are used to write.

Although neuropsychological evidence suggests that writing may not be completely dependent on the internal generation of phonology, several researchers have argued that writing may require some sublexical phonological processing (e.g. Dodd, 1980; Frith, 1980; Nolan & Caramazza, 1983; see Barry, 1994; and Ellis, 1988, for reviews). For example, Nolan and Caramazza argued that portions of familiar irregular words, whose spelling does not correspond to their phonology, are stored in memory. The orthographic fragments provide the framework for writing the word. Sublexical phoneme-to-grapheme conversion processes then "fill in" the predictable parts of the word. One problem for this argument is that only a few word elements can be predicted with phoneme-

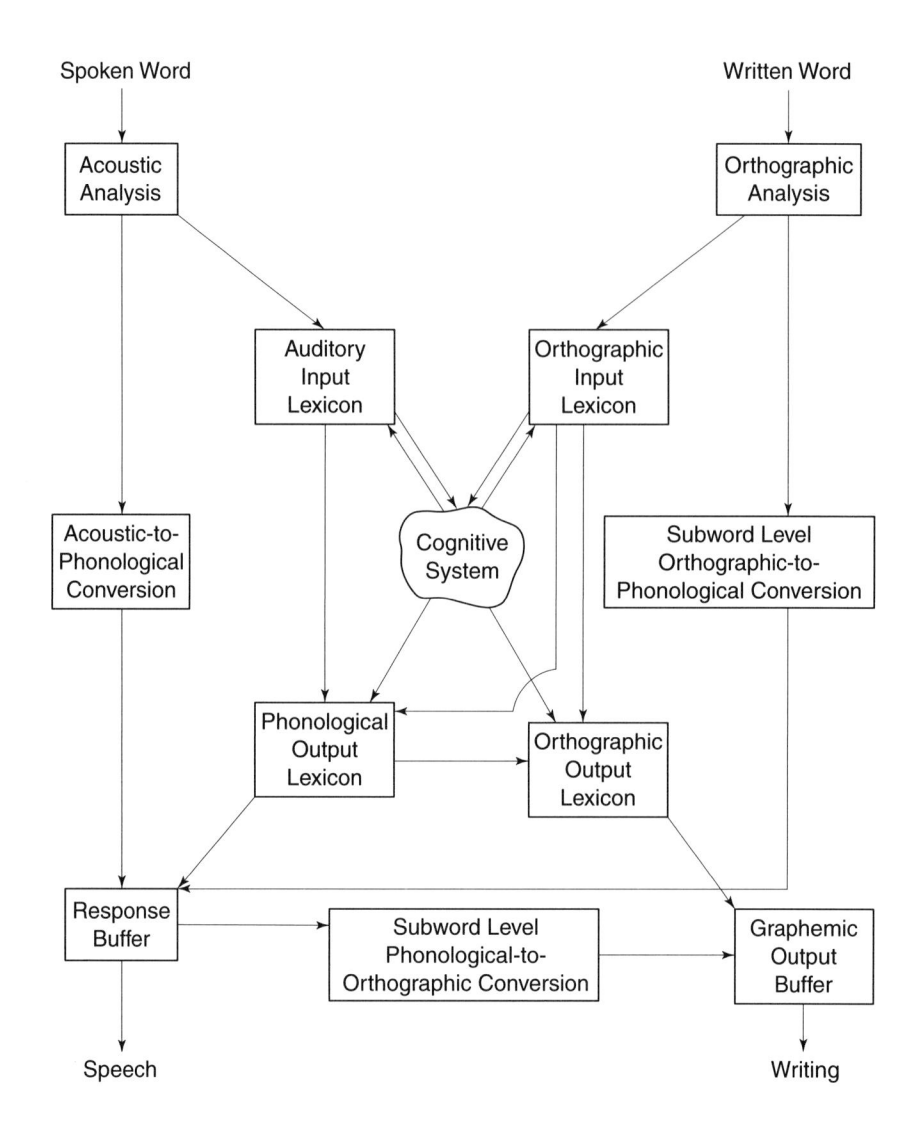

FIG. 1. A processing model of word and nonword recognition, comprehension, and production, taken from Patterson and Shewell (1987).

to-grapheme conversion processes (Ellis, 1988). A second problem for this argument comes from the data reported for the patient described earlier, who writes words successfully but cannot write nonwords (Shallice, 1981).

Barry (1994) points out, however, that there have been no reports of patients who are completely successful in word writing and completely unsuccessful in nonword writing, suggesting that some contribution of phonology might be required in word writing. The few successful written nonword productions achieved by previously reported patients do not necessarily rule out this possibility. That is, the patients must have had some sublexical phonological conversion abilities to produce a correct nonword, even though these abilities were extremely limited. Nevertheless, it is commonly believed that sublexical phonological processing abilities are not a critical support for successful word writing (see Ellis, 1988).

A second issue surrounding the role of phonology in writing concerns the activation of information in the orthographic output lexicon via activation of information in the phonological output lexicon. According to the model presented in Fig. 1, writing could be achieved by activating a phonological form from semantics and subsequently activating the orthographic form corresponding to the phonological form. Thus, a patient could have impaired sublexical phonological abilities yet writing would still be mediated phonologically, through support from the phonological output lexicon. As argued by others in this issue (see Miceli, Benvegnù, Capasso, & Caramazza; Rapp, Benzing, & Caramazza), if writing is supported by information from the phonological output lexicon, damage to the phonological output lexicon should result in similar performance in speaking and writing. If, however, writing can be achieved independently of the generation of phonology, damage that is localised at both lexical and sublexical phonological output processing should have little or no influence on writing performance (and/or responses should be different for writing and reading—see Miceli et al. and Rapp et al., this issue, for arguments concerning inconsistent responses between the two production modalities).

The patient described in this paper (EA) demonstrates successful *written* naming of pictured items but very poor *oral* naming of these same items. Further, he fails *completely* at writing nonwords to dictation, suggesting no need for support of sublexical phonological conversion abilities to write words successfully. No patients, to date, have been reported who cannot write any nonwords to dictation. His difficulty in spoken word production is argued to result from damage to phonological output, damage either in accessing information in the lexicon and/or to the lexicon itself. Previous reports of patients who present with superior written naming as opposed to verbal naming have not demonstrated explicitly that the level of damage is to the lexical output lexicon, thus leaving open the suggestion that poor verbal naming results from a postlexical deficit(s). EA's word and nonword naming abilities are extremely limited but word and nonword repetition performance is much better. Writing words to dictation is very impaired. Finally, the patient's auditory and reading comprehension are quite good.

Given this pattern of performance, we will argue that orthographic output is *not* dependent on sublexical or lexical-phonologic mediation. EA's oral picture naming deficit will be argued to result from a deficit at the lexical-phonological output level and sublexical phonological procedures will be argued to be nonexistent due to a complete inability to write nonwords to dictation (even though it is clear that EA understood the task). This finding eliminates any role of sublexical phoneme-to-grapheme conversion in writing, either by itself or in some way combined with impoverished lexical phonological output processing. Thus, EA is argued to have severely impaired lexical and sublexical phonological output processing capabilities, but still successfully writes picture names, indicating that writing can be achieved independently of phonological mediation.

In addition to providing evidence for orthographic autonomy in writing, EA's data may address the issue of phonologic mediation in reading. Van Orden and colleagues (e.g. Van Orden, 1991; Van Orden, Johnston, & Hale, 1988) have argued that phonologic mediation is "fundamental" (Van Orden, 1991) to reading comprehension. Van Orden et al. (1988) present several experiments demonstrating that subjects falsely classify nonword homophones (e.g. sute) into semantic categories (e.g. article of clothing) significantly more often than visually related controls (e.g. surt). Based on this result, and other evidence concerning processing of phonologically related word homophones, Van Orden et al. argue that phonologic mediation is necessarily involved in reading. Further, they suggest that no unambiguous evidence exists to support the evidence of a direct connection between an orthographic input lexicon and semantics.

EA's data can provide some evidence that specifically addresses the issue of obligatory phonologic mediation in reading. His reading comprehension will be shown to be quite good, whereas nonword reading will be shown to be extremely impaired. Moreover, the nonword reading difficulties cannot be the result of either poor spoken output, as we will demonstrate that EA can repeat words and nonwords, or the result of poor orthographic input processing, as we will demonstrate that EA's reading comprehension is quite good. We will argue that EA has difficulty accessing semantics from the phonological input lexicon, since he demonstrates impaired writing to dictation that is improved when the target word is presented in context. If phonologic mediation is fundamental to reading, we would expect that damage to phonological input processing to result in poor reading comprehension, especially when sublexical phonological processing is so severely impaired. We will argue that EA's data provide evidence that an orthographic input lexicon is directly connected to semantics, as shown in the model presented in Fig. 1.

PATIENT DESCRIPTION

EA is a 64-year-old right-handed male who suffered a cerebral vascular accident in 1983. CT scans revealed damage to the posterior left frontal lobe extending into the left anterior temporal lobe and ventral aspect of the basal gangliar region; this lesion also extends into the left parietal lobe. EA suffers from a severe nonfluent aphasia and right upper and lower hemiparesis. Although he has some limitations in his right limbs, EA drives himself to our lab, delivers food for Meals on Wheels, and delivers blood to various sites for the Red Cross. EA holds a master's degree in engineering and was CEO of an engineering firm at the time of his stroke.

Prior to this study, EA had undergone extensive speech therapy in a number of settings, including a residential 9-month programme, and several psycholinguistic treatments (Haendiges, Berndt, & Mitchum, 1996; Mitchum, Haendiges, & Berndt, 1993; Weinrich, Shelton, Cox, & McCall, in press; Weinrich, Shelton, McCall, & Cox, in press). Despite making positive changes specific to the treatment context, EA remains nonfluent, only producing several stereotypical phrases (e.g. "how are you"; "good morning"). He commonly writes a single word when communicating but cannot orally produce the words that he writes. EA's oral single word and sentence production have been investigated previously (Berndt, Haendiges, Mitchum, & Sandson, 1997; Berndt, Mitchum, Haendiges, & Sandson, 1997). Also, EA's oral picture naming in response to semantic cueing has been examined (McCall, Cox, Shelton, & Weinrich, in press). This report is an analysis of EA's pattern of spared and impaired performance across a number of processing tasks. In this paper, the focus is on those items that remain relatively undamaged: highly imageable/concrete nouns and verbs[3].

SINGLE WORD PRODUCTION TASKS

Several picture naming, reading, writing to dictation, and repetition tasks were administered to examine differences in EA's ability to produce written and spoken language.

---

[3] EA has substantial processing problems with low-imageable/abstract concepts and demonstrates these deficits in a number of language processing domains. For example, EA has serious reading difficulties when presented with low-imageable words (Berndt, Haendiges, Mitchum, & Wayland, 1996) and demonstrates a similar pattern of performance in writing these same items to dictation. For example, writing to dictation performance (proportion correct) on stimuli other than concrete items is as follows: adjectives: .08, low-imageability: .03, functors: .10. In addition, initial investigation of EA's comprehension of low-imageability items indicates impaired comprehension of abstract words. In a relatedness judgement task, EA was presented with three words and asked to pick the word that was the least related of the group. EA performed very well with concrete items (25/26 = .96) but not with abstract items (14/26 = .54).

PALPA Production Tasks

Five production tasks from the PALPA (Kay, Lesser, & Coltheart, 1992) that use the same stimuli were administered. These tasks include: oral picture naming, written picture naming, repetition, oral reading, and writing to dictation. There are 40 concrete nouns, 20 with regular spellings and 20 with irregular spellings. These tasks were administered over several testing sessions.

EA's level of performance on these tasks is presented in Table 1. Written naming and repetition were nearly perfect, and there was no regularity effect. There was a large difference between EA's oral and written naming abilities ($z = 6.34$, $p < .05$)[4]. Further, written naming was much better than writing to dictation ($z = 5.04$, $p < .05$). There was no difference in performance between oral naming, oral reading, and writing to dictation (all ps $> .15$). Production errors will be discussed following presentation of two other tasks.

Philadelphia Naming Task (PNT)

This task consists of 175 items representing high-, medium-, and low-frequency concrete nouns that range in length from 1 to 4 syllables (Roach, Schwartz, Martin, Grewal, & Brecher, in press). EA was required to produce oral and written names for each picture, read and write to dictation the word corresponding to each picture, and repeat the first 40 items in the assessment. These tasks were administered over several testing sessions.

EA's level of performance is presented in Table 2. As with the PALPA, EA performed much better with written naming of pictures than with oral naming of pictures ($z = 8.31$, $p < .05$). In addition, his performance on oral naming, oral reading, and writing to dictation tasks was similar (all ps $> .15$). As shown in the bottom half of Table 2, there was no effect of frequency or word length on

TABLE 1
Performance on PALPA Production Tasks: Proportion Correct (Number Correct in Parentheses)[a]

Task	Overall	Regular	Irregular
Oral naming	.30 (12)	.30 (6)	.30 (6)
Written naming	.89 (39)	.95 (19)	1.0 (20)
Oral reading	.40 (16)	.35 (7)	.45 (9)
Writing to dictation	.48 (19)	.50 (10)	.45 (9)
Repetition	.98 (39)	1.0 (20)	.95 (19)

[a] Proportion: $N = 40$/task condition.

---

[4] z scores resulted from a difference between two proportions test (Bruning & Kintz, 1987).

TABLE 2
Performance on PNT Production Tasks: Proportion Correct (Number Correct in Parentheses: N = 175/Task Condition: N = 40/Repetition)

Task	Overall			
Oral naming	.35 (61)			
Written naming	.79 (138)			
Oral reading	.41 (72)			
Writing to dictation	.40 (70)			
Repetition	1.0 (40)			

Performance by Frequency Conditions

Frequency (N)	Oral Naming	Written Naming	Reading	Writing to Dictation
High (31)	.36 (12)	.82 (25)	.45 (14)	.39 (12)
Medium (44)	.36 (17)	.82 (35)	.35 (17)	.37 (15)
Low (100)	.32 (32)	.78 (78)	.39 (41)	.43 (43)

Performance by Syllable Length Conditions

Length (N)	Oral Naming	Written Naming	Reading	Writing to Dictation
1 syll (103)	.37 (38)	.84 (41)	.30 (38)	.43 (43)
2 syll (49)	.34 (16)	.78 (36)	.25 (12)	.59 (26)
3&4 syll (23)	.30 (7)	.78 (17)	.70 (17)	.15 (3)

his performance[5]. EA's nearly perfect repetition performance on both the PALPA and PNT indicates that his spoken word production is not the result of secondary damage to motor programming (i.e. dysarthria or apraxia).

Noun and Verb Naming

A noun and verb naming task (Berndt et al., 1997) was also administered. The stimuli consist of 30 high-frequency nouns, 30 low-frequency nouns, and 30 verbs, which are matched in base and cumulative frequency to the low- and high-frequency nouns, respectively. The stimuli from these tasks were presented to EA for oral and written picture naming, reading, and writing to dictation. These tasks were administered over several testing sessions.

---

[5] We have not determined EA's performance in terms of syllable length × frequency. The number of items in the three- and four-syllable conditions is quite small (e.g. $N = 23$ across both conditions) and becomes even smaller when it is subdivided by frequency. There was no evidence that EA showed any significant main effects of either frequency or number of syllables. Although there is a trend for EA to perform worse on longer words in some conditions (e.g. writing to dictation and oral naming), these differences are not significant. Moreover, this trend in performance is not necessarily the result of his poor overall performance (e.g. consider reading: EA is extremely impaired at word reading but actually reads correctly the highest proportion of stimuli in the three-and four-syllable condition).

The proportion of correct responses for each condition are presented in Table 3. As with the PALPA and PNT, EA was much better at written naming than he was at oral naming for both nouns and verbs ($zs > 2.1$). EA was much better at written noun naming than written verb naming ($z > 2.0$). As shown in Table 3, there is no effect of frequency on naming performance in any condition (consistent with findings from Berndt et al., in press). Once again, his oral naming, oral reading, and writing to dictation abilities were similar (all $ps > .25$).

Error Analysis for All Production Tasks[6]

Classification of error types was determined using a system based on Mitchum, Ritgert, Sandson, and Berndt (1990). Errors are classified in the following way—*semantic (S)*: coordinate or associate, superordinate or subordinate, circumlocution, definition or semantic rejection; *phonological (P)*: having at least 50% phonemes in common with the target; *unrelated (UR)*: real or nonsense word bearing no semantic or phonological relationship to the target; *no-response (NR)*: silence, statement of no response, or an empty comment. We added the category *semantic+phonological (S+P)* in which the response and the target share both semantic similarity and at least 50% phonemes. EA's

TABLE 3
Performance on the Noun–Verb Naming Task: Proportion Correct (Number Correct in Parentheses)

	Oral Naming	Written Naming
Noun Picture Naming[a]		
High frequency	.38 (11)	.88 (26)
Low frequency	.43 (13)	.83 (25)
Verb Picture Naming[b]	.30 (9)	.53 (16)

	Reading	Writing to Dictation
Noun	.35 (21)	.28 (17)
High frequency	.40 (12)	.20 (6)
Low frequency	.30 (9)	.36 (11)
Verb	.23 (7)	.33 (10)

[a] $N = 30$/frequency condition.
[b] $N = 30$.

---

[6] Errors were not tabulated for PALPA written naming or for any of the word repetition tasks, given his almost perfect level of performance.

errors fell clearly into these categories and there was little ambiguity concerning how errors should be classified. A summary of the error classifications is presented in Table 4.

Analysis of EA's errors revealed that he made a majority of semantic errors and no-response errors. In oral production, EA often produced a semantic error that was conceptually related but not phonologically related to the target (e.g. strawberries → grapes; foot → socks). His no-response errors in oral production often consisted of the statement, "I don't know," even though he gestured and said "I know inside." On oral picture naming tasks, he often wrote the word with his finger on the table to indicate he knew the name but could not produce

TABLE 4
Error Classification across Production Tasks: Proportion of All Errors (Number of Errors in Parentheses)

	No. of Errors	S	S+P	P	UR	NR
PALPA						+
Oral picture naming	(28)	.52 (15)	0	0	.17 (5)	.31 (8)
Reading	(24)	.65 (16)	0	.04 (1)	.09 (2)	.22 (5)
Writing to dictation	(21)	.29 (6)	0	.05 (1)	0	.67 (14)
Philadelphia Naming Test						+
Oral picture naming	(114)	.43 (49)	.02 (2)	.02 (2)	.08 (9)	.45 (52)
Written picture naming	(37)	.54 (20)	.03 (1)	.08 (3)	.03 (1)	.32 (12)
Reading	(103)	.52 (54)	0	.06 (6)	.12 (12)	.30 (31)
Writing to dictation	(105)	.28 (29)	0	.09 (9)	.13 (13)	.52 (54)
Noun–Verb Naming Test						
Oral picture naming						
Noun	(36)	.66 (24)	0	0	.17 (6)	.17 (6)
Verb	(21)	.50 (11)	0	0	.35 (7)	.15 (4)
Written picture naming						
Noun	(9)	.89 (8)	0	0	0	.11 (1)
Verb	(14)	.88 (12)	0	0	0	.12 (2)
Reading						
Noun	(39)	.46 (19)	0	0	.17 (6)	.37 (14)
Verb	(23)	.50 (12)	0	0	.09 (2)	.41 (9)
Writing to dictation						
Noun	(43)	.22 (10)	0	0	.12 (5)	.66 (28)
Verb	(20)	.29 (6)	0	0	.06 (1)	.65 (13)

S=semantic; S+P=semantic and phonological; P=phonological (and orthographic); UR=unrelated; NR=no response.

it orally[7]. His few errors in written naming were almost always semantically related to the target.

Unlike the oral production tasks, and written naming, EA's writing to dictation produced more no-response errors than semantic errors. When writing to dictation, EA either wrote a word immediately (even if the word was incorrect and was usually a semantic error; e.g. ambulance → hospital; pencil → write) or repeated the word several times and said, "I don't know." For example, when the target "shoe" was presented, EA repeated the word several times out loud, looked puzzled, questioned "shoe" (with rising inflection to indicate a question), and finally said, "I don't know." When the experimenter pointed to her shoe, EA said, "aha" and wrote the correct response.

EA's errors in writing to dictation suggest that he cannot rely on the auditory input when producing a written response, but must instead rely on the meaning of the word. Thus, EA appears to have difficulty contacting the correct item in the phonological input lexicon or contacting the meaning of the item from the phonological input lexicon. EA's good written picture naming indicates he can successfully contact the orthographic output lexicon from semantics. Thus, his writing to dictation problem does not result from an inability to write. We return to this issue after first determining the extent to which EA can use sublexical processes to produce written and spoken language (i.e. his ability to convert phonemes to graphemes and graphemes to phonemes).

Reading/Writing to Dictation: Pseudohomophones and Nonwords

If EA can rely on phoneme-to-grapheme conversion and grapheme-to-phoneme conversion processes, one would expect much better performance on word reading and writing for regularly spelled words. EA's poor word reading and writing to dictation performance, and the lack of a regularity effect, suggest that he does not rely on sublexical conversion processes to carry out these tasks.

---

[7] An informal record was kept when EA produced different responses in speaking and writing, *at the time* he was performing one or the other of these tasks. Unfortunately, this record was informal and was not kept for every task, so the numbers may actually underestimate the number of times different responses would occur between the two output modalities. When producing names orally in response to the pictures included in the noun/verb naming task, 32% (18/57) of EA's incorrect oral responses accompanied different written responses. Some examples are: target: sun; oral production: *moon and stars*, written production: *sun*; target: radio; oral production: *telephone*; written production: *radio*; target: sharpen; oral production: *I don't know*; written production: *pencil*; target: badge; oral production: *fire engine*; written production: *patrol*. EA also showed an asymmetry between the two output modalities when the task was written picture naming. Although the number of errors in this task is fairly low, 26% (6/23) of EA's incorrect written responses accompanied correct oral responses. Some examples are: target: shave; oral production: *shaving*; written production: *moustch*; target: melt; oral production: *melting*; written production: *snow*; target: ball; oral production: *ball*, written production: *soccer*.

EA was required to read 20 pseudohomophones and 20 nonwords matched orthographically to the pseudohomophones, and to read and write to dictation 55 nonwords (stimuli are from Berndt et al., 1996). His score on nonwords was near zero for reading (2/55 = .04) and zero for writing to dictation. In reading, 30/187 (.16) individual target phonemes were produced. In writing to dictation, 2/187 (.01) individual target graphemes were produced. In oral nonword reading, EA made 17 lexicalisation errors (e.g. homins → quiet), 8 lexicalisation/phonological errors (e.g. ceach → seat); 7 phonological nonword errors (e.g. feep → feef), 13 unrelated nonword errors (e.g. teep → rafe), and 8 no-response errors. In nonword writing, EA rarely produced the first letter of the nonword ($N = 2$); all other errors were no-response errors (he responded, "I can't," "I don't"). He understood the task, but indicated he had no idea what the correct response was.

EA did not orally read any pseudohomophone correctly, and only 11/140 (.08) individual target phonemes were produced correctly. He produced 13 lexicalisation errors (e.g. trooth → cave), 4 lexicalisation/phonological errors (e.g. kwality → quite), 8 lexicalisation/semantic errors (e.g. erth → moon), 12 unrelated nonword errors (e.g. stewdint → veesher), and 3 no-response errors. His lexical errors were not necessarily related to the sound of the word (e.g. *raydeo* → horse (presumably via rodeo); *atitood* → climbing [presumably via altitude]). As evidenced by his performance, EA suffers from a severe impairment converting graphemes to phonemes and phonemes to graphemes. Thus, his success in written picture names does not appear to be supported by the generation of the phonology of the target name and a conversion of the phonetic information to the appropriate graphemes.

Word and Nonword Repetition

Although EA's poor oral naming and reading may result from a deficit to phonological output processing, his oral repetition of the stimuli he cannot produce verbally is quite good. As noted earlier, this indicates that EA's poor oral production is not the result of a deficit to peripheral motor processing. In a second repetition task, we wished to determine whether or not EA's repetition would be influenced by lexical-semantic factors. These factors include lexicality, frequency, and imageability. If EA is relying on a sublexical route to repeat words (auditory input to phonological output), repetition of nonwords should be good. If EA is relying on a lexical-semantic route to repeat words, effects of frequency and/or imageability might be expected, since these factors can only be represented for pre-existing items (i.e. known words).

EA was required to repeat 240 words, consisting of 2–3-syllable items that varied in frequency (high: +50/million occurrences; low: < 50/million occurrences) and imageability (picturable and not picturable). EA was also required to repeat 100 one- to three-syllable nonwords that were created by changing one letter from a word to create a nonsense word. He was allowed to view the experimenter's mouth during presentation of these stimuli.

The proportion of correct word repetitions is presented in Table 5. Overall, EA correctly repeated 85% (204/240) of the words. EA performed much better with high-imageability words than low-imageability words ($z = 2.30, p < .05$), and showed no frequency effect ($z < 1.3$). These factors do not interact ($\chi^2 < .12$). This pattern of performance suggests that EA was relying on a lexical-semantic route to carry out word repetition. EA's errors consisted of 20 phonologically related nonwords (reaction → rejection), 10 phonologically related words (vanity → sanity), 2 morphologically related words (session → sessions), 3 unrelated words (conquest → fluster), and 1 no response.

EA correctly repeated 80% (80/100) of nonwords, and made 7/20 (.35) phonological/lexicalisation errors (goverder → governor). The rest of his errors (13/20 = .65) consisted of phonologically related nonword responses (captiss → bactiss). EA's nonword repetition performance was slightly impaired (normal performance ranges from 88%–100% correct), indicating a deficit in the ability to convert auditory input to oral output.

Discussion of Production Tasks

EA's performance was remarkably consistent across a variety of stimuli. Written picture naming was vastly superior to oral picture naming. The majority of EA's errors in oral picture naming were semantically related (43%–66%) to the target rather than phonologically related (0–2%) to the target (see Table 4). If EA's problems in oral picture naming were due to damage *beyond* the level of the phonological output lexicon (e.g. phonological buffer or motor programming), we would expect the majority of his errors to be phonetic paraphasias related to the correct target name. Further, since EA performs so well with written picture naming, his oral picture naming difficulties cannot be localised completely within the semantic system (and comprehension is examined in more detail later to further the claim that EA's semantic system is mostly intact). Thus, EA's oral naming deficit must result from damage at the level of the

TABLE 5
Repetition Performance for Words: Proportion Correct
(Number Correct in Parentheses)

Imageability[a]	Frequency[a]		
	High	Low	Total
High	.95 (57)	.90 (54)	.925 (111)
Low	.84 (50)	.72 (43)	.78 (93)
Total	.895 (107)	.81 (97)	.85 (204)

[a] $N = 120$/condition.

phonological output lexicon (either in accessing these forms and/or to the forms themselves). Given this assumption, EA's written naming performance suggests that there are distinct phonological and orthographic lexicons that do not necessarily interact to support successful writing. This point will be returned to in the General Discussion.

EA's ability to write to dictation was poor for both words and nonwords. His complete inability to write nonwords from dictation, in the face of successful written picture naming, provides strong evidence against the hypothesis that writing is mediated by sublexical phonological mechanisms (see Barry, 1994; Ellis, 1988, for reviews). EA's inability to write nonwords did not result from an inability to perform the task. EA was always willing to perform any task, even though he knew he would have trouble and would make mistakes. Instead, EA reported that he had absolutely no idea what letters might make up the word presented to him, even after the experimenter presented examples of correct written productions to him. Further, EA's poor nonword reading performance indicates that he has severe difficulties in converting graphemes to phonemes. These results suggest that EA's sublexical grapheme-to-phoneme and phoneme-to-grapheme abilities are very severely impaired.

EA's good performance with written picture naming indicates that his poor writing to dictation is not a result of contacting orthographic output from semantics (or as a result of other problems in writing, e.g. motor programming). One possible reason for the discrepancy between written naming and writing to dictation abilities could be that EA cannot contact semantics from auditory input. If this were the case, EA should perform poorly on auditory comprehension tasks, but successfully on auditory lexical decision. That is, if EA can contact information in the phonological input lexicon successfully, he should do well in determining if a heard stimulus is an English word. Alternatively, his inability to write to dictation could be attributed to impairments in phonological analysis or contact with the phonological input lexicon. If so, he should perform poorly on an auditory lexical decision task. There are already two findings that argue against the second explanation. First, EA is relatively good at repeating words. Second, the effect of imageability on repetition indicates that he can analyse auditory input and contact the phonological input lexicon. Thus, we expect excellent performance on auditory lexical decision. This is examined next.

SINGLE WORD COMPREHENSION TASKS

A number of tasks assessing auditory and visual single word comprehension were administered to determine the integrity of EA's semantic knowledge. Auditory comprehension was assessed to determine how well EA can analyse auditory input to contact the phonological input lexicon and semantic system.

Visual comprehension was tested to provide a comparison of reading aloud and reading comprehension, and a comparison to auditory comprehension.

Lexical Decision—PALPA

EA saw a letter string or heard the same letter string pronounced aloud. He was instructed to decide if the stimulus was a real word. Both imageability and frequency were manipulated, with 15 words in each of the following conditions: high imageability/high frequency, high imageability/low frequency, low imageability/high frequency, and low imageability/low frequency. There were 60 pronounceable nonwords randomly intermixed in the overall stimulus list. Stimuli were presented once aurally and once visually, in separate testing sessions.

EA correctly rejected all aurally presented nonwords (60/60), but committed three misses on words (57/60). Two of these errors were on low frequency/low imageability words, and one error was on a low frequency/high imageability word. EA performed perfectly on visually presented words (60/60), but committed two false alarms on nonwords (58/60). Although performance was not perfect, EA does very well at determining if letter strings represent real words, indicating relatively well-preserved phonological and orthographic input representations.

Auditory Word–Picture Matching—PALPA

EA saw five pictures arranged on a sheet of paper and was instructed to pick the picture that matched the aurally presented target word. The four distracter pictures consisted of a close semantic distracter, a distant semantic distracter, a semantically unrelated visual distracter, and an unrelated distracter.

EA missed one item on this task (39/40 = .98), picking the picture "finger" for the target word "thumb." A second task was developed to look more closely at EA's ability to determine if a target word matched a presented picture, with both auditory and visual input.

Word Verification for Nouns and Verbs: Auditory and Visual Comprehension

Thirty noun targets and 30 verb targets were selected. Comprehension was assessed under three conditions: *matching target condition*—the word matched the picture; *related target condition*—the word and picture were semantically related; and *unrelated target condition*—the word and picture were unrelated. Unrelated targets were created by rearranging the nonmatching targets used in the related target condition (i.e. "nose" was the related target for "ear" but served as the unrelated target for "door").

Three stimulus lists were developed for both nouns and verbs such that comprehension of each target was assessed once within each stimulus list presentation. Ten matching targets, 10 related targets, and 10 unrelated targets made up each stimulus list. In addition, 10 matching filler trials were added to each list to equalise the number of "yes" and "no" responses in each list. The filler trials remained the same across the stimulus lists. Within each stimulus list, presentation of the targets was randomised. Lists were presented over several sessions in both auditory and visual modalities. EA was required to indicate whether or not the target and picture represented the same concept.

An item was scored as correct only if EA accepted the matching target and rejected the nonmatching targets on all three presentations of an item. EA's auditory comprehension of nouns was good, as he comprehended 26/30 (.87) items correctly. Visual comprehension was also very good, as he comprehended 28/30 (.97) items correctly. There was no difference in his auditory and visual comprehension performance ($p > .25$).

EA's auditory comprehension of verbs was numerically worse than his auditory comprehension of nouns (20/30 = .67), but failed to reach significance ($z = 1.80, p = .07$). Visual comprehension of verbs also resulted in numerically worse performance with verbs than nouns (26/30 = .87), but the difference was not significant ($p > .25$). Taken together with the results from the PALPA, EA appears to have a mild semantic deficit that becomes more pronounced for verbs (see also footnote 3, p. 111).

Spoken Word–Written Word Matching

If EA cannot use phonological information to match auditory and visual input (due to an inability to perform grapheme-to-phoneme conversion, and vice versa), he may rely on the meaning of the word to match spoken to written words. If auditory word processing is impaired, and little contextual information in the form of a picture is available, we would expect EA to make a number of errors on this task.

The noun and verb stimuli described in the word–picture verification task were used to assess EA's ability to match a spoken word to a written word. On each trial, a sheet of paper containing the target, a semantically related foil (that was not phonologically related to the target), and an unrelated foil was presented along with the spoken target. EA was asked to select the word that matched the spoken target. Nouns and verbs were tested in separate blocks. Presentation of items was randomised. This task was administered several sessions after completion of the word–picture verification task.

There was no significant difference ($p > .30$) in EA's ability to comprehend nouns (24/30 = .80) and verbs (21/30 = .70). All of EA's errors on this task resulted from selection of the semantically related distractor. EA's level of performance on this task was slightly worse than his level of performance on the word–picture verification task, but not significantly so.

Discussion of Single Word Comprehension Tasks

EA's pattern of performance indicates that he has a mild deficit to semantic knowledge; but his reading comprehension is quite good, especially for concrete nouns, indicating that the deficit is rather mild. Also, given his poor pattern of performance with sublexical phonological processing, it is evident that EA does not rely on sublexical phonologic mediation for reading comprehension. His mild semantic deficit could result in the production of some semantic errors (see Table 4). However, the semantic errors in oral naming cannot only be the result of a semantic deficit, since he can produce a written name for a picture that he cannot orally name. It has been argued that multiple phonological output representations could be activated by the semantic information and that semantic errors can result from a problem in selecting the correct phonological output form (Caramazza & Hillis, 1990). Thus, it appears that EA's semantic errors in oral naming result mostly from accessing a phonological output form from the correct semantic information.

There is no significant difference between EA's comprehension of nouns and verbs and no significant difference between EA's oral production of nouns and verbs, indicating that his poorer performance in writing picture names of verbs as compared to nouns does not result from damage to the semantic representations but rather to output processing (see Caramazza & Hillis, 1990, 1991). However, EA always comprehended nouns better than verbs (79/90 vs. 67/90, respectively, across all tasks assessing noun and verb comprehension) and orally he did produce slightly more nouns than verbs (11 high-frequency nouns, 13 low-frequency nouns vs. 9 verbs). These data suggest that EA may have damage to his semantic knowledge that differentially affects verbs more than nouns, and that this damage is responsible for his poorer performance in written naming of verbs as compared to nouns. The data reported here do not allow us to decide unequivocally between the two possibilities.

EA's level of performance on auditory comprehension tasks indicates that he can make use of auditory information to contact the semantic system in some, but not all, cases. It would appear that EA's inability to write to dictation is not entirely due to an inability to determine the semantic concept represented by the phonological input, since his auditory comprehension is much better than would be expected from his performance in writing to dictation. However, the contextual information provided in the comprehension tasks may be enough to allow EA to determine the meaning of the phonological input. That is, the contextual information in the pictures may interact with the phonological input to specify the meaning of the aurally presented word. If this is the case, EA's performance on writing to dictation should improve when the target word is presented with contextual information.

CONTEXTUAL EFFECTS ON WRITING TO DICTATION

If EA's inability to write to dictation results from a deficit in determining the meaning of the auditory input, context would be expected to improve his writing to dictation. The exact influence of contextual effects on auditory and visual comprehension is underspecified in most models of language processing and we make no claims as to the specific processes that may interact in situations where language is processed in context. However, we hypothesised that a sentential context that provided semantic details about the target word might influence EA's writing to dictation by helping him determine the exact target. In testing, it was noticed that EA would often not understand the target word when writing to dictation but would successfully write the word when it was presented in a sentence. Thus, we formally tested whether or not the context (i.e. the sentence) improved his ability to write to dictation.

Noun Targets Embedded in Sentences: Provision of a Target

The high- and low-frequency noun targets from the noun–verb naming test were presented again for writing to dictation with the target embedded in a sentence frame that was semantically biased towards the target. The frames were designed so that the target was predictable from the sentence (see Zingeser & Berndt, 1988, for a description of development and norming of the sentence frames). First, the target word was presented. Next, the sentence frame was presented with the target in the word final position, and then the target was presented again. For example, the target word "moon" was presented, followed by "the round bright object in the night sky is the *moon*," then the word "moon" was presented a second time. The target and sentence were repeated upon request.

As presented earlier, EA wrote 17/60 (.28) noun targets when the words were presented in isolation. He produced many more of the same targets when they were embedded in a sentence (48/60 = .80). Thus, EA's writing to dictation improved significantly when the target was embedded in a sentence ($z > 4.0$), indicating that he is highly dependent on contextual information to identify the target word. In the sentence-embedded target condition, his level of writing performance was almost identical to his written picture naming performance (49/60 = .82).

To examine the impact of providing additional auditory context on oral picture naming, EA was presented with the same sentence completions used earlier (without provision of the target word) and the accompanying picture, and asked to name the picture following the sentence prompt. The sentence prompt was repeated upon request. This task can be considered a "pseudo-analogue" to the task described earlier; that is, EA was provided with a contextual cue *and* the "target" and was required to produce the target name. The "target" in this case was the picture.

Unlike the improvement afforded when writing to dictation, EA's oral picture naming in response to sentence cues (29/60 = .48) improved very little over oral picture naming without any cues, reported earlier (25/60 = .42). Contextual information did not help EA generate the oral picture name, but did help him write a dictated word.

Discussion of Contextual Effects on Writing

When provided with contextual information and the target item, EA's ability to write to dictation is at the same level as his ability to write picture names. This pattern suggests that EA's poor writing to dictation results from his inability to determine the meaning of the target word. That is, without the support of semantic information, EA is unable to produce a written target (and cannot do so using a phoneme-to-grapheme conversion system, given his *abolished* nonword writing). EA's error pattern in "noncontextual" writing to dictation tasks would also support this conclusion, since the majority of his errors are "no-response." EA's few semantic errors indicate that he can sometimes access information in the semantic system from auditory input without the addition of contextual information. For the most part, however, EA appears to have little idea about the meaning of the isolated aurally presented words[8].

---

[8] EA's difficulty in contacting semantics from auditory input resembles, in some respects, a pattern of performance termed "word meaning deafness" (e.g. Ellis, 1984; Kohn & Friedman, 1986). Word meaning deafness has been described as an inability to understand the meaning of an aurally presented word when the patient can successfully repeat it and write it to dictation. Often, the patient understands the aurally presented word once they have written it down (Ellis, 1984). Like "word meaning deaf" patients, EA does not appear to understand aurally presented words in isolation. However, his pattern of performance does not conform to a pure "word meaning deaf" patient, since his writing to dictation is poor and auditory comprehension is quite good when he hears the word in context. EA may be more similar to the case (DRB) described by Franklin, Howard, and Patterson (1994). According to Franklin et al., DRB suffers from "abstract word meaning deafness." DRB could not understand abstract words but showed good lexical decision performance with these words. Further, DRB could not write to dictation or repeat nonwords, and produced semantic errors in word repetition. Writing to dictation of abstract words was also poor. Visual comprehension was good for all word types. Franklin et al. argue that DRB's pattern of results are consistent with a deficit in contacting semantics from the phonological input lexicon that is specific to abstract words. EA's pattern of performance on auditory input processing tasks can be interpreted similarly; however, his "word meaning deafness" is apparent for concrete words.

Given his good performance on auditory lexical decision, it is likely that EA has relatively intact phonological input representations but has difficulty accessing the meaning of those representations. The same contextual information that improved his ability to write to dictation did not improve his ability to name a picture orally. This implies that nonpictorial semantic information and the pictured target were not sufficient to support retrieval of the lexical-phonological output form.

GENERAL DISCUSSION

Detailed examination of EA's language comprehension and production abilities revealed an array of relatively spared and damaged processes. EA demonstrated significantly better written than spoken picture naming, an infrequent pattern of performance in aphasic patients (Kertesz, 1979). As Patterson and Shewell (1987, p. 291) point out, writing is often considered to be the most vulnerable skill in aphasia, and preserved writing in the face of impaired spoken output is "sufficiently rare to allow interest in some further case studies." Both EA's oral word and nonword reading, as well as his writing to dictation abilities for both words and nonwords, are extremely impaired. Writing to dictation improved when contextual information was provided with the target item. Auditory and visual comprehension of concrete items is quite good and performance was normal on auditory and visual lexical decision tasks.

The most relevant aspect of EA's performance for the issues being discussed in this forum is significantly impaired oral naming in conjunction with relatively spared written naming. EA cannot name pictures and cannot read words or nonwords, but comprehends the words he cannot produce orally. As argued earlier, given that the majority of EA's errors in oral output (across picture naming and reading tasks) are *semantic* and not phonological strongly suggests that the damage is located at *lexical*-phonological output processing, rather than postlexical-phonological output processing. Thus, based on the model presented in Fig. 1, EA appears to have damage on the phonological output side of processing, either to the connection from the semantic system to the phonological output lexicon, or to the representations in the output lexicon itself (or to both).

However, one piece of evidence from EA's word repetition performance might be used to argue against this conclusion. His good word repetition, and especially the effects of imageability on repetition, suggest that EA makes use of a route from semantics to phonological output to repeat words. If EA makes use of the route from semantics to output phonology to repeat, how can damage in oral output be localised at the output lexical-phonological level? Recall, however, that the majority of his repetition errors were phonological errors (and there were *no* semantic errors), suggesting that EA is relying mainly on phonological information in *repetition* (this conclusion is also supported by his ability to repeat 80% of the nonwords). This error pattern is completely different from his error pattern in oral picture naming and reading, which resulted in a majority of semantic errors and few phonological errors. EA's *oral naming* error pattern suggests that he is unable to generate the phonology of the target name from pictorial or visual word input.

Recall, also, EA's poor writing to dictation when the word is presented in isolation. This suggests that he cannot activate a complete semantic representation from phonological input (and *writing to dictation* is impaired because of abolished phoneme-to-grapheme conversion procedures). Therefore, the effect of imageability on EA's repetition could be interpreted as partial semantic activation coupled with relatively spared acoustic-to-phonological conversion procedures. This interpretation does not undermine the conclusion that EA has damage to lexical-phonological output processing, which impairs EA's ability to generate a phonological target when presented with a picture or a written word.

If we accept the conclusion that EA's oral naming impairment results from damage to phonological output processing, then his data provide strong evidence against the idea that phonological information is required for correct written production, since EA can successfully write the names of items for which he cannot successfully generate the phonological output. Thus, the generation of lexical-orthographic output representations does not appear to depend on the generation of lexical-phonological output representations.

Furthermore, EA's data argue against the notion that writing is mediated by sublexical phonological mechanisms. EA does not appear to be able to do *any* phoneme-to-grapheme conversion, yet he can write single words accurately. Thus, his data suggest that writing can be carried out completely independently of sublexical phonological generation, a conclusion contrary to previous arguments (e.g. Barry, 1994; Dodd, 1980; Frith, 1980; Nolan & Caramazza, 1983). Although lexical and sublexical phonological output information does not appear necessary to support successful writing, it may be the case that this information is used, when available, to facilitate writing. Evidence suggesting that writing can be influenced by phonological factors does not undermine the conclusion that writing is not *obligated* to make use of phonological information, as in the case of EA.

Evidence concerning the role of phonologic mediation in reading comprehension also emerged from EA's pattern of performance. His inability to carry out sublexical phonological conversion provides support for a direct connection between the orthographic input lexicon and semantics. EA has nearly perfect reading comprehension for concrete stimuli, indicating an ability to contact the semantic system from an orthographic input string *without* needing to rely on sublexical conversion of this string to a phonological representation. That is, EA's extremely poor nonword reading and the small number of phonological errors (11/83 phonological errors; 63/83 errors were completely unrelated to the target phonologically) suggest that his ability to convert graphemes to phonemes is severely restricted[9]. Moreover, the small number of phonological errors he commits in word reading (see Table 4) indicates he cannot generate the phonology associated with the target word. Finally, performance on the spoken word–written word matching test should have been perfect if EA used phonological mediation to determine the meaning of the written stimulus. That is, if he could use grapheme-to-phoneme conversion processes plus good phonological input analysis, he should not make semantic errors on this task (13/13 semantic errors). We have argued that EA has problems with phonological input processing and can activate some but not all the semantic information associated with the auditory input. The absence of grapheme-to-phoneme conversion processes cannot help him reconcile the auditory input with the visual input, thus leading to errors on the spoken word–written word matching task. Taken together, EA's pattern of performance on sublexical and lexical-phonological processing tasks suggests that reading comprehension can occur without the generation and support of phonology. This finding is in direct contradiction to Van Orden's proposal that phonologic mediation is fundamental to written word identification (e.g. Van Orden, 1991; Van Orden et al., 1988). Phonological factors might influence reading in certain situations but do not appear to be necessary (or "fundamental") for reading comprehension.

EA presents with multiple deficits to his language processing system that result in several dissociations between language processing abilities. EA can successfully write single words from pictorial input but is unable to produce these same items orally. Writing is not supported by the generation of a sublexical phonological representation, as evidenced by his inability to write nonwords. Also, writing is not supported by the generation of a lexical-phonological representation, as evidenced by the fact that his pattern of errors in oral naming tasks (i.e. semantic rather than phonological errors) indicates damage at lexical-phonological output processing. EA's reading comprehension is quite good, in spite of an inability to perform grapheme-to-phoneme conversion and in the face of damage to phonological input processing. The most obvious explanation of this pattern of performance is that orthographic and phonological representations are represented separately in the cognitive system and each has direct connections between semantics and the corresponding input/output lexicons. Writing and reading comprehension are not dependent on the generation of a lexical or sublexical phonological code.

---

[9] We have not included lexicalisation/phonological errors ($N = 8$) in this summary, since although we labelled these errors lexicalisation/*phonological* errors, it is impossible to determine whether or not they result from *visual* similarity between the target and the response (e.g. ceach → seat). Also, we have not included "no-response" errors in this summary.

REFERENCES

Allport, D.A. (1984). Speech production and comprehension: One lexicon or two? In W. Prinz & A.F. Sanders (Eds.), *Cognition and motor processes*. Berlin: Springer.
Assal, G., Buttet, J., & Jolivet, R. (1981). Dissociations in aphasia: A case report. *Brain and Language, 13*, 223–240.
Barry, C. (1994). Spelling routes (or roots or rutes). In G.D.A. Brown & N.C. Ellis (Eds.), *Handbook of spelling: Theory, process and intervention*. New York: John Wiley.
Berndt, R.S., Haendiges, A.N., Mitchum, C.C., & Wayland, S.C. (1996). An investigation of nonlexical reading impairments. *Cognitive Neuropsychology, 13*, 763–801.
Berndt, R.S., Haendiges, A.N., Mitchum, C.C., & Sandson, J. (1997). Verb retrieval in aphasia: 2. Relationship to sentence processing. *Brain and Language, 56*, 107–137.
Berndt, R.S., Mitchum, C.C., Haendiges, A.N., & Sandson, J. (1997). Verb retrieval in aphasia: 1. Characterising single word impairments. *Brain and Language, 56*, 68–106.
Blanken, G., de Langen, E.G., Dittmann, J., & Wallesch, C.W. (1989). Implications of preserved written language abilities for the functional basis of speech automatisms (recurring utterances): A single case study. *Cognitive Neuropsychology, 6*, 211–249.
Bruning, J.L., & Kintz, B.L. (1987). *Computational handbook of statistics* (3rd edn.). Glenview, IL: Scott, Foresman, & Company.
Bub, D., & Chertkow, H. (1988). Agraphia. In J. Boller & J. Grafman (Eds.), *Handbook of neuropsychology, Vol. 1*. Amsterdam: Elsevier Science Publishers.
Bub, D., & Kertesz, A. (1982). Evidence of lexicographic processing in a patient with preserved written over oral single word naming. *Brain, 105*, 697–717.
Caramazza, A., Berndt, R.S., & Basili, A.G. (1983). The selective impairment of phonological processing: A case study. *Brain and Language, 18*, 128–174.
Caramazza, A., & Hillis, A.E. (1990). Where do semantic errors come from? *Cortex, 26*, 95–122.
Caramazza, A., & Hillis, A.E. (1991). Lexical organization of nouns and verbs in the brain. *Nature, 349*, 788–790.
Coltheart, M., & Funnell, E. (1987). Reading and writing: One lexicon or two? In A. Allport, D.G. MacKay, W. Prinz, & E. Scheerer (Eds.), *Language perception and production: Relationships between speaking, reading and writing*. London: Lawrence Erlbaum Associates Ltd.
Davies, P. (Ed.) (1978). *American heritage dictionary* (Paperback edn.) New York: Dell Publishing.
Dodd, B. (1980). The spelling abilities of profoundly pre-lingually deaf children. In U. Frith (Ed.), *Cognitive processes in spelling*. London: Academic Press.
Ellis, A.W. (1984). Introduction to Bramwell's (1987) case of word meaning deafness. *Cognitive Neuropsychology, 1*, 245–258.
Ellis, A.W. (1988). Modelling the writing process. In C. Denes, C. Semenza, & P. Bisiacchi (Eds.), *Perspectives in cognitive neuropsychology*. London: Lawrence Erlbaum Associates Ltd.
Ellis, A.W., Miller, D., & Sin, G. .(1983). Wernicke's aphasia and normal language processing: A case study in cognitive neuropsychology. *Cognition, 15*, 111–144.
Franklin, S., Howard, D., & Patterson, K. (1994). Abstract word meaning deafness. *Cognitive Neuropsychology, 11*, 1–34.
Frith, U. (1980). Unexpected spelling problems. In U. Frith (Ed.), *Cognitive processes in spelling*. London: Academic Press.
Haendiges, A.N., Berndt, R.S., & Mitchum, C.C. (1996). Assessing the elements contributing to a "mapping" deficit: A targeted treatment study. *Brain and Language, 52*, 276–302.
Hatfield, F.M., & Patterson, K.E. (1983). Phonological spelling. *Quarterly Journal of Experimental Psychology, 35A*, 451–468.
Hier, D.B., & Mohr, J.P. (1977). Incongruous oral and written naming: Evidence for a subdivision of the syndrome Wernicke's aphasia. *Brain and Language, 4*, 115–126.

Howard, D., & Franklin, S. (1988). *Missing the meaning*. Cambridge, MA: MIT Press.
Kay, J., Lesser, R., & Coltheart, M. (1992). *Psycholinguistic assessments of language processing in aphasia (PALPA)*. London: Lawrence Erlbaum Associates Ltd.
Kertesz, A. (1979). *Aphasia and associated disorders: Taxonomy, localization, and recovery*. New York: Grune & Stratton.
Kohn, S., & Friedman, R. (1986). Word meaning deafness: A phonological-semantic dissociation. *Cognitive Neuropsychology, 3*, 291–308.
Kremin, H. (1987). Is there more than ah-oh-oh? Alternative strategies for writing and repeating lexically. In M. Coltheart, G. Sartori, & R. Job (Eds.), *The cognitive neuropsychology of language*. London: Lawrence Erlbaum Associates Ltd.
Levine, D.N., Calvanio, R., & Popovics, A. (1982). Language in the absence of inner speech. *Neuropsychologia, 20*, 391–409.
McCall, D., Cox, D.M., Shelton, J.R., & Weinrich, M. (in press). The influence of semantic and syntactic information on picture naming in aphasia. *Aphasiology*.
Mitchum, C.C., Haendiges, A.N., & Berndt, R.S. (1993). Model-guided treatment to improve written sentence production: A case study. *Aphasiology, 7*, 71–109.
Mitchum, C.C., Ritgert, B.A., Sandson, J., & Berndt, R.S. (1990). The use of response analysis in confrontation naming. *Aphasiology, 4*, 261–280.
Monsell, S. (1987). On the relation between lexical input and output pathways for speech. In A. Allport, D.G. MacKay, W. Prinz, & E. Scheerer (Eds.), *Language perception and production: Relationships between speaking, reading and writing*. London: Lawrence Erlbaum Associates Ltd.
Nolan, K.A., & Caramazza, A. (1983). An analysis of writing in a case of deep dyslexia. *Brain and Language, 20*, 305–328.
Patterson, K.E., & Shewell, C. (1987). Speak and spell: Dissociations and word class effects. In M. Coltheart, G. Sartori, & R. Job (Eds.), *The cognitive neuropsychology of language*. London: Lawrence Erlbaum Associates Ltd.
Roach, A., Schwartz, M.F., Martin, N., Grewal, R.S., & Brecher, A. (in press). The Philadelphia Naming Test: Scoring and rationale. *Clinical Aphasiology*.
Shallice, T. (1981). Phonological agraphia and the lexical route in writing. *Brain, 104*, 413–429.
Shallice, T. (1988). *From neuropsychology to mental structure*. Cambridge: Cambridge University Press.
Van Orden, G.C. (1991). Phonologic mediation is fundamental to reading. In D. Besner & G.W. Humphreys (Eds.), *Basic processes in reading: Visual word recognition*. Hillsdale, NJ: Lawrence Erlbaum Associates Inc.
Van Orden, G.C., Johnston, J.C., & Hale, B.L. (1988). Word identification in reading proceeds from spelling to sound to meaning. *Journal of Experimental Psychology: Learning, Memory and Cognition, 14*, 371–386.
Weinrich, M., Shelton, J.R., Cox, D.M., & McCall, D. (in press). Remediating production of tense morphology improved verb production in chronic aphasia. *Brain and Language*.
Weinrich, M., Shelton, J.R., McCall, D., & Cox, D.M. (in press). Generalization from single sentence to multi-sentence production in severely aphasic patients. *Brain and Language*.
Zingeser, L., & Berndt, R.S. (1988). Grammatical class and context effects in a case of pure anomia: Implications for models of language processing. *Cognitive Neuropsychology, 5*, 473–516.

Complex Dynamic Systems also Predict Dissociations, but They Do Not Reduce to Autonomous Components

Guy C. Van Orden and Marian A. Jansen op de Haar
Arizona State University, Tempe, USA

Anna M. T. Bosman
University of Nijmegen, The Netherlands

Dissociations, according to the target articles, are due to damaged autonomous phonologic (or spelling) representations. However, a damaged recurrent network model may also produce dissociations. Recurrent networks do not entail autonomous components. They are strongly nonlinear dynamic systems that self-organise through recurrent feedback. A simple model with these properties that produces both regularisation errors (PINT named to rhyme with MINT) and semantic errors (BUSH named as TREE) is described. It may also produce dissociations between "spoken" responses and "written" responses. The mathematical basis of this model is motivated by contemporary neurobiological accounts that also derive from dynamic systems theory. The mathematical basis may also predict *multistability* and *metastability*. These are indicated by *hysteresis* and *1/f noise*, respectively, and we review recent reports of these phenomena in speech perception and word recognition. In addition, feedback has been corroborated in the feedback consistency effect. Reported generic behaviours of a complex system, the simulated dissociation of errors, and the established bidirectional nature of perception all demonstrate the utility of a cognitive systems approach to cognitive phenomena.

Requests for reprints should be addressed to Guy Van Orden, Cognitive Systems Group, Department of Psychology, Arizona State University, Tempe, AZ 85287–1104, USA (email: guy.van.orden@asu.edu).

Preparation of this commentary was supported by a FIRST Award (CMS 5 R29 NS26247) and an Independent Scientist Award (1 K02 NS 01905) to Guy Van Orden from the National Institute of Neurological Disorders and Stroke. We thank Peter Killeen for a brief tutorial on *metastability*.

© 1997 Psychology Press, an imprint of Erlbaum (UK) Taylor & Francis Ltd

INTRODUCTION

This special issue of Cognitive Neuropsychology showcases four careful and detailed case studies. All four converge on a common conclusion: Autonomous spelling representations may affect behaviour associated with literacy. By inference, automotous spelling representations must be included in a proper account of intact reading and writing. The following performance profiles motivate this conclusion.

PS, a patient described in Hanley and McDonnell (this issue), produces the correct written response when presented with the picture of a BEAR, but cannot produce the correct spoken name of the picture. Generally, PS had great difficulty with tasks that required spoken responses relative to tasks that allowed written responses. Similarly, his performance was better when he could point at the correct alternative, as in matching a picture with a written word. His difficulty with spoken responses is due to a general deficit in phonology. For example, he is sometimes unable to produce the sound-alike alternative of a homophonic word (although most errors in this and other tasks are constrained by the spelling and phonology of the correct responses). A similar case is described by Shelton and Weinrich (this issue). The patient EA's picture naming was better when the task allowed a written response than when it required a spoken response. However, EA had great difficulty writing words to dictation, and was essentially incapable of writing nonwords to dictation. As in the previous case, EA performs poorly on many tasks that require a spoken response, but unlike the previous case, EA can correctly repeat spoken words.

The patients PW (Rapp, Benzing, & Caramazza, this issue) and WMA (Miceli, Benvegnù, Capasso, & Caramazza, this issue), produced overall profiles that were similar to each other, but different from the previous two patients. Both PW and WMA were better at reading words aloud than at writing words to dictation, an asymmetry that is also found in intact reading and writing. Their overall picture naming was also better when the task allowed spoken responses compared to written responses. However, like PS and EA, both patients occasionally produced a correct written response when they did not produce a correct spoken response. This occasional pattern is the key dissociation. Consider WMA, for example. When asked to name a picture, WMA may provide one name if the response is spoken and a different name if the response is written. Two different responses to the same picture! Sometimes the correct response is the written response, sometimes it is the spoken response, and sometimes neither is correct.

Each of the previous patients produces a dissociation between written responses and spoken responses. A traditional logic licenses a formulaic interpretation of dissociations. For example, writing one name and saying a different name to the same picture indicates that the separate responses have separate causal origins. The causal basis of a spoken name is a phonologic representation. By implication, if phonologic representations affect the written response, then the written response should be the same as the spoken response. Consequently, when the written name diverges from the spoken name it cannot have originated in phonology. And yet a written response is produced, which implies that some intact representation is still present, perhaps an orthographic representation. Thus, by default, we infer the presence of spelling representations that are independent of phonologic representations. This inference is then extended backward in time. We project back in time to before these men had brain damage and infer that the same orthographic representations were autonomous in an intact specialised reading (writing) process.

We were invited to describe a different perspective on the previous patients' data. Our account is not more correct than those offered in the target articles. The framework that we work within cannot be discriminated from traditional computational models of cognitive performance on the basis of correspondence to data (see Stone & Van Orden, 1993, 1994). Instead, the value of our account derives from two simple propositions: Things can look a bit different from a different perspective, and multiple perspectives on phenomena may yield more general understandings of those phenomena.

The difference in perspective is fundamental. To understand why, we must back up the traditional logic and explore its root assumptions—i.e. how it is that one infers cognitive structures from observed behaviour. Next we discuss these root assumptions of the standard practice of cognitive neuropsychology. Past that point, we briefly review contemporary hypotheses concerning the neurological basis of behaviour. Our goal in that review is to motivate an alternative neurobiological metaphor that does not entail the root assumptions of conventional cognitive neuropsychology. Following that, we describe a simple recurrent network model of intact word perception that is congruent with contemporary neurobiology, and explain how this simple network begins to account for key findings from the target articles. The simple model is strictly grounded in the theoretical basis of the neurobiological metaphor. Finally, we review several recent findings that demonstrate the utility of our approach.

THE EFFECT = STRUCTURE ASSUMPTION

Standard computational models are usually laid out in a flow chart of processes that transform one cognitive structure into another, as when a spelling representation is transformed into a phonologic representation. Two of the target articles include flow chart illustrations that track the cognitive structures of reading and writing. In this section, we look closely at the theoretical method that licenses the discovery of these cognitive structures.

Orthographic representations and other cognitive structures are induced from reliable features of human behaviour. We observe specific patterns in behaviours, but our goal is to induce general structures of a cognitive architecture. However, no guaranteed formula exists for this generalisation, because an objective God's-eye-view of cognition is not possible. Instead we rely on plausible a priori assumptions, which we trust as though they were true. In contemporary cognitive psychology, for example, we assume that careful laboratory studies can reveal the presence of cognitive structures. Observed performance in laboratory tasks (e.g. the overall variability in response times or errors) is divided into component effects using linear statistical methods (e.g. ANOVA), and these component effects originate in causal components of mind. Thus, behaviour is assumed to be the *sum* of strictly separable pieces, *plus* some noise.

For example, in a categorisation task, subjects miscategorise homophones like ROWS as a *flower*, more often than control words like ROBS. This main effect of homophone phonology is treated as a separate piece of overall behaviour. The isolated piece is thought to originate in a distinct causal structure of the cognitive architecture, namely, a representation of /roz/. The contrast between the experimental condition (ROWS) and the control condition (ROBS) reduces behaviour (categorisation errors) to pieces (effects) that, in turn, indicate the pieces of mind (causal structures) in which the behaviour originates. In other words, *the presence of an effect equals the presence of a structure*.

In cognitive psychology, this logic usually ends as we left it in the previous paragraph—a positive demonstration of a reliable effect ends in the inference of a cognitive structure. However, it is just as important for this logic that the opposite side of this inference is reliable, namely, *the absence of an effect equals the absence of a structure* (Mackie, 1974; Mill, 1974). This logical entailment is not always made explicit by cognitive psychologists; it is more prominent in neuropsychology. Cognitive neuropsychologists must infer the nature of cognition prior to brain damage from the shape of behaviour after brain damage. They take careful note of the missing pieces of behaviour and use these observations to reconstruct the previously intact system. This is the basis for the standard dissociation logic of cognitive neuropsychology.

When the patient PW fails to name a picture of a PEAR correctly (Rapp et al., this issue), his error deviates from the response that would be expected from intact naming. Apparently, a causal structure that would be present in intact naming is absent in PW. The standard dissociation logic licenses the inference that a particular causal structure is missing and that this causal structure would have had isolable effects in the intact architecture. The failure to produce the spoken word *pear* thus indicates the absence of output phonology or some other linking structure in a causal chain with output phonology. All discussion in the target articles concerns precisely which structures are absent from a patient's behaviour. Cognitive neuropsychologists must always infer which or what kind of cognitive structures were present, prior to a lesion, from behaviour's missing pieces after the lesion (Patterson, 1981). Thus, they require a reliable basis to infer that *the absence of an effect equals the absence of a structure*. We refer to the *presence* and *absence* sides of this inference together as *effect = structure* (Van Orden, Holdend, Podgornik, & Aitchison, submitted; cf. Lakoff, 1987).

Assuming that *effect = structure*, the case studies described in the target articles supply compelling evidence that the complex writing and naming behaviour of these patients may be reduced to classes of behaviour or functions (e.g. writing versus naming), and that these functions may be reduced further to more elementary causal structures (e.g. orthographic and phonologic representations). Thus behaviour originates in isolable cognitive structures or *single causes*). Single causes entail the familiar notion of "domino causality." Push the first domino in a chain of standing dominos and each will fall in its turn. The input to this causal chain, a shove on the first domino, is linked to the output, the force of the first domino as it falls. In turn, this output becomes the input to the second domino, and so on, for each trailing domino down the chain. It is this notion of causality that is assumed in flow charts of cognition. A stimulus input is linked by causal rules through a hierarchical chain of representations, and the final output of this causal chain is the observed datum in a laboratory task.

Now comes the tricky part. Given that we may only observe the final output datum, how do we get inside this causal chain to discover its components? The solution is to choose tasks and manipulations that differ from each other by the causal equivalent of one domino (or one branch off a forked chain of dominos). The extensive test batteries in the target articles are designed for exactly this purpose. The problem that arises, however, is how to decide which tasks differ by exactly one single cause, or by one branch of single causes. One requires objective knowledge of how tasks are accomplished to know reliably which or how many components each task entails. Thus, we face an inescapable problem of circularity. Our goal is to induce general cognitive components entailed in a specific task from observed behaviour, but the method by which we induce these components requires reliable a priori knowledge of the self-same cognitive components.

No theoretical approach escapes this problem. Every act of induction derives from a set of a priori assumptions, and no act of induction can validate the assumptions from which it derives (cf. Duhem, 1954; Quine, 1961). No matter how compelling the apparent confirmation of single causes, we must resist accepting this confirmation as conclusive. Objective knowledge of single causes is required, a priori, to induce single causes reliably from observed behaviour. Consequently, the successful induction of single causes cannot be turned around to validate the root assumption. The simple danger here is that scientists may be seduced by their own success. The danger of this seduction is complacency, by which we mean the exclusion of other possibilities. The history of science is littered with previously successful paradigms that, in their time, were practised to the exclusion of other possibilities. With respect to the target articles, the conclusion that the observed pattern of dissociations demonstrates autonomous or independent representations (single causes) simply affirms the inevitable consequent of assuming there were autonomous representations in the first place (Shallice, 1988; Van Orden, Pennington, & Stone, submitted).

To this point, we have not questioned the utility of continuing in the standard practice of cognitive neuropsychology. We merely suggest that it is wise to maintain a sceptical stance with respect to a priori assumptions such as *effect = structure*.

NEUROBIOLOGY AND BEHAVIOUR

So why are we so concerned with a version of causality that, on the surface, seems so plausible? After all, causality, at our natural scale of experience, seems to agree with this intuition—dominos do knock each other down. Although intuitive causality may serve us in ordinary circumstances, it may nevertheless distort our view of cognitive systems. By comparison, many other areas of contemporary science have been reframed by taking an alternative perspective that does not simply entail single causes (e.g. see Cohen & Stuart, 1994; Freeman, 1995; Goodwin, 1994). This alternative also invokes a reciprocal form of causality in which every part of a system is always present in each behaviour of that system. Each of these parts continuously affects every other part, to the point that their independent contributions cannot be sorted out in the behaviour of the whole. Most important, this perspective has usefully been applied to neuroscience, which is pertinent to our present concerns. The educated guesses that we make concerning brain damage are informed by our knowledge of how brains work in the first place. We will illustrate this notion of reciprocal causality by describing contemporary hypotheses concerning the neurobiological basis of behaviour.

At one time, Hubel and Wiesel's classic experiments seemed to provide a reasonable basis in neurobiology for single causes. They demonstrated reliable correlations between stimulus events and individual neuronal activity (Hubel & Wiesel, 1962, 1965, 1968). Flow-chart theories often extrapolate from Hubel and Wiesel's findings. "Feature detectors" are extended metaphorically to cognitive systems where they become hierarchies of representations. In perception, hierarchies of stimulus features, and combinations of features, culminate in explicit representations of whole stimulus forms ("grandmother cells"). This qualitatively linear scheme assumes a causal chain between real-world objects, their stimulus forms, and their consequent representations. Access to representations may depend on weakly nonlinear mechanisms such as thresholds, but they are laid out in a linear chain of single causes from proximal stimulus to intermediate representations to observed behaviour.

The previous causal chain was composed of isolable representations that correspond to behaviourally meaningful information. In its simplest form, this metaphor implies representations with binary states analogous to neural detectors that are either above or below their thresholds (alternatively, a continuous change in neural response amplitude eventually yields a discontinuous change in representation). Recent findings, however, suggest that neural activity undergoes a more complex qualitative change than crossing a threshold. This qualitative change entails the reciprocal causality that we mentioned earlier.

Presently, behaviour is thought to originate in neural activity that self-organises through recurrent feedback into interdependent, context-sensitive, dynamic patterns. Observable behaviour derives from complex coordinated activity among populations of *sensory* and *motor* neurons (Bressler, Coppola, & Nakamura, 1993; Freeman, 1991a, 1991b, 1995; Singer, 1993; Skarda & Freeman, 1987; von der Malsburg & Schneider, 1986). Although, initially, a stimulus pattern may activate specific neural ensembles (Livingstone & Hubel, 1988), this local activation is subsequently transformed into a global pattern as the system self-organises in recurrent feedback dynamics (Freeman, 1995; Skarda & Freeman, 1987). Input conditions of local activation become complex oscillating patterns in which the character of "input" activity is a strongly nonlinear function of "output" activity. These complex patterns are not strictly tied to the local tissue that serves as their excitable medium. Global patterns of neural activation are related to neurons in (very) roughly the same way that global patterns of ocean waves are related to water molecules. (See Goodwin, 1994, for more precise but less mundane analogies.) Nevertheless, each global pattern maintains an identifiable but highly context-sensitive profile in the amplitude "waves" of neural activity.

We may find utility in the contemporary neurobiological metaphor for understanding cognitive performance. However, we must accommodate the *nonlinear* qualitative transformation of *sensory* and *motor* activation into subsequent, behaviourally meaningful, *sensorimotor* dynamics. By implication, the performance of cognitive systems is not reduced to local chains of independent feature hierarchies; behaviour emerges in coordinated activity among interdependent *sensorimotor ensembles*. This strongly nonlinear, qualitative transformation leaves no practical possibility of reducing cognitive performance to singularly causal neural ensembles, nor even singularly causal component oscillations. Within this metaphor, sensory and motor activation are combined and transformed as their dynamic trajectory traces a path of *metastable states*.

Metastability implies that a nervous system never settles fully on a dominant percept or action (attractor). In a sense, this means that the system is always entertaining alternative possibilities, albeit only one alternative may be expressed in perception and action. Consequently this system is always slightly unstable. This instability makes it more flexible. By (very) rough analogy, a person who *always* has an alternative "plan B," or plans B, C, and D, at *every* juncture, would appear more flexible (metastable) than a single-minded person who cannot deviate from plan A. Crucially, however, if metastable neural states are the basis of observable behaviour, then no basis exists in observable behaviour for inducing causal chains of representations. The metastable basis of behaviour is antithetical to discovering implacable single causes that run from input to output.

In such strongly nonlinear complex systems, it is impossible to track backwards from observable, contextually embedded, stimulus-response, attractor states to initial conditions. Consequently, it is not possible to discover a causally distinct "input" component. Performance with few degrees of freedom emerges in patterns of sensorimotor activity with moderate degrees of freedom, which originate in prior patterns of sensory and motor activation with vast degrees of freedom. Each reduction in the degrees of freedom is a loss of information about previous states of the system. The loss of information creates an impenetrable *barrier of uncertainty* (Abraham & Shaw, 1992; Prigogine & Stengers, 1984). This barrier blocks any possibility of discovering linear causal chains running between proximal stimuli and performance (Uttal, 1990). Rather, "stimulus" and "response" are better viewed as an irreducible whole that self-organises through recurrent feedback (Freeman, 1995; Van Orden & Goldinger, 1994, 1996; Varela, Thompson, & Rosch, 1991). This self-organising gestalt allows fluid continuity between action and perception, and organism and environment (Gibson, 1986; Turvey & Carello, 1981). Coincidentally, the striking competence of behaviour is fluid accommodation of continuous changes in the environment (Gibbs & Van Orden, submitted; Stone & Van Orden, 1993; Thelen & Smith, 1994; Van Orden, Holden, et al., submitted).

Contemporary models of nervous systems are specific applications of mathematical dynamic systems theory, the most general formal framework available to scientists. Dynamic systems theory concerns how behaviour of complex systems changes over time. This mathematical theory promises someday to provide a common metalanguage for diverse areas of science (Abraham & Shaw, 1992; Haken, 1984). Today, it provides new theoretical and methodological tools for scientific enquiry. This framework is so general as to include previous flow-chart models as a subset of possibilities. Giunti (1995) describes how computational models (Turing machines) form a narrow subset of dynamic systems. Our discussion requires a related point: The products of linear reductive analyses (reliable intercorrelations between independent and dependent variables) may always be redescribed ("regraphed") to coincide with the trajectory of a dynamic system. Consequently, behaviour thought to be characteristic of linear systems may always be reframed in terms of more general nonlinear systems. The simple point here is that dynamic systems theory is sufficient to account for any behavioural phenomenon that was previously formalised in a flow-chart model. What remains to be determined is whether it will have utility over and above the traditional approach (Carello, Turvey, & Lukatela, 1992).

In the next section, we describe a model system in which behaviour is organised by recurrent feedback. Our model system is not reducible to a neural account, although it is strictly in line with the contemporary metaphor. As Thelen and Smith (1994, p. 130) note: "While mechanisms of change for mental processes most certainly do involve changes in neurotransmission, satisfactory explanations need not reside only at this level. Nonetheless . . . explanation at every level must be consistent and ultimately reconcilable . . . the dynamics of behavioural phenomena must be consistent with the dynamics of the neural phenomena."

We propose that many behavioural and neural phenomena may be reconciled with respect to a common mathematical basis, as found in dynamic systems theory. Respective choices for models within this framework, however, are mostly determined by the observed complexity of the behaviour to be modelled. For example, we model performance in simple reading tasks. Simple reading tasks provide punctate data measured at a single point in time (response time) and scored for accuracy. Thus, we may begin with models appropriate for "fixed-point" data—i.e. models that converge on point attractors. The network that we describe is not superficially isomorphic to a neurobiological model (e.g. Freeman, 1987). At most, it traces a low-dimensional "shadow" of the vastly higher dimensional description of nervous systems.

Our goal is to illustrate how the behavioural trajectory of a fully interdependent dynamic system may simulate the behaviour that is characteristic of dissociations. In the service of this goal (Freeman, 1995, p. 53): " . . . we move conceptually from the local neural network and its clearly defined properties out to the limits of its utility, multiply the network to infinity, and then awaken into a new local network in which the infinities of components are collapsed into the emergent elements at the next higher hierarchical level." Our simple model mimics intact behaviour and the behaviour characteristic of dissociations. Eventually, we explain how this simple model could fail to name a "picture" of a pear and yet produce a "written" response, or produce different "spoken" and written responses to the same picture.

PHONOLOGIC MEDIATION IN READING AND SPELLING

The emphasis in much reading research is on the perception of single words, as this is the most predictive aspect of reading skill. A poor aptitude for word perception severely limits the development of skilled reading and reading comprehension (Pennington, 1991; Perfetti, 1985). As noted in the target articles, a perennial question in such research is whether a word's phonology always mediates visual word perception. For reading, a recent proliferation of phonology effects in laboratory paradigms suggests that phonology's role is fundamental (for overviews, see Berent & Perfetti, 1995; Carello et al., 1992; Frost, submitted; Katz & Frost, 1992; Perfetti, Zhang, & Berent, 1992; Van Orden et al., 1990). For writing, systematic misspellings, like substituting ROZE or ROWS for ROSE, are common (for an overview, see Bosman & Van Orden, in press). Phonologic constraints are also apparent in patients' spelling performance, as when a patient spells YACHT as YOT (Hatfield & Patterson, 1983). Moreover, patients who exhibit substantially disrupted phonology almost always also exhibit bizarre reading performance.

Phonology effects are found with readers and writers spanning the full range of reading skill. They are found across languages (in both alphabetic and nonalphabetic writing systems), and across laboratory tasks. All these phenomena converge on the straightforward conclusion that phonology is fundamental to intact reading and spelling. Why is phonology so involved in reading or spelling? In the next section, we describe a recurrent network model of word perception and spelling that explains phonology's fundamental role. The description pertains to a very simple model that has been implemented (Farrar & Van Orden, 1994), but the principled basis of our account is not tied to the specifics of our simulation (see Stone & Van Orden, 1994; Van Orden & Goldinger, 1994).

We do not propose a connectionist network that is causally in between a stimulus and a response. The nodes of our model cannot be localised within a mind or brain separate from its environment (see also Saltzman, 1995). At first this may sound paradoxical, but recurrent dynamics are plausibly described as occurring directly, between an organism and its environment (Turvey & Carello, 1981; Van Orden & Goldinger, 1994). Perhaps this theoretical entailment will appear less paradoxical if we take into account the pragmatic entailments of behavioural research. Behavioural data cannot apportion effects between environments and organisms because behaviour always occurs at their interface. Consequently, with respect to behavioural data, there is no reliable way to determine where the environment leaves off and the organism begins (Shanon, 1993; Varela et al., 1991). Organism and environment are always both "present" in every instance of behaviour. Nevertheless, to make our story more concrete we tell it with respect to a fictitious nervous system.

A SIMPLE MODEL

Imagine a fictitious nervous system that perceives printed words. This system consists of three families of neurons: letter neurons, phoneme neurons, and semantic neurons. Every neuron in each family is (potentially) bidirectionally connected to every neuron of the other two families. Bidirectional connectivity means that if a feedforward connection exists from neuron "x" to neuron "y," there is also a feedback connection from neuron "y" to neuron "x." Now, imagine a specific pattern of activation across the letter neurons, due to the presence of a printed word. This letter pattern feeds activation forward through a matrix of "synaptic" connections, creating patterns of activation across phoneme and semantic neurons. The phoneme and semantic neurons, in turn, feed activation back through a top-down matrix of connections, transforming their patterns back into letter patterns. Whenever the feedback patterns match the original letter pattern, top-down activation *conserves* bottom-up activation. Consequently, the "matched" letter neurons conserve their capacity to reactivate matching phoneme and semantic neurons that, in turn, reactivate the letter neurons, and so on. This feedback cycle is temporarily stable, resulting in a coherent dynamic whole—a *resonance*.

This neural network is only for exposition. It is helpful to consider word perception in terms of artificial neural activity, but the more precise analogy between nervous systems and cognitive systems is a hypothetical trajectory of sensorimotor dynamics (alternatively, a perception-action trajectory) that is correlated with cognitive performance. No claim is made concerning the "correct" architecture (see Stone & Van Orden, 1994; Van Orden & Goldinger, 1994; Van Orden et al, 1990; Van Orden, Holden, et al., submitted; Van Orden, Pennington, et al., submitted). Thus, with respect to the model's nodes, we are free to discuss word perception in cognitive system's terms. Figure 1 illustrates cognitive macrodynamics of word perception (Van Orden & Goldinger, 1994, 1996) and spelling (Bosman & Van Orden, in press), and Fig. 2 illustrates microdynamics.

Figure 1 portrays a recurrent network with three families of fully interdependent nodes (letter nodes, phoneme nodes, and semantic nodes). On average, the connections between node families differ in strength; the rank order of

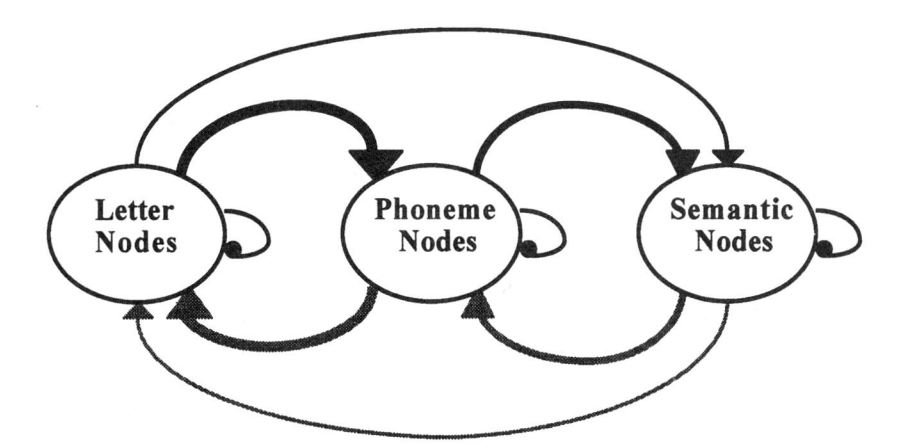

FIG. 1. Macrodynamics of reading and spelling performance emergent in a recurrent network. The boldness of the arrows indicates the overall strength of the relations between letter, phoneme, and semantic node families (see text).

overall strength is illustrated by the relative boldness of arrows in the figure. In alphabetic languages, letters and phonemes correlate quite strongly. For example, the letter B is almost always pronounced as [b], and the phoneme [b] is always written with a B. Correlations between phonemes and semantic features, or letters and semantic features, are far weaker than correlations between letters and phonemes. Knowing that a word begins with the letter B indicates almost nothing about its meaning, but much about its initial pronunciation.

Notice also that phoneme-semantic relations are depicted as stronger correlations than letter-semantic relations, primarily because we speak before and more often than we read. Once in place, this asymmetry is self-perpetuating. Reading strengthens phoneme-semantic connections, because phonology functions in every instance of printed word perception. Thus, even the exceptional condition of people who read more than they speak would support phoneme-semantic connections that are at least as strong as letter-semantic connections. Also, if a coherent positive feedback loop forms between phoneme and semantic nodes, before the feedback loop between letter and semantic nodes, then printed or spoken discourse may proceed without resolving the feedback loop between letter and semantic nodes. The absence of resonance in the latter feedback loop may preclude strengthening the connections between letter and semantic nodes (Grossberg & Stone, 1986). Thus, at this macro-level of description, node families differ in overall strength of relations with other node families. These differences in overall correlational structure are illustrated in the relative boldness of the arrows in Fig. 1.

The strong bidirectional connections between letter and phoneme nodes, as compared to those with semantic nodes, causes the letter-phoneme dynamic to cohere (resonate) before all others. This is the *phonologic coherence hypothesis*. The relatively consistent bidirectional covariance between letters (form) and phonemes (function) explains how phonology comes to be so fundamental in reading and spelling. Stated differently, it explains why sound-alike words (ROSE and ROWS) may be confused in reading (Van Orden, 1987); it explains why the majority of spelling errors (ROZE instead of ROSE) are phonologically acceptable; and it explains why patients' spoken and written errors often resemble the spelling and pronunciations of the correct response that was not produced. (Van Orden & Goldinger, 1994, 1996; Van Orden, Pennington, et al., submitted, describe various other phenomena that derive from the bidirectional covariance between spelling and phonology.)

In a model analogous to Fig. 1, presentation of a printed word activates letter nodes, which, in turn, activate phoneme and semantic nodes. Following initial activation, recurrent feedback begins among all these node families. Similarly, presentation of a spoken word activates phoneme nodes, which, in turn, activate semantic and letter nodes (and "picture naming" might be simulated with activation of semantic nodes which, in turn, activate phoneme and letter nodes, cf. Dell, Schwartz, Martin, Saffran, & Gagnon, in press). In all these cases, initial activation leads to recurrent feedback among all node families. However, the strongest recurrent dynamic is between letter and phoneme nodes, which creates the common basis of reading and spelling. The strength of a recurrent dynamic is a function of *self-consistency*—the capacity of a node or a family of nodes to conserve their own activation (Smolensky, 1986; Van Orden et al., 1990). Nodes conserve their activation when they "send" it to other nodes that "return" it in relatively exclusive recurrent feedback. This capacity to conserve activation derives from relatively consistent bidirectional covariance between nodes or node families—i.e. a history of structural coupling (cf. Varela et al., 1991). The bidirectional relation between letter and phoneme nodes is more self-consistent than other pairings of node families. Consequently, letter-phoneme dynamics supply the strongest and most generally reliable constraints on the model's performance.

Notice the difference between the description of phonologic mediation in the target articles and the phonologic coherence hypothesis. Linear flow-chart models use the term *phonologic mediation* to refer to a causally intermediate phonologic representation that is activated by spelling representations and, in turn, activates semantic representations (for example)[1]. This is why phonologic

---

[1] My (Van Orden's) view of phonologic mediation has changed in the last decade, as I have learned more of mathematical dynamic systems theory. I have moved from a representational connectionist view (e.g. Van Orden, 1987) to a "nonrepresentational" cognitive systems view (e.g. Van Orden & Goldinger, 1994). However, I do not recall proposing the straw man account that is attributed to me in the target articles. A more careful reading of my cited articles would find the following quotes:

> The extent to which phonology affects performance . . . is underscored by the simple verification model's relatively comprehensive account of [these] results . . . even though it lacked a mechanism of direct access. This is not to say that I deny the possibility of direct access (Van Orden, 1987, p. 192).

> A mechanism of covariant learning can also accomplish direct access in the same way that it accomplishes phonological coding . . . any linguistic features that frequently covary with orthographic features will become associated. The consequence . . . for any subsequent instance of lexical coding will be that, initially, a representation of the spelling of a word will activate most strongly those linguistic features (i.e. semantic, syntactic, and phonological features) that covary to the highest degree with its orthographic features (Van Orden, 1987, p. 194).

> This is not to say that we deny the possibility of direct bottom-up activation of lexical features by orthographic features. Rather, it may be useful to abandon the notion of separate, independent routes of lexical access. A potential alternative . . . is a connectionist mechanism . . . that . . . comes to reflect the covariance between all linguistic features (syntactic, semantic, and phonological) and orthographic features in its associative weights . . . (Van Orden, Johnston, & Hale, 1988, p. 382).

Continued overleaf

mediation has appeared inefficient and counterintuitive (Van Orden & Goldinger, 1994). Why should information processing traverse the same psychological distance in two steps (step one: orthography to phonology; step two: phonology to semantics), rather than one step (orthography to semantics)? By contrast, the phonologic coherence hypothesis implies that phonology's mediating effect in reading and writing is economical and efficient. Self-consistent feedback from phonology rapidly organises the system, and strongly constrains local competitions that would organise the visual stimulus. Subsequently, a coherent visual-phonologic dynamic "mediates" competitions among alternative global interpretations—their chances for survival are enhanced if they conform to extant, visual-phonologic dynamics. Phonologic "mediation" is inescapable in the simple model, due to the powerfully self-consistent relation between letter nodes and phoneme nodes.

Figure 2 illustrates microdynamics. Now we zoom in on the connectivity between letter and phoneme nodes (and ignore, for now, phoneme-semantic and letter-semantic connectivity). In Fig. 2a, reading the printed word HI includes activation of letter nodes H_1 and I_2, which activate the phoneme nodes $[h_1]$ and $[a^I_2]$, but also competing correlated nodes such as $[I_2]$ (as in [hIt]) which must be inhibited. (The subscripts refer to the positions of the letters or phonemes in words.) Figure 2b shows how, in turn, phoneme nodes feed activation back to letter nodes (illustrated for the phoneme nodes $[h_1]$ and $[a^I_2]$). The phoneme node $[a^I_2]$ activates the correct letter nodes H_1 and I_2 and also competing letter nodes, for example, the letter node Y_2 as in MY or BY. Thus, early patterns of activation are loosely structured. They include the activation of correct, but also many incorrect, candidates for resonance. This is due to *multistability*, a defining characteristic of dynamic systems. In our simple model, the dynamics from this point select a combination of nodes through cooperative-competitive dynamics.

Reliable performance emerges if the overall bidirectional configuration of connections favours mutual activation between the letter nodes H_1 and I_2 and the phoneme nodes $[h_1]$ and $[a^I_2]$. This advantage grows over time as the "strong grow stronger" and the "weak grow weaker" (cf. McClelland & Rumelhart,

---

Name (phonologic) codes have a . . . processing advantage over other lexical codes. This advantage is not, however, an advantage in the relative time course of phonologic activation; phonologic codes are activated in parallel with other linguistic codes. Rather, relatively invariant phonologic codes are relatively stable pockets of lexical activity, and other lexical codes congeal around this relative stability (Van Orden et al., 1990, p. 513).

Once again, we emphasize that it is not a difference in the time course of initial activation that distinguishes phonologic codes: All lexical codes are activated in parallel. Instead it is the difference in coherence times that constrains processing (Van Orden et al., 1990, p. 514).

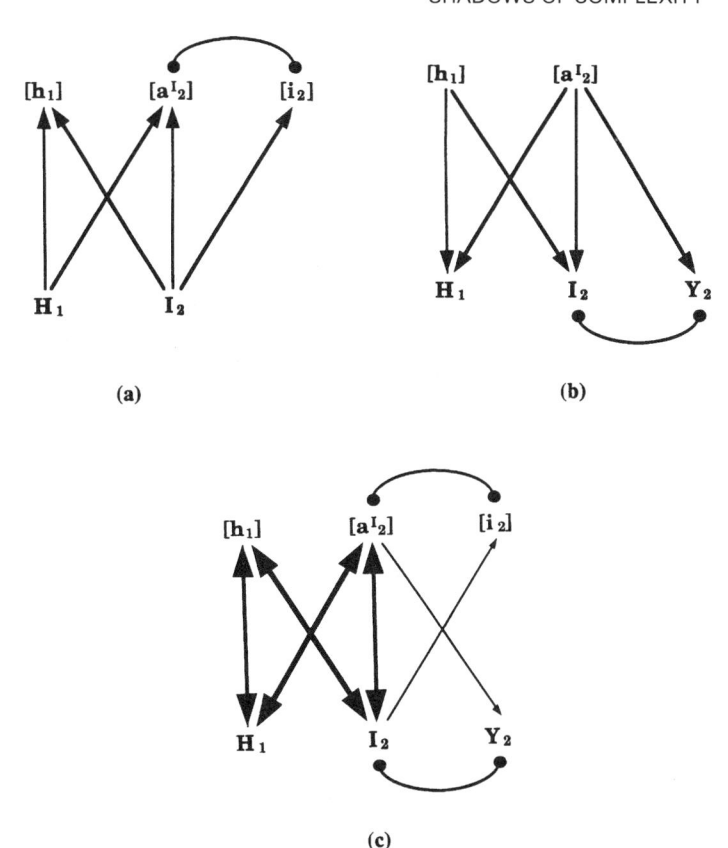

FIG. 2. A simplified illustration of microdynamics that "read aloud" the word HI. (a) Presented with HI, activation feeds forward from letter nodes to phoneme nodes. (b) In turn, phoneme nodes feed activation back to letter nodes. (c) A resonance that emerges between letter and phoneme nodes corresponding to HI. To reduce the number of lines in the figure, bidirectional connections are depicted with single double-headed arrows.

1981). This is illustrated in Fig. 2c, which combines the flow of activation from letter nodes to phoneme nodes and from phoneme nodes back to letter nodes, as assumed in a recurrent network. Presentation of the spoken word /ha^I/ to the network (as in a spelling task) leads to a similar dynamic between phoneme and letter nodes. Thus, activation initiated in phoneme nodes may generate a coherent pattern of activity across letter nodes.

THE DISSOCIATION BETWEEN READING AND SPELLING

Anyone who writes in English will experience occasional doubts about how to spell a word, but we almost never forget how a word should be read aloud. This dissociation of intact naming from intact spelling is evident for a variety of languages, at all levels of skill (Bosman & Van Orden, in press). This dissociation is also present, although exaggerated, in the performance of PW (Rapp et al., this issue) and WMA (Micelli et al., this issue). Both these patients correctly read aloud many more words than they correctly spell in written picture naming or to dictation. We do not suggest that their spelling performance is not affected by their lesions, just that this pattern respects the topology of intact naming and spelling. The discussion of these patients in the target articles does not take into account the topological properties of intact performance, but we eventually discuss why this concern is more salient from our perspective.

Our account explains why people find spelling more difficult than reading aloud. This dissociation illustrates one basis for dissociations in a "lesioned" recurrent network. The model may behave one way if activation of letter nodes drives a naming response, but differently if activation of phoneme nodes drives a spelling response. This dissociation may be described simply with respect to the previous illustrations of microdynamics (letter-phoneme dynamics), and macrodynamics (dynamics among node families).

Returning to Fig. 2, reading the word HI not only activates phoneme nodes $[h_1]$ and $[a^I_2]$, and the letter nodes H_1 and I_2, but also all possible pronunciations of H_1 and I_2 and all possible spellings of $[h_1]$ and $[a^I_2]$. Again, this is due to multistability. The same stimulus supports multiple percepts and actions. Multistability implies that reading a word correctly must include inhibition of incorrect phoneme nodes, and spelling a word correctly must include inhibition of incorrect letter nodes. In the case of reading, the letters are presented to the model (or reader). As a consequence, phoneme → letter ambiguity is highly unlikely to result in full activation of incorrect letter nodes, because persistent and stable environmental constraints (visible letters) accelerate correct feedback loops with phoneme and semantic nodes (as illustrated by bold arrows in Fig 2c). In the case of spelling, however, one must generate this resonant pattern from phonologic and semantic activation alone. In this case, the environment does not include explicit support for correct letter nodes.

Differences in environmental constraints strongly affect performance. For example, a patient may be much better at repeating auditorily presented pseudowords—i.e. explicit environmental support for phonology—than at reading pseudowords aloud—i.e. only implicit environmental support for phonology (Funnell, 1983). Likewise, a patient may be much better at copying printed words than at writing to dictation. This point is also more salient from a perspective that emphasises a history of covariance (structural coupling) between environmental forms and their cognitive functions. From a traditional view, the environment is equally relevant or irrelevant in both cases, because it must be represented symbolically.

The crux of spelling is that English orthography, generally, has more possible spellings for any given word than possible readings, and this is true of most writing systems (e.g. Stone, Vanhoy, & Van Orden, in press; Ziegler, Stone, & Jacobs, in press). Consider, for example, the multiple inconsistent "spelling bodies" that may correspond to the "rime" [__ûrch], __IRCH as in BIRCH, __ERCH as in PERCH, __URCH as in LURCH, and __EARCH as in SEARCH. Stone et al. (in press) estimated that 31% of low-frequency English one-syllable words are spelling → phonology inconsistent (at the grain-size of spelling-bodies and rimes), but fully 72% are phonology → spelling inconsistent (at the same grain-size). This estimate was corroborated in a larger sample, including both low- and high-frequency one-syllable words. Again, 72% of all spelling → phonology consistent words were phonology → spelling inconsistent. These linguistic analyses clearly indicate that phonology → spelling inconsistency is the rule for English (see also Ziegler, Jacobs, & Stone, in press, concerning French).

Although both reading and spelling are powerfully constrained by the strong correlational structure of letter-phoneme relations, the occasional inconsistencies in these relations are resolved by different sources of constraint. Now, we refer again to the illustration of macrodynamics in Fig. 1. When a model "reads" a low-frequency, spelling → phonology *inconsistent word* such as PINT, the more consistent letter-phoneme relation would rhyme with MINT (and HINT, LINT, TINT). Similarly, the letter-phoneme dynamic would yield two correct pronunciations for words like WIND (although it would typically favour the more regular pronunciation, Kawamoto & Zemblidge, 1992). In both these cases, relatively strong semantic-phoneme relations may supply sufficient secondary constraints to encourage the appropriate letter-phoneme dynamic. In the case of WIND, semantic constraints may also be due to context. In the model, contextual and stimulus sources of semantic constraints contribute via the relatively strong connections between semantic and phoneme nodes. Highly imageable or concrete words have stronger semantic correlations to letters and phonemes, which promotes better intact and patient performance (cf. Plaut & Shallice, 1993; Strain, Patterson, & Seidenberg, 1995). Also, added contextual support for correct performance contributes directly through semantic connections to activation of letter and phoneme nodes.

In the case of spelling, a model must resolve the inverted patterns of ambiguity in the phoneme-letter dynamic. To spell a low-frequency phonology → spelling inconsistent word such as HEAP, the rime [__ip]'s correct spelling would compete with a more strongly correlated incorrect spelling-body __EEP (as in DEEP, BEEP, KEEP, PEEP, SEEP, and WEEP). Additionally, the phoneme-letter dynamic yields two correct spellings for homophones (e.g. ROSE/ROWS). In either case, correct spelling must rely on relatively weak semantic-letter constraints (as illustrated in Fig. 1) to activate the appropriate letter nodes sufficiently—even contextual support is filtered through the weak letter-semantic connections. This weaker support for spelling, compared to the strong support for reading (i.e. phoneme-semantic constraints) is the "macro-basis" for the asymmetry between reading and spelling. Spelling is thus more difficult than reading for two reasons: microdynamic phoneme → letter relations are more inconsistent than letter → phoneme relations, and macrodynamic support for spelling (i.e. letter-semantic connections) is weaker than macrodynamic support for reading (i.e. phoneme-semantic connections).

SIMULATED BRAIN DAMAGE

The previous section demonstrates the utility of our model for understanding intact performance. In this section, we discuss how this approach may be extended to patient data. Our focus will be limited to a few theoretically important phenomena associated with acquired dyslexia, and a few key performance phenomena from the target articles. Marshall and Newcombe's (1973) classic article described distinct syndromes of acquired dyslexia: *surface dyslexia* and *deep dyslexia*. These syndromes are defined by characteristic profiles of naming errors. For example, deep dyslexics sometimes produce bizarre semantic errors (e.g. BUSH named as TREE), and surface dyslexics sometimes produce regularisation errors (e.g. PINT named to rhyme with MINT). Next, we describe how to produce similar errors in "lesioned" models that previously produced patterns of skilled naming performance.

Regularisation errors are characteristic of surface dyslexic patients, occurring when words such as PINT, with irregular pronunciations, are read aloud incorrectly to rhyme with similar regular words (e.g. MINT, HINT, and LINT). Although skilled readers also make regularisation errors in speeded naming tasks (Kawamoto & Zemblidge, 1992), surface dyslexic patients make many more. Regularisation errors are symptoms of multistable dynamics in intact naming. Multistability implies that multiple percepts and actions may arise to the same stimulus. For example, intact dynamics that lead to a correct pronunciation of PINT include the rhyme with MINT, which must be inhibited. The rhyme with MINT is locally more self-consistent because it is favoured by overall letter-phoneme covariance. In a model, the relatively late phoneme-semantic resonance strengthens the correct pronunciation of PINT and allows it to inhibit the "regularisation error" (Van Orden & Goldinger, 1994). Thus, regularisation errors in intact performance are much more likely when naming is speeded using a deadline procedure, and when a phoneme-semantic resonance is weaker as in low-frequency words. Also, regularisation errors in patient performance are correlated with semantic deficits that may imply reduced semantic constraints for inconsistent pronunciations (Patterson & Hodges, 1992; Patterson, Marshall, & Coltheart, 1985; Warrington, 1975). In a model, the reduced constraints from phoneme-semantic dynamics release the more regular pronunciation from the inhibition, resulting in a regularisation error.

Semantic errors are characteristic of deep dyslexic patients, occurring when words are read aloud incorrectly as semantically related words. For example, the word BUSH might be read aloud incorrectly as TREE. Semantic errors are also symptoms of multistable dynamics and release from inhibition. In a model, activation of semantic nodes leads, in the next time step, to activation of all letter and phoneme nodes which have previously covaried with any active semantic node. This allows the surface features of a competitor, such as TREE, to be activated by a semantically related stimulus word, such as BUSH. An intact model is saved from semantic errors because the letter nodes of BUSH are explicit in the environment and they are powerfully correlated with the phoneme nodes of BUSH. Thus, BUSH's letter-phoneme dynamic readily inhibits the surface features of TREE in intact performance.

The separate occurrence of semantic and regularisation errors has been incorrectly interpreted to be evidence against recurrent network models (see Van Orden, Pennington, et al., submitted, for a review and counter-argument). Farrar and Van Orden (1994) refuted this claim with an existence proof—i.e. a recurrent network model that produces these two error types. They began with a network very similar in structure to the simple illustrations presented in this commentary. Three families of nodes (see Fig. 1) were "taught" a sample of English words using a Hebbian-type learning algorithm (10 learning trials each for "high-frequency" words and 1 each for "low-frequency" words), until the model produced patterns of naming performance similar to those of skilled readers. The "naming response" was taken from the pattern of most active phonemes and "naming time" was defined as the number of cycles required to generate a coherent pattern of phonemes.) In particular, the model produced a frequency × consistency interaction. Low-frequency inconsistent words such as PINT were named more slowly than low-frequency consistent words such as DUCK, whereas all high-frequency words were named quickly (see Waters & Seidenberg, 1985).

To simulate the regularisation error, they added noise to the intact network. Noise was implemented as a uniform distribution of small increments of positive or negative activation added in each cycle to the activation values of randomly chosen nodes. The noise eroded the strength of phoneme-semantic attractors. In turn, this eroded the network's capacity for inhibiting regularisation errors. For example, instead of PINT's correct phonemes, the network produced activation on phoneme nodes that regularised PINT to rhyme with MINT. Specifically, noise destabilised the weakest phoneme-semantic attractors, which released from inhibition the powerful local constraints of "regular" letter-phoneme attractors. Because letter-phoneme dynamics primarily reflect the strongest correlations between letters and phonemes, they are naturally drawn into regularisation errors.

Importantly, Farrar and Van Orden (1994) could have simulated regularisation errors in several ways. A "lesion" could be implemented by reducing top-down activation from semantic nodes to phonologic nodes (Patterson et al., in press; Plaut, McClelland, Seidenberg, & Patterson, 1996). Their more subtle implementation added a uniform distribution of noise, which erodes the model's capacity to enter weakly self-consistent resonances (compare Lewenstein & Nowak, 1989). Alternatively, they could have introduced small changes in randomly chosen connection strengths. Similarly, the *locus* of noise need not be crucial. Bidirectional flow of activation means that noise introduced anywhere in the model spreads throughout the model in the next time step (although noise reduction does occur due to remote local inhibition). Because weaker "coarse-grain" phoneme-semantic relations yield less self-consistent dynamic structures, they are more vulnerable. Performances that rely on similar coarse-grain, visual-phoneme-semantic constraints include naming of irregular words, object and picture naming, and comprehension. These performances are typically deficient in surface dyslexia.

To simulate semantic errors, Farrar and Van Orden (1994) further "lesioned" the noisy network that previously produced regularisation errors. They set all of the letter-phoneme connections at zero, effectively "cutting" the connections (they could have cut fewer connections with the same effect; the minimum proportion that would produce semantic errors is interdependent with other modelling choices such as the amount of noise). Subsequently, the network produced semantic errors. When presented with BUSH, the network produced a relatively unstable pattern of activity across phoneme nodes corresponding to TREE. Setting the letter-phoneme connections to zero creates a highly unstable network, causing it to rely heavily on semantic-phoneme dynamics, the most reliable remaining source of constraints. However, in the absence of letter-phoneme constraints, semantic-phoneme dynamics are sometimes misled into a semantic error, and the relatively weaker letter-semantic dynamics cannot rescue the network from this error. Semantic errors are especially likely when semantic nodes of one word (BUSH) are strongly correlated with phoneme nodes of a different word (TREE) (see also Plaut & Shallice, 1993).

The Dissociation of Writing and Naming

So, how might we simulate dissociations of written and spoken responses in picture naming? Farrar and Van Orden (1994) did not construct a model of picture naming, but we can understand how such a model would behave by thinking of picture naming as a dynamic initiated from semantic nodes to letter and phoneme nodes. The crux of the present articles is that a dissociation between written and spoken picture names forces the inference that *intact* writing and naming include causally independent orthographic representations. Thus, any lesioned model that mimics this dissociation, but does not entail causally independent orthographic nodes, contradicts the basis of this inference. In this regard, we point out that the previous simulation of semantic errors already exhibits a dissociation of "written" letter node activation from "spoken" phoneme node activation, as we describe next.

Suppose that we presented "pictures" to a model that already produces semantic errors. An artificial lesion has disconnected letter and phoneme nodes and also generated a uniform distribution of noise. This results in a highly unstable system with no direct constraints between phoneme and letter nodes (however, they are still causally interdependent through indirect recurrent connections). Such a system may generate the same written and spoken names when a complete, relatively familiar semantic pattern resonates with phoneme and letter nodes. Alternatively, if the semantic pattern that initiates dynamics is incomplete then it may support different letter nodes and phoneme nodes. This is especially likely if the history of semantic-phoneme covariance favours a different response than the history of semantic-letter covariance (compare the previous dissociation of spelling and naming in intact performance). Of course, ablating a portion of the phoneme nodes would further degrade explicitly phonologic performance. (See Dell et al., in press, for additional modelling choices.)

We have described how an overly-simple recurrent network can dissociate written responses from spoken responses, but the intact version of this model does not include autonomous spelling representations. Moreover, it would be a mistake to imagine that the simple model is the only possible choice within the cognitive systems framework, or that "falsification" of the simple model impugnes our more general claims concerning causality. That reasoning would ignore the strong and broad theoretical basis of this framework in mathematical dynamic systems theory. Just as one may always construct a flow-chart model of performance, one may also always construct a theoretically meaningful recurrent network to mimic any performance profile of any complexity (Stone & Van Orden, 1994). We have described a minimal model that was trained to embody a subset of visual-phonologic-semantic covariant structure. Once trained, that model's behavioural trajectories suffice to mimic theoretically important intact performance, and to produce dissociations when lesioned.

The Topology of Performance

Empirical constraints on the construction of cognitive systems models are primarily derived from generic patterns in behaviour (Abraham & Shaw, 1992). This basis for rigorous qualitative analysis may be very useful for cognitive neuropsychology, which deals mostly with qualitative effects. For example, we have discussed generic predictions for intact naming and spelling that derive from self-consistency between spelling, phonology, and meaning (e.g. Bosman & Van Orden, in press; Van Orden & Goldinger, 1994). This performance topology may be tested against the behaviour of patients. Table 1 summarises the patients' performance from the target articles on six key tasks. Macro- and

TABLE 1
Representative Performance in Each of Six Tasks by the Patients PW, WMA, PS, and EA[a] (Proportion Correct)

Task	Stimulus	Response	PW	WMA	PS	EA
Copying	Printed word	Printed word	.94	.94	—	—
Repetition	Spoken word	Spoken word	.99	.97	.40	.98
Reading aloud	Printed word	Spoken word	.89	.78	.42	.40
Writing to dictation	Spoken word	Printed word	.44	.55	.76	.48
Picture naming: Spoken response	Picture	Spoken word	.72	.60	.51	.30
Picture naming: Written response	Picture	Printed word	.46	.44	.90	.98

[a]PW (Rapp et al., this issue); WMA (Miceli et al., this issue); PS (Hanley & McDonnell, this issue); EA (Shelton & Weinrich, this issue).

micropatterns of self-consistency supply qualitative predictions for several contrasts between tasks. The utility of this approach is illustrated using the overall profiles of PW (Rapp et al., this issue) and WMA (Miceli et al., this issue), so we will discuss their profiles first. Following that we discuss how this approach might accommodate the less agreeable profiles of PS (Hanley & McDonnell, this issue) and EA (Shelton & Weinrich, this issue).

In Fig. 1, we described the macrodynamics of naming and spelling; dynamics between phonology and semantics are more self-consistent than dynamics between spelling and semantics. In Fig. 2, we described the microdynamics that pertain to naming and spelling; English spelling-to-phonology is more consistent than phonology-to-spelling. We also noted several times that our approach assumes explicit direct constraint from the environment (Gibson, 1986; Turvey & Carello, 1981; van Leeuwen, Steyvers, & Nooter, submitted; Van Orden & Goldinger, 1994). Copying printed words or repeating spoken words both have relatively transparent relations between performance and environmental constraints. In the case of repetition, acoustic form and articulatory function have an ancient history of structural coupling, which explains why the two modalities have virtually isomorphic descriptive features. The practice of copying printed words doesn't go quite so far back in the history of our species, but there is a more general ancient structural coupling entailed by copying, as in drawing. Moreover, the presence of the stimulus during performance explicitly supports memory, as well as feedback for error correction. Thus, all other things equal, we expect performance on these tasks to be relatively less vulnerable to brain damage. PW and WMA demonstrate virtual ceiling performance on these tasks, but on no other tasks (see Table 1).

The relation between spelling and phonology is more consistent than the relation between phonology and spelling. Also, printed letters are explicit in the environment, but phonology is derived. Consequently, the relation that supports naming is more self-consistent, and reading aloud is superior to writing to dictation. The predicted direction of this contrast agrees with the performance of PW and WMA. They both show better performance when reading aloud than when writing to dictation.

Likewise, because we speak before and more often than we write, the history of structural coupling that supports spoken responses in picture naming is more self-consistent than the support for written responses in picture naming. The predicted direction of this contrast also agrees with the performance of PW and WMA. Additionally, spoken responses in picture naming are supported by less self-consistent relations than spoken responses in printed word naming. The predicted direction of this contrast also agrees with the performance of PW and WMA. Altogether, these outcomes weave an agreeable web of support in line with the described topology of intact behaviour.

Less Agreeable Patterns

PS (Hanley & McDonnell, this issue) and EA (Shelton & Weinrich, this issue) present us with patterns more complex than the performance topology of our simple model. It is important to understand why this does not falsify our approach, and what it means for fleshing out the topology of a more inclusive model. For example, PS is generally poorer in tasks that require spoken responses than in tasks that require written responses; even repetition performance is very poor. Specifically, PS's profile contradicts three natural predictions: (1) repetition $\geq$ reading aloud, writing to dictation, and both forms of picture naming; (2) reading aloud $\geq$ writing to dictation; (3) picture naming with spoken response $\geq$ picture naming with written response. However, the model is readily expanded to become more inclusive.

For example, the phoneme nodes would be more appropriately reconstituted as emergent properties of recurrent acoustic-articulatory dynamics. Then we could "lesion" the connections between acoustic nodes and articulatory nodes, or add noise to randomly chosen connections, or ablate selected articulatory nodes. We could even reconstitute the model to allow complex oscillations, as in dynamic models of speech production (Browman & Goldstein, 1995). Clearly we are not short of options, and all these options are directly in line with the principled basis of our analysis. Any of our options for damaging phonology would suffice to accommodate the overall dissociation in PS's profile. Namely, performance that requires a spoken response is worse than performance that allows a written response (see Table 1).

EA presents another interesting and complex profile. EA had extensive speech therapy, but he remains nonfluent. He only produces sentences like

"How are you" and "Good morning." He writes single words to communicate, but he cannot read them aloud. He is nonfluent and yet performs well in repetition. Except for repetition, EA's performance is low on any task that involves a spoken word response. To simulate EA's profile we would need the previous reconstituted model. We could then add weak uniform noise to acoustic-articulatory dynamics, cut the connections to letter nodes, and cut a portion of connections to semantic nodes. Subsequently, any relatively weak acoustic-articulatory attractors are isolated from sources of constraint other than the preserved semantic constraints, consonant with better repetition performance for imageable/concrete words. Like all other effects, imageability/concreteness effects are predicted in terms of self-consistency. In this case, self-consistency results from covariance of words with contexts. Highly imageable/concrete words vary less in meaning across contexts, which builds more self-consistent relations with their surface forms (Van Orden, Pennington, et al., submitted, and cf. Jones, 1985; Saffran, Schwartz, & Marin, 1979; Shallice, 1988). Nonword repetition is possible, but nonwords would not have the words' advantage of learned whole-word attractors, including phoneme-semantic attractors, so a slight deficit in nonword repetition is not surprising.

Please don't get the impression that building an actual model is a piece of cake; it is not. When all parts of a model are interdependent it can take quite a bit of work to explore the parameter space of the model and arrive at the empirical topology (just ask our friend Bill Farrar). However, success is assured for any reliable empirical topology. The explanatory power of these models does not reside in specific parameter settings; it resides in the general topological principles from which they are constructed.

The profiles of PS and EA have not exhausted our options. We may continue to reconstitute nodes, making use of reliable finer-grain relations among stimulus forms and cognitive functions, without doing any violence to the overarching framework. As we noted, it is even possible to reconstitute point attractors to accommodate complex time-varying behaviour such as that entailed by on-line articulatory gestures. Likewise, the node activation denoted as *semantic* could be expanded as emergent sensorimotor ensembles, including visual-acoustic-articulatory-postural-gestural-etc. ensembles (Allport, 1983; compare *image schemas* in Gibbs, 1994; Johnson, 1987; Lakoff, 1987). The crux of our analysis is not the discovery of correct nodes, nor correct oscillations; it is the utility of general mathematical (topological) principles at all scales of analysis (Abraham & Shaw, 1992).

The circular relation between the way we view data and the theoretical basis of our analysis presents no more problems than the circular relation between a linear reduction of data and the linear componential models that are then inferred. Data cannot decide between linear and nonlinear approaches to human performance. Consequently, claims that require the "truth" of one or the other perspective can only be supported by acts of faith. The implication is simply this: We retain an explicit and healthy scepticism toward the theories we propose, keeping one eye open for alternative workable frameworks. We shrug off tyrannical "objective" truth, exercise pluralism, and keep pragmatic concerns foremost (Lakoff, 1987).

MULTISTABILITY, METASTABILITY, AND INTACT PERFORMANCE

So far, we have described intact naming and spelling, and dissociations between naming and spelling, in ways that are as plausible as any flow-chart model, but not more plausible. One pragmatic test of a theoretical framework is whether we may learn something new about the systems we study—something that we might not have learned without the guiding framework. The flow-chart models described in the target articles have already passed this test (Carello et al., 1992). We need only track the history of reading research from the seminal articles of Coltheart (1978) and Marshall and Newcombe (1973), to validate the utility of flow-chart models for oganising and generating new findings. An explosion of studies have described important and reliable patterns in human performance. Recurrent network models and their entailed cognitive systems framework have also begun to demonstrate this utility. As we describe next, this framework has produced remarkable findings that are highly unlikely from a traditional perspective.

The phenomena we describe are not widely appreciated in cognitive psychology and neuropsychology. Consequently, it is easy to miss the fact that they converge within a cognitive systems approach. Each of the phenomena that we will describe pertain to printed and spoken word perception. However, this narrow convergence is only a small set of the large variety of reported findings that motivate this framework. From the broader perspective, an exciting possibility has taken shape. Perception and action may be generally and usefully described as the products of a self-organising complex dynamic system (Kelso et al., 1995).

Feedback and Multistability

The simple model described in the previous sections predicts a rather non-intuitive microeffect. This prediction derives from a common feature of dynamic systems—recurrent feedback. The specific prediction concerns multistability in the performance of tasks related to letters and phonemes, operationalised as ambiguity or *inconsistency*. Until recently, all discussion of consistency has concerned a classic, feedforward, spelling → phonology effect. _INT is inconsistent in PINT because it may be pronounced as in MINT; UCK is pronounced consistently as in DUCK. Inconsistent words such as PINT are named more slowly than consistent words such as DUCK. Thus, the feedforward consistency effect answers the question: Does it matter in *visual* word perception that a spelling may have more than one *pronunciation*? From the perspective of flow-chart models or feedforward connectionism, this is the only sensible question: The letter string is unambiguous to subjects (it is right in front of their eyes); the only potential ambiguity arises with respect to derived phonology. Once we consider perception as a product of recurrent feedback, however, the concept of perceptual ambiguity must be generalised—we must consider consistency in the *feedback* direction as well. Now we ask the feedback question: Does it matter in *visual* word perception that a *pronunciation* may have more than one *spelling*? From the perspective of resonant dynamics, feedback consistency should affect performance as strongly as classic, feedforward consistency.

Stone et al. (in press) tested for both feedforward and feedback consistency effects in a lexical decision task. They used a factorial design that included four types of words. In bidirectionally consistent words such as DUCK, the spelling body (__UCK) can only be pronounced one way, and the pronunciation body (/__uk/) is only spelled one way. In spelling → phonology inconsistent words such as MOTH, the spelling body can be pronounced in multiple ways (e.g. BOTH), but the pronunciation body (/__ôth/) is only spelled one way. In phonology → spelling inconsistent words such as HURL, the spelling body is pronounced in only one way, but the pronunciation body can be spelled in more than one way (e.g. GIRL). In bidirectionally inconsistent words such as WORM, the spelling body can be pronounced in multiple ways (e.g. DORM), and the pronunciation body can be spelled in multiple ways (e.g. FIRM). Stone et al. found strong evidence for perception as a "two-way street." Correct response times were equally (and strongly) slowed by both feedforward and feedback inconsistency. Additionally, they found a reliable interaction; all inconsistent words produced approximately equal response times, even those that were inconsistent in both directions. Only words that were bidirectionally consistent produced faster and more accurate performance.

The feedback consistency effect is compelling, for several reasons. First, it underscores the importance of bidirectional dynamics in perception. Second, it demonstrates that stimulus function (in this case, a word's "name function") lends perceptual structure to stimulus form. Again, note the nonintuitive nature of this phenomenon. The letter string is clearly visible to the subject, and it remains visible until a response is recorded. However, if feedback from phonology suggests that some *other* letter-string *could have* been presented, performance is slower. Third, it could only be predicted by a theory emphasising bidirectional dynamics. It is straightforward corroboration for bidirectional multistability in subword dynamics. In a simple model, multistable (ambiguous) pronunciations and spellings are resolved through successive cycles of cooperative (excitatory) and competitive (inhibitory) feedback.

Ziegler and his colleagues observed a similar counter-intuitive effect in a letter-search task (Ziegler & Jacobs, 1995; Ziegler, Van Orden, & Jacobs, in press). Subjects in this experiment were briefly presented with a letter string such as BRANE (a pseudohomophone of the word "brain"), followed by a pattern mask (#####). The subjects were instructed to respond whether a predesignated letter was present in the masked letter string, for example the letter "i". In the case of BRANE, they (mis)reported having seen the letter "i" more often than in a control stimulus. Similarly, they failed to report the letter "i" in the letter string TAIP (a pseudohomophone of the word "tape"), more often than in a control stimulus. Presumably, the phonology of the pseudo-homophones BRANE or TAIP suggested that "brain" or "tape" were presented, causing subjects to misreport the presence or absence of the letter "i." These results also corroborate the description of word perception as a multistable dynamic system.

Hysteresis and Multistability

Betty Tuller and her colleagues have demonstrated hysteresis in speech perception (Tuller, Case, Ding, & Kelso, 1994). Hysteresis effects are a well-defined signature of multistability in nonlinear systems. In the present example, this means there are multiple perceptions of the same spoken stimulus. Tuller et al. focused on the classic phenomenon of categorical speech perception (Liberman, Harris, Hoffman, & Griffith, 1957). In one experiment, they manipulated the presentation order of speech stimuli. These stimuli were constructed to morph between the words SAY and STAY—their acoustic properties changed incrementally along a continuum from SAY to STAY (cf. Best, Morrongiello, & Robson, 1981; Hodgson & Miller, 1992). Each run of Tuller et al.'s experiment presented a subject with this continuum running from SAY to STAY and back again (or vice versa). Hysteresis was observed on 41% of runs across subjects and conditions. Specifically, for some intermediate range of stimuli, a subject perceived this range of stimuli as SAY if it had been preceded by SAY stimuli, but they perceived the identical range as STAY if it had been preceded by STAY stimuli. The intermediate range is thus multistable.

As noted, identical stimuli were perceived as SAY or STAY depending on preceding stimuli. Tuller et al. (1994) were not concerned with which reported stimulus identity is the "true" representation. They explored instead the interdependence of context and stimulus. They asked: What is the pattern of interaction between perceivers and contexts that characterises categorical speech perception? The hysteresis pattern is a generic pattern that is observed widely in physical, chemical, biological, and cognitive systems. Historically, in psychology, hysteresis has been considered a nuisance effect. For example, it motivated Fechner's *method of limits* in classical psychophysics—effectively, a statistical technique to make hysteresis disappear. Currently, hysteresis is better understood with respect to multistability. Thus, although Tuller et al.'s results were not derived from the simple model we described, hysteresis is convergent on the theoretical basis of this model. This fundamental construct provides a general and natural basis for understanding ubiquitous multistability in language, e.g. feedforward and feedback inconsistency, homography (LEAD or WIND), homophony (ROWS vs. ROSE), polysemy (Pete Rose is OVER the hill. vs. There were flies all OVER the ceiling—from Lakoff, 1987), and syntactic/semantic ambiguity (The church pardons very few people. vs. The church pardons are difficult to obtain—adapted from Rayner & Pollatsek, 1989).

1/f Noise and Metastability

David Gilden and his colleagues have demonstrated a complex interdependence between trial-by-trial response times in several cognitive tasks, including a word recognition task (Gilden, in press; Gilden, Thornton, & Mallon, 1995). The source of this interdependence is fully cognitive in affiliation (it does not arise in a "noncognitive" simple reaction time task, for example—Gilden et al., 1995). Also, mundane sources of priming such as DOCTOR ⇒ NURSE semantic priming, MINT ⇒ HINT form priming, or successions of identical responses were ruled out as potential sources (Gilden, in press). Instead, the source may be a metastable complex dynamic process. Metastability implies that a system never settles fully in a dominant attractor, and is thus more flexible. Remember the rough analogy from the earlier section on neurobiology: A person who *always* has alternative plans B, C, and D at the ready, is more flexible (metastable) than a person who is stuck in plan A. Metastability has been proposed to explain the smooth flexibility of perception and action.

Metastability in response time (and neural activity) is revealed in a rather esoteric phenomenon—*1/f noise*—observed in the "error" variance of response time (the variance left over when treatment effects are partitioned out). This phenomenon can be very difficult to grasp because it goes so strongly against the grain of typical psychological analyses. After all, we're used to discarding error variance, not analysing it for structure. 1/f noise is a mathematically generic pattern expressed here in trial by trial response time. If we graph each response time in a sequence, the data points will oscillate between fast and slow response times throughout the series of trials. If we "connect the dots," they form a complex waveform. In turn, this complex waveform may be viewed as a composite of waves that span a large range of frequencies. 1/f noise is a weak inverse relation between "power" (amplitude of change in response time) and the frequency of composite waves.

This correlation exists between changes in response time separated by small, intermediate, or large intervals. These nested correlations comprise a well-defined mathematical object from fractal geometry. Fractal objects are self-similar. So far, 1/f noise is only seen in the time domain, but self-similarity is easier to grasp in terms of ordinary objects that are extended in space. For example, a coastline is self-similar; it has a ragged structure of the same complexity when viewed from outer space, from an aeroplane, or from a cliff above the shore.

So what do we make of this rarefied phenomenon? On the down side, the presence of 1/f noise in response time is inconsistent with the conventional logic of partitioning response time into independent sources of variance, as in ANOVA. Virtually every study in which response time is the dependent measure averages response times across trials, items, and subjects. Comparisons are always conducted between means. One key assumption of this practice is that the response time in each trial is independent of the response times in other trials. The assumption of independence is at the heart of the linear statistical models that are used to discover independent sources of variance. The presence of 1/f noise contradicts this assumption. Thus, generally, we may have to rework the relation between data, method, and theory in response time studies. And, specifically, we are justified in our scepticism concerning the *effect = structure* assumption. It requires that data may be strictly carved at their joints to yield independent effects.

On the up side, 1/f noise may be a signature of metastability. If so, then it converges with the previous phenomena in this section to corroborate the utility of our approach. 1/f noise accounts for a stunning 70% (or more) of subjects' variance in response time for each of the cognitive tasks that were evaluated (Gilden, in press). By comparison, the best conventional models of word naming account for 3–12% of variance in average naming times (Besner, in press).

We wish to stress two caveats before we leave this section. First, 1/f noise does not confirm our simple model of naming. In fact, our simple model does not produce this phenomenon. The corroboration is for the cognitive systems framework that we work within. The simple model produces lower-dimensional behaviour than a more inclusive model that would produce 1/f noise. Once again, each trajectory produced by the simple model is a low-dimensional shadow of a trajectory that would be produced by a higher-dimensional model.

Second, our main point in reviewing these phenomena was to add some meat to the utility of our approach. The previous findings do not falsify the more conventional linear analyses of cognitive systems. Nonlinear accounts cannot be distinguished from linear accounts on the basis of correspondence to data —even data as compelling as those of Gilden (in press; Gilden et al., 1995) and Tuller et al. (1994). A linear componential model could be constructed for any data set, given enough components (Stone & Van Orden, 1993). Even the analytic difficulties raised by Gilden's data could be overcome if one wished to ignore the nonlinear perspective. Data can always be "corrected" to eliminate interdependence between successive trials (West & Hepworth, 1991). This practice can be very useful depending upon the goals of the analysis. However, in the case of Gilden's data, it would effectively send to the trash can 70% (or more) of theoretically meaningful variance.

Our general point is simply this: The basis for applying any particular framework is exclusively pragmatic. The practical utility of strongly nonlinear models is demonstrated as they become successful guides to a more general and inclusive understanding of cognitive phenomena. The practical utility of linear models is questioned if they would fail to discover theoretically meaningful phenomena. In that regard, the phenomena reviewed in this section question the utility of the *effect = structure* assumption. These phenomena are antithetical to that assumption, and they could never have been anticipated from the standard approach to patient data.

SUMMARY AND CONCLUSIONS

Dissociations cannot be trusted to isolate independent representations. The existence of plausible alternatives undermines their reliability for reducing performance phenomena to single causes (Van Orden, Pennington, et al., submitted). Induction of single causes required a priori the truth of single causes. Still, it is natural to prefer the familiar relation between componential methods, theory, and data. Moreover, there seems to be a general utility in such a pursuit, at least initially. Bechtel and Richardson (1993) review historic analyses in which, initially, scientists find it useful to assume linear *independence* (single causes) as a working hypothesis. Be that as it may, behaviour characteristics of linear independence are a small subset of the generic behaviours characteristic of complex dynamic systems (Abraham & Shaw, 1992; Giunti, 1995); they cannot be trusted to validate the *effect = structure* assumption.

Some readers might be tempted to claim that letter, phoneme, and semantic nodes are themselves independent representations. But that would imbue these notational distinctions with causal properties that they cannot bear (cf. Anderson, 1991; Perrone & Basti, 1995; Putnam, 1981). At most, nodes denote emergent form-function dynamics (structural couplings) that are not explicit in a model. As we noted, the node activation denoted as *phonologic* could emerge in recurrent acoustic-articulatory dynamics, and the node activation denoted as *semantic* could be effected in metastable sensorimotor trajectories, including visual-acoustic-articulatory-postural-gestural-etc. trajectories. Thus, the activation trajectories denoted as semantic emerge from the same stuff—i.e. the same excitable medium—as letter and phoneme "nodes." The simple model system is not real, except in its capacity to produce a trajectory that mimics human performance. It is plausibly interpreted as a low-dimensional projection—again, the shadow—of a vastly higher-dimensional description of readers, writers, texts, and laboratories.

No reliable basis exists for the discovery of primitive causal structures in human performance (Uttal, 1990; Van Orden, Holden, et al., submitted; Van Orden, Pennington, et al., submitted). Complex natural systems may not give up the true bases of their behaviour (Cohen & Stewart, 1994; Goodwin, 1994; Lindley, 1993). We accept this complexity and refuse to reify modelling notations such as nodes. Nodes are chosen to accommodate the grain-size of organism-environment coupling that predicts behavioural phenomena (Van Orden et al., 1990; Van Orden & Goldinger, 1994, and cf. Varela et al., 1991). Again, the explanatory isomorphism runs from described performance to a model's dynamic trajectory. Data make reference to such trajectories, exclusively; there are no data leftovers from which to deduce static atomic structures in an observed behaviour. Consequently, from a cognitive systems' perspective, the *effect = structure* assumption is not wrong; it is simply impracticable.

REFERENCES

Abraham, R.H., & Shaw, C.D. (1992). *Dynamics: The geometry of behavior*. Redwood City, CA: Addison-Wesley.

Allport, D.A. (1983). Distributed memory, modular subsystems and dysphasia. In S. Newman & R. Epstein (Eds.), *Current perspectives in dysphasia* (pp. 32–60). London: Churchill Livingstone.

Anderson, J.R. (1991). The place of cognitive architectures in a rational analysis. In K. VanLehn (Ed.), *Architectures for intelligence: The twenty-second Carnegie symposium on cognition* (pp. 1–24). Hillsdale, NJ: Lawrence Erlbaum Associates Inc.

Bechtel, W., & Richardson, R.C. (1993). *Discovering complexity: Decomposition and localization as strategies in scientific research*. Princeton, NJ: Princeton University Press.

Berent, I., & Perfetti, C.A. (1995). A rose is a REEZ: The two-cycles model of phonology assembly in reading English. *Psychological Review, 102*, 146–184.

Besner, D. (in press). Basic processes in reading: Multiple routines in localist and connectionist models. To appear in P.A. McMullen & R.M. Klein (Eds.), *Converging methods for understanding reading and dyslexia*. Cambridge, MA: MIT Press.

Best, C., Morrongiello, B., & Robson, R. (1981). Perceptual equivalence of acoustic cues in speech and nonspeech perception. *Perception and Psychophysics, 29*, 191–211.

Bosman, A.M.T., & Van Orden, G.C. (in press). Why spelling is more difficult than reading. In C.A. Perfetti, M. Fayol, & L. Rieben (Eds.), *Learning to spell*. Hillsdale, NJ: Lawrence Erlbaum Associates Inc.

Bressler, S.L., Coppola, R., & Nakamura, R. (1993). Episodic multiregional cortical coherence at multiple frequencies during visual task performance. *Nature, 366*, 153–156.

Browman, C.P., & Goldstein, L. (1995). Dynamics and articulatory phonology. In R.F. Port & T. van Gelder (Eds.), *Mind as motion: Explorations in the dynamics of cognition* (pp. 175–193). Cambridge, MA: MIT Press.

Carello, C., Turvey, M.T., & Lukatela, G. (1992). Can theories of word recognition remain stubbornly nonphonological? In R. Frost & L. Katz (Eds.), *Orthography, phonology, morphology, and meaning* (pp. 211–226). Amsterdam: North-Holland.

Cohen, J., & Stewart, I. (1994). *The collapse of chaos: Discovering simplicity in a complex world*. New York: Viking.

Coltheart, M. (1978). Lexical access in simple reading tasks. In G. Underwood (Ed.), *Strategies in information processing* (pp. 151–216). London: Academic Press.

Dell, G.S., Schwartz, M.F., Martin, N., Saffran, E.M., & Gagnon, D.A. (in press). Lexical access in aphasic and nonaphasic speakers. *Psychological Review.*
Duhem, P. (1954). *Aim and structure of physical theory.* York: Antheneum. (Originally published in 1906.)
Farrar, W.T., & Van Orden, G.C. (1994). *Simulation of surface and deep dyslexia in a unified network.* Poster presented at the Annual Meeting of the Psychonomic Society, St. Louis, November.
Freeman, W.J. (1987). Simulation of chaotic EEG patterns with a dynamic model of the olfactory system. *Biological Cybernetics, 56,* 139–150.
Freeman, W.J. (1991a). The physiology of perception. *Scientific American, 264,* 78–85.
Freeman, W.J. (1991b). What are the state variables for modeling brain dynamics with neural networks? In H.G. Schuster (Ed.), *Nonlinear dynamics and neuronal networks* (pp. 243–255). New York: VCH Publishers.
Freeman, W.J. (1995). *Societies of brains: A study in the neuroscience of love and hate.* Hillsdale, NJ: Lawrence Erlbaum Associates Inc.
Frost, R. (submitted). *Toward a strong phonological model of reading: True issues and false trails.* Manuscript submitted for publication.
Funnell, E. (1983). Phonological processes in reading: New evidence from acquired dyslexia. *British Journal of Psychology, 74,* 159–180.
Gibbs, P., & Van Orden, G.C. (submitted). *Pathway selection's utility for control of word recognition.* Manuscript submitted for publication.
Gibbs, R.W. (1994). *The poetics of mind: Figurative thought, language, and understanding.* New York: Cambridge University Press.
Gibson, J.J. (1986). *An ecological approach to visual perception.* (Original work published 1979.) Hillsdale, NJ: Lawrence Erlbaum Associates Inc.
Gilden, D.L. (in press). Fluctuations in the time required for elementary decisions. *Psychological Science.*
Gilden, D.L., Thornton, T., & Mallon, M.W. (1995). 1/f noise in human cognition. *Science, 267,* 1837–1839.
Giunti, M. (1995). Dynamical models of cognition. In R.F. Port & T. van Gelder (Eds.), *Mind as motion: Explorations in the dynamics of cognition* (pp. 549–571). Cambridge, MA: MIT Press.
Goodwin, B. (1994). *How the leopard changed its spots: The evolution of complexity.* New York: Scribner.
Grossberg, S., & Stone, G.O. (1986). Neural dynamics of word recognition and recall: Priming, learning, and resonance. *Psychological Review, 93,* 46–74.
Haken, H. (1984). *The science of structure: Synergetics.* New York: Van Nostrand Reinhold.
Hatfield, F.M., & Patterson, K.E. (1983). Phonological spelling. *Quarterly Journal of Experimental Psychology, 35A,* 451–468.
Hodgson, P., & Miller, J.L. (1992). Internal phonetic category structure depends on multiple acoustic properties: Evidence for within-category trading relations (abstract). *Journal of the Acoustical Society of America, 92,* 2464.
Hubel, D.H., & Wiesel, T.N. (1962). Receptive fields, binocular interaction and functional architecture in the cat's visual cortex. *Journal of Physiology (London), 160,* 106–154.
Hubel, D.H., & Wiesel, T.N. (1965). Receptive fields and functional architecture in two nonstriate visual areas (18 and 19) of the cat. *Journal of Neurophysiology, 28,* 229–289.
Hubel, D.H., & Wiesel, T.N. (1968). Receptive fields and functional architecture of monkey striate cortex. *Journal of Physiology (London), 195,* 215–243.
Johnson, M. (1987). *The body in the mind: The bodily basis of meaning, imagination, and reason.* Chicago, IL: University of Chicago Press.
Jones, G.V. (1985). Deep dyslexia, imageability, and ease of predication. *Brain and Language, 24,* 1–19.

Katz, L., & Frost, R. (1992). The reading process is different for different orthographies: The orthographic depth hypothesis. In R. Frost & L. Katz (Eds.), *Orthography, phonology, morphology, and meaning* (pp. 67–84). Amsterdam: North-Holland.

Kawamoto, A., & Zemblidge, J. (1992). Pronunciation of homographs. *Journal of Memory and Language, 31*, 349–374.

Kelso, J.A.S., Case, P., Holroyd, T., Horvath, E., Raczaszek, J., Tuller, B., & Ding, M. (1995). Multistability and metastability in perceptual and brain dynamics. In P. Kruse & M. Stadler (Eds.), *Ambiguity in mind and nature* (pp. 159–184). Berlin: Springer-Verlag.

Lakoff, G. (1987). *Women, fire, and dangerous things: What categories reveal about the mind.* Chicago, IL: University of Chicago Press.

Lewenstein, M., & Nowak, A. (1989). Recognition with self-control in neural networks. *Physical Review A, 40*, 4652–4664.

Liberman, A.M., Harris, K.S., Hoffman, H.S., & Griffith, B.C. (1957). The discrimination of speech sounds within and across phoneme boundaries. *Journal of Experimental Psychology, 54*, 358–368.

Lindley, D. (1993). *The end of physics: The myth of a unified theory.* New York: Basic Books.

Livingstone, M.S., & Hubel, D.H. (1988). Segregation of form, colour, movement and depth: Anatomy, physiology and perception. *Science, 240*, 740–749.

Mackie, J.L. (1974). *The cement of the universe.* Oxford: Oxford University Press.

Marshall, J.C., & Newcombe, F. (1973). Patterns of paralexia: A psycholinguistic approach. *Journal of Psycholinguistic Research, 2*, 175–199.

McClelland, J.L., & Rumelhart, D.E. (1981). An interactive-activation model of context effects in letter perception. Part 1: An account of basic findings. *Psychological Review, 88*, 375–407.

Mill, J.S. (1974). A system of logic. J.M. Robson (Ed.), *Collected works of John Stuart Mill, Vol. VII.* Toronto: University of Toronto Press.

Patterson, K.E. (1981). Neuropsychological approaches to the study of reading. *British Journal of Psychology, 72*, 151–174.

Patterson, K.E., & Hodges, J.R. (1992). Deterioration of word meaning: Implications for reading. *Neuropsychologia, 30*, 1025–1040.

Patterson, K.E., Marshall, J.C., & Coltheart, M. (Eds.) (1985). *Surface dyslexia.* London: Lawrence Erlbaum Associates Inc.

Patterson, K.E., Plaut, D.C., McClelland, J.L., Seidenberg, M.S., Behrman, M., & Hodges, J. (in press). Connections and disconnections: A connectionist account of surface dyslexia. To appear in J. Reggia, R. Berndt, & E. Ruppin (Eds.), *Neural modeling of cognitive and brain disorders.* New York: World Scientific.

Pennington, B.F. (1991). *Diagnosing learning disorders: A neuropsychological framework.* New York: Guilford Press.

Perfetti, C.A. (1985). *Reading ability.* New York: Oxford University Press.

Perfetti, C.A., Zhang, S., & Berent, I. (1992). Reading in English and Chinese: Evidence for a "universal" phonological principle. In R. Frost & L. Katz (Eds.), *Orthography, phonology, morphology, and meaning* (pp. 227–248). Amsterdam: North-Holland.

Perrone, A.L., & Basti, G. (1995). Neural images and neural coding. *Behavioral and Brain Sciences, 18*, 368–369.

Plaut, D.C., McClelland, J.L., Seidenberg, M.S., & Patterson, K. (1996). Understanding normal and impaired word reading: Computational principles in quasi-regular domains. *Psychological Review, 103*, 56–115.

Plaut, D.C., & Shallice, T. (1993). Deep dyslexia: A case study of connectionist neuropsychology. *Cognitive Neuropsychology, 10*, 377–500.

Prigogine, I., & Stengers, I. (1984). *Order out of chaos: Man's new dialogue with nature.* New York: Bantam Books.

Putnam, H. (1981). Reductionism and the nature of psychology. In J. Haugeland (Ed.), *Mind design* (pp. 205–219). Cambridge, MA: MIT Press.

Quine, W.V.O. (1961). Two dogmas of empiricism. In W.V.O. Quine (Ed.), *From a logical point of view* (pp. 20–46). (Originally published in 1953.) New York: Harper & Row.
Rayner, K., & Pollatsek, A. (1989). *The psychology of reading.* Englewood Cliffs, NJ: Prentice Hall.
Saffran, E.M., Schwartz, M.F., & Marin, O.S.M. (1979). Neuropsychological evidence for mechanisms of reading: 1. Deep dyslexia. Paper presented to the Seventh International Neuropsychology Society Meeting, New York.
Saltzman, E.L. (1995). Dynamics and coordinate systems in skilled sensorimotor activity. In R.F. Port & T. van Gelder (Eds.), *Mind as motion: Explorations in the dynamics of cognition* (pp. 149–173). Cambridge, MA: MIT Press.
Shallice, T. (1988). *From neuropsychology to mental structure.* New York: Cambridge University Press.
Shanon, B. (1993). *The representational and the presentational: An essay on cognition and the study of the mind.* New York: Harvester Wheatsheaf.
Singer, W. (1993). Synchronization of cortical activity and its putative role in information processing and learning. *Annual Review of Physiology, 55,* 349–374.
Skarda, C.A., & Freeman, W.J. (1987). How brains make chaos in order to make sense of the world. *Behavioral and Brain Sciences, 10,* 161–195.
Smolensky, P. (1986). Information processing in dynamical systems: Foundations of harmony theory. In D.E. Rumelhart, J.L. McClelland, & the PDP Research Group, *Parallel distributed processing: Explorations in the microstructure of cognition: Vol. 1. Foundations* (pp. 194–281). Cambridge, MA: MIT Press.
Stone, G.O., Vanhoy, M., & Van Orden, G.C. (in press). Perception is a two-way street: Feedforward and feedback phonology in visual word recognition. *Journal of Memory and Language.*
Stone, G.O., & Van Orden, G.C. (1993). Strategic processes in printed word recognition. *Journal of Experimental Psychology: Human Perception and Performance, 19,* 744–774.
Stone, G.O., & Van Orden, G.C. (1994). Building a resonance framework for word recognition using design and system principles. *Journal of Experimental Psychology: Human Perception and Performance, 20,* 1248–1268.
Strain, E., Patterson, K., & Seidenberg, M.S. (1995). Semantic effects in single-word naming. *Journal of Experimental Psychology: Learning, Memory and Cognition, 21,* 1140–1154.
Thelen, E., & Smith, L. (1994). *A dynamic systems approach to the development of cognition and action.* Cambridge, MA: Harvard Press.
Tuller, B., Case, P., Ding, M., & Kelso, J.A.S. (1994). The nonlinear dynamics of speech categorization. *Journal of Experimental Psychology: Human Perception and Performance, 20,* 3–16.
Turvey, M.T., & Carello, C. (1981). Cognition: The view from ecological realism. *Cognition, 10,* 313–321.
Uttal, W.R. (1990). On some two-way barriers between models and mechanisms. *Perception and Psychophysics, 48,* 188–203.
van Leeuwen, C., Steyvers, M., & Nooter, M. (submitted). *Stability and intermittency in high-dimensional dynamical models for perceptual grouping.* Manuscript submitted for publication.
Van Orden, G.C. (1987). A ROWS is a ROSE: Spelling, sound, and reading. *Memory and Cognition, 15,* 181–198.
Van Orden, G.C., Holden, J.G., Podgornik, M.N., & Aitchison, C.S., (submitted). *When a ROWS is not a ROSE: Null effects and the absence of mental structure.* Manuscript submitted for publication.
Van Orden, G.C., & Goldinger, S.D. (1994). Interdependence of form and function in cognitive systems explains perception of printed words. *Journal of Experimental Psychology: Human Perception and Performance, 20,* 1269–1291.

Van Orden, G.C., & Goldinger, S.D. (1996). Phonologic mediation in skilled and dyslexic reading. In C. Chase, G. Rosen, & G. Sherman (Eds.), *Developmental dyslexia: Neuro, cognitive, and genetic mechanisms* (pp. 185–223). Timonium, MA: York Press.

Van Orden, G.C., Johnston, J.C., & Hale, B.L. (1988). Word identification in reading proceeds from spelling to sound to meaning. *Journal of Experimental Psychology: Learning, Memory, and Cognition, 14*, 371–385.

Van Orden, G.C., Pennington, B.F., & Stone, G.O. (1990). Word identification in reading and the promise of subsymbolic psycholinguistics. *Psychological Review, 97*, 488–522.

Van Orden, G.C., Pennington, B.F., & Stone, G.O. (submitted). *What do double dissociations prove? Modularity yields a degenerating research program*. Manuscript submitted for publication.

Varela, F.J., Thompson, E., & Rosch, E. (1991). *The embodied mind*. Cambridge, MA: MIT Press.

von der Malsburg, C., & Schneider, W. (1986). A neural cocktail-party processor. *Biological Cybernetics, 54*, 29–40.

Warrington, E.K. (1975). The selective impairment of semantic memory. *Quarterly Journal of Experimental Psychology, 27*, 635–657.

Waters, G.S., & Seidenberg, M.S. (1985). Spelling-sound effects in reading: Time course and decision criteria. *Memory and Cognition, 13*, 557–572.

West, S.G., & Hepworth, J.T. (1991). Statistical issues in the study of temporal data: Daily experiences. *Journal of Personality, 59*, 609–662.

Ziegler, J.C., & Jacobs, A.M. (1995). Phonological information provides early sources of constraint in the processing of letter strings. *Journal of Memory and Language, 34*, 567–593.

Ziegler, J.C., Jacobs, A.M., & Stone, G.O. (in press). Statistical analysis of the bidirectional inconsistency of spelling and sound in French. *Behavioral Research Methods, Instruments, and Computers*.

Ziegler, J.C., Stone, G.O., & Jacobs, A.M. (in press). What's the pronunciation for OUGH and the spelling for /u/?: A database for computing feedforward and feedback inconsistency in English. *Behavioral Research Methods, Instruments and Computers*.

Ziegler, J.C., Van Orden, G.C., & Jacobs, A.M. (in press). Phonology can help or hurt the perception of print. *Journal of Experimental Psychology: Human Perception and Performance*.

Reading Comprehension Is Not Exclusively Reliant upon Phonological Representation

Max Coltheart and Veronika Coltheart

Macquarie University, Sydney, Australia

Some recent theorists have argued that reading comprehension is exclusively reliant upon phonological recoding of print prior to semantic access. We argued that neuropsychological data reported in this *Special Issue*, and data from intact subjects, are inconsistent with this claim.

The role played by phonology in single-word reading comprehension has been debated for more than a century. M. Coltheart (1980) cited some of the conflicting views that have accumulated concerning this issue; he also came to the conclusion at that time that there was little or no evidence in the literature to support the view that phonological representations played any crucial role in single-word reading comprehension.

Subsequently, however, some authors have advocated a diametrically opposed view, namely, that single-word reading comprehension is exclusively mediated by phonology—that the only route from orthography to semantics is via phonology.

Analogous views have also been raised about the role of phonology in spelling, with some authors arguing that it is entirely phonologically mediated and others stressing the importance of retrieval of orthographic representations.

Our paper focuses on these issues as they apply to reading, but much or all of what we claim we believe applies equally well to spelling.

With respect to reading, in recent years two groups of investigators have been advocating the strong claim that reading comprehension depends entirely upon phonological mediation.

The first of these is Van Orden and his colleagues, according to whom (Van Orden, Johnston, & Hale, 1988, p. 371), "word identification in reading

---

Requests for reprints should be addressed to Professor Max Coltheart, School of Psychology, Macquarie University, Sydney, NSW 2109, Australia.

© 1997 Psychology Press, an imprint of Erlbaum (UK) Taylor & Francis Ltd

proceeds from spelling to sound to meaning" (see also Van Orden, 1987, 1991; Van Orden, Pennington, & Stone, 1990; Van Orden et al., 1992). The technique they have mainly used is single-word semantic categorisation, in which the reader is provided with a category (e.g. A VEGETABLE) and then a printed letter string (e.g. BEETS or HORSE) to verify against the category. An influence of phonological representation in this reading comprehension task is indicated by the finding that nontargets that are homophonic with targets (e.g. BEATS when the category is A VEGETABLE) generate high error rates (false acceptances) and/or slow response latencies (see, e.g., Meyer, & Gutschera, 1975). A critical result is that this effect is just as large when the homophonic target is a nonword (e.g. A FOUR-FOOT ANIMAL with the target SHEAP). If there were any purely orthographic processing of the targets, one would expect this to reduce error rates with the pseudohomophones, as this orthographic processing would reveal that the target is not a word and so NO must be the correct answer. It is because word and nonword foils yielded equivalent error rates that Van Orden and colleagues argued that targets are represented solely in phonological form in this reading comprehension experiment.

The second group of investigators who have advocated a purely phonological account of single-word reading comprehension is Lukatela and Turvey (1991, 1993, 1994a, 1994b). They propose (see, e.g., Lukatela & Turvey, 1994b, p. 349) that the first step in reading is that a letter string is converted to phonological form (regardless of whether it is a word or not). This prelexical phonological representation is then used to access a phonological lexicon: Such access will occur if the stimulus is a word or a pseudohomophone, but not if it is a nonpseudohomophonic nonword.

If access succeeds, the semantic representation(s) appropriate to the phonological form that generated this access is (are) activated; in addition, retrieval of the spelling(s) corresponding to the accessed entry (entries) occurs. Then there is a check of the retrieved spelling(s) against the orthographic input. If the spelling of any entry matches the input, all other entries that were accessed are turned off, leaving only the correct entry activated. If no spelling matches (which will happen if the input is a pseudohomophone), all activated entries are left activated.

The task Lukatela and Turvey have mainly used here is semantic priming of word reading. They report (Lukatela & Turvey, 1994b) that the reading aloud of a target word (e.g. FROG) is primed by prior presentation of a semantically related word (e.g. TOAD) but also by the prior presentation of a pseudohomophone of a semantically related word (e.g. TODE). These two types of prime have equal effects. So there appears to be no contribution of orthography here, just a contribution from phonology. If the orthography of the prime were considered at all, then the priming by TODE should be reduced or eliminated, since the pseudohomophone would not access the lexical entry for the word TOAD. That is a major reason for these authors taking the view that the route from print to meaning is exclusively via phonology ("Each word and each nonword homophonic with a word is able to bring about the full activation of a lexical entry, including its spelling"—Lukatela & Turvey, 1994a, p. 122).

The hypothesis that the only way from print to meaning in reading comprehension is via phonology, the hypothesis advanced by Van Orden and colleagues and by Lukatela and Turvey, is traditionally distinguished from two other hypotheses:

1. The direct-access or orthographic hypothesis, according to which the phonological representation of a printed word has no influence at all when single-word reading comprehension is occurring, because there is direct contact between lexical-orthographic word representations and semantics.

2. The dual-route hypothesis (M. Coltheart, 1980). The claim here is that there is a processing route that runs directly from orthography to semantics, and that there must also be a processing route that runs from orthography to phonology and then from phonology to semantics. Otherwise, how could a reader, viewing a pseudohomophone such as PHOCKS, answer the question "Does that sound exactly like the name of an animal?". Indeed, it can be argued (M. Coltheart, Masterson, Byng, Prior, & Riddoch, 1983) that there are *two* such routes from orthography via phonology to semantics. One uses nonlexically computed phonology (computed, for example, by grapheme-phoneme rules) and so supports the performance of the PHOCKS task. If that were the only such route, however, one would not observe the following reading comprehension error: *bury*—"A fruit on a tree" (M. Coltheart et al., 1983). The critical point here is that *bury* is an exception word, so that its phonology could not be computed nonlexically. Hence the word's phonology must have been retrieved from a lexical-phonological store—and yet the word's semantic representation was not correctly retrieved. Here semantic access resulted from the use of a lexical-phonological rather than a lexical-orthographic representation. This claim of two different phonologically mediated routes from orthography to semantics is consistent with such models of reading as that of Patterson and Shewell (1987; reproduced as Fig. 1 in the papers by Shelton & Weinrich and by Hanley & McDonnell, this issue).

There are many theoretical complexities associated with this dual-route view of semantic access from print, but they need not concern us here, since we mention this view only to contrast it with the pure-phonology view of reading comprehension. Our aim in this paper is to consider the implications for the latter view of some of the neuropsychological data reported elsewhere in this issue.

Consider, for example, patient EA (Shelton & Weinrich). His ability to derive phonology from orthography was severely impaired, as assessed by the task of nonword reading. He was correct in reading only 2 out of 55 nonwords.

It cannot be argued that this is an output effect (i.e. a difficulty in uttering nonwords) for two reasons: First, EA could utter nonwords; he scored 80% in a nonword repetition task, which is not normal but far superior to his ability to read nonwords. Second, and more critically, EA could not read nonwords even when the task did not require him to utter nonwords. A task with this property is pseudohomophone reading, where the input is a nonword but the output is a word. EA scored 0/20 on this task.

Now, notice that on both the Van Orden and Lukatela–Turvey accounts we have discussed, the process by which orthography is converted to phonology is the same for words and for nonwords; and reading comprehension cannot be achieved until this process is successfully completed. The process is grossly disturbed in EA, and so it follows from their accounts that EA's single-word reading comprehension must also be grossly disturbed.

However, this was not the case at all. EA performed extremely well in various single-word reading comprehension tasks. He scored 29/30 on matching single written nouns to pictures in the presence of semantic distractors; and he performed well in a task of comprehending printed verbs (26/30 correct—numerically superior to performance on auditory comprehension of the same verbs).

It might be argued here that EA's difficulty in deriving phonology from orthography was confined to the situation where the stimulus was a nonword; perhaps he could do this well as long as the stimulus was a word: Could he therefore still be carrying out the reading comprehension task via phonology? We make two points here. First, on the Van Orden and Lukatela–Turvey views, it is by no means clear how one could see a patient who could read words aloud normally but nonwords hardly at all, since the mechanism for computing phonology from orthography is the same for words and nonwords, according to these authors. Second, in any case EA was not competent at reading words aloud: In a variety of tests of word reading, he scored around 40% correct (even though he scored 95%–100% in repeating these words).

We conclude, then, that the reading aloud, reading comprehension, and repetition data reported by Shelton and Weinrich are inconsistent with the view that reading comprehension is solely phonologically mediated.

Consider next the patient PS, described in the paper by Hanley and McDonnell in this issue. His nonword reading was also extremely poor: 4/24 correct with short monosyllabic nonwords. However, unlike EA, PS was better at reading pseudohomophones than nonpseudohomophonic nonwords, and was also impaired at repetition. Hence it could be argued that his nonword reading impairment was an output problem; the superior reading of pseudohomophones could be attributed to semantic support of an impaired phonological system, which would help pseudohomophones but not nonpseudohomophonic nonwords (as argued by, for example, Patterson, Suzuki, & Wydell, 1996; Sasanuma, Ito, Patterson, & Ito, 1996), and hence account for the difference in reading levels here. Therefore, if it turned out that PS had intact reading comprehension in the presence of poor nonword reading, this might not be strong evidence against the Van Orden and Lukatela–Turvey position.

PS did indeed have intact single-word reading comprehension, and even intact written sentence comprehension. Could he have been translating orthography to phonology flawlessly so as to achieve this comprehension, even though impaired at producing such phonology subsequently (as in reading aloud)? Hanley and McDonnell (this issue) report several results that are relevant here.

1. PS was completely at chance at the task of distinguishing printed pseudo-homophones from printed nonpseudohomophonic nonwords (note that no overt production is needed here).
2. He was very poor at judging whether printed word pairs rhymed or not.
3. He was very poor at judging whether printed word pairs were homophonic or not.
4. Most convincing here are the results from a test in which PS was shown a homophonic word such as *symbol* and asked to give a semantic associate to the other member of the homophone pair (e.g. "drum"). Once again, performance was extremely poor.

These four tests establish that PS was very impaired at deriving phonology from orthography even when no phonological output was needed; yet his reading comprehension was normal.

We consider, then, that both of these neuropsychological studies have provided very clear evidence that reading comprehension is not entirely reliant upon phonological representation. We consider that this phonology-only hypothesis is also refuted by data from studies of normal readers, particularly by the following findings.

1. If reading comprehension relied solely upon phonological representation of print, then it would not matter, with phonological foils that have the same pronunciation as genuine category exemplars, how orthographically similar foil and exemplar are; yet this turns out to be a critical variable. When orthographic overlap of foil to genuine exemplar is low (e.g. A TYPE OF FLOWER—ROWS), the homophone effect is small (Van Orden, 1987) or nonsignificant (V. Coltheart, Patterson, & Leahy, 1994; Jared & Seidenberg, 1991). The finding of a smaller effect might be explained as due to facilitation of a post-access spelling check when stimulus and potential exemplar are orthographically dissimilar, but the failure to find any effect at all cannot be explained in this way.

2. Van Orden (1987) used extremely narrow categories, including A SPHERICAL OBJECT, A FEATURE OF A PERSON'S ABDOMEN, A

FEATURE OF AN OCEAN SHORE, A BIBLICAL RELIGIOUS LEADER, A MEMBER OF A CONVENT or A BREAKFAST FOOD; here it is easy for the subject to narrow down potential targets to a few possibilities (or even one: We invite the reader to predict the targets for the categories just listed). Jared and Seidenberg (1991) used much larger categories such as LIVING THING or OBJECT, and under these conditions found no homophone effects for high-frequency foils, suggesting that comprehension via phonology is not obligatory, and that phonology only influences performance when access is slow because frequency is low.

3. The critical finding that the homophone effect is just as large with pseudohomophones—which is the cornerstone of Van Orden's claim that orthography does not contribute at all to reading comprehension—was not replicated by V. Coltheart, Avons, Masterson, and Laxon (1991). Indeed, when these authors explicitly instructed subjects only to accept correctly spelled category exemplars, there was no homophony effect at all for pseudohomophones (though the effect still occurred with homophones).

In subsequent work in which subjects were instructed to reject misspellings, and in which the nonwords were pseudohomophones of homophones, rather than merely pseudohomophones of ordinary words (V. Coltheart et al., 1994), homophone effects with nonwords occurred, but were substantially smaller than the effects seen with words. The pseudohomophones included a wide range of spelling substitutions, unlike those used by Van Orden et al., 1988, which used a high proportion of EE/EA substitutions. In Van Orden's research, up to 50–60% of the small set of critical items typically involve EE/EA substitutions (DEER/DEAR, SHEAP/SHEEP), and these generate disproportionately high error rates on word and nonword homophone foils (V. Coltheart et al., 1994). English contains thousands of homophone pairs, and it seems injudicious to make claims about written word recognition on the basis of experiments based on a very small subset of words embodying very few orthographic spelling patterns. Item analyses based on such studies can hardly be claimed to generalise over English words.

Thus, considering both the neuropsychological data presented in other papers in this issue, and the data from normal subjects to which we have just referred, we agree entirely with the conclusion reached by Wydell, Patterson, and Humphreys (1993, p. 530): "we prefer to maintain the view (as do most other reading theorists, e.g. Coltheart, 1985; Monsell, Patterson, Graham, Hughes, & Milroy, 1992; Pollatsek et al., 1992; Seidenberg, & McClelland, 1989) that both orthographic and phonological representations contribute to word comprehension in reading."

Exactly what form do these contributions take? M. Coltheart and Rastle (1994) discussed this question in relation to the pseudohomophone effect in visual lexical decision, presenting an illustrative simulation using the Dual-route Cascaded (DRC) model, a computational implementation of the Patterson–Shewell model referred to earlier (M. Coltheart, Curtis, Atkins, & Haller, 1993). This model operates according to the principles of interactive activation, which means that representations in adjacent modules of the model bidirectionally activate or inhibit each other. For example, a representation at the phoneme output level of the model that has been computed by the nonlexical component of the model (the grapheme-phoneme rule system) will, if the stimulus is a pseudohomophone, activate a lexical entry in the model's phonological output lexicon, and that in turn will activate a lexical entry in the model's orthographic input lexicon. Thus the pseudohomophone KOAT will eventually engender some activation in the COAT entry in the orthographic input lexicon, and it is because of this lexical activation that it is difficult to respond NO to KOAT in a lexical decision task. However, when a pseudohomophone is orthographically very different from its parent word (e.g. KOTE), this activation does not occur because of the large degree of letter-to-word inhibition exerted by KOTE upon COAT. Hence this provides an explanation of why there is a pseudohomophone effect in lexical decision, and why this occurs only when the pseudohomophone is orthographically close to its parent.

The extension of this reasoning to the semantic classification task is obvious. Consider an interactive-activation version of the model shown in Fig. 1 of the papers by Shelton and Weinrich and by Hanley and McDonnell in this issue (that is, imagine that each arrow in these figures transmits activation in both directions): That is the DRC model. A word homophone can incorrectly activate the semantics of its homophonous mate via the route from orthographic input lexicon to phonological output lexicon to semantics, and simultaneously (if it is a regular word) by the route from subword level orthographic-to-phonological conversion to response buffer to auditory input lexicon to semantics. A pseudohomophone can produce this spurious semantic activation only by the second of these two routes. These effects will interact with the degree to which the homophonic or pseudohomophonic foil is orthographically similar to the target with which the foil is phonologically identical; the smaller this similarity, the more the orthographic lexical entry for the target will be inhibited, and so the less its semantic representation will be (spuriously) activated.

As is evident from the other papers in this issue, exactly analogous questions arise with respect to spelling rather than reading, since phonology-only claims have been made there too. In this case, however, unlike the case of reading, useful data from studies of normal spellers is sparse. Hence the neuropsychological data are of special significance here, and these data strongly support the analogous conclusion: Spelling is certainly not a solely phonologically mediated process, but it is a process over which phonological representations exert some influence. The joint orthographic and phonological processes affecting spelling can be described in just the same interactive-activation way as we have done for reading.

REFERENCES

Coltheart, M. (1980). Reading, phonological recoding and deep dyslexia. In M. Coltheart, K.E. Patterson, & J. Marshall (Eds.), *Deep dyslexia* (pp. 197–226). London: Routledge & Kegan Paul.

Coltheart, M. (1985). Cognitive neuropsychology and the study of reading. In M.I. Posner & O.S.M. Marin (Eds.), Attention and performance XI (pp. 3–37). Hillsdale, NJ: Lawrence Erlbaum Associates Inc.

Coltheart, M., Masterson, J., Byng, S., Prior, M., & Riddoch, M.J. (1983). Surface dyslexia. *Quarterly Journal of Experimental Psychology, 35A*, 469–495.

Coltheart, M., Curtis, B., Atkins, P., & Haller, M. (1993). Models of reading aloud: Dual-route and parallel distributed processing approaches. *Psychological Review, 100*, 589–608.

Coltheart, M., Patterson, K.E., & Marshall, J. (Eds.) (1980). *Deep dyslexia*. London: Routledge & Kegan Paul.

Coltheart, M., & Rastle, K. (1994). A left-to-right serial process in reading aloud. *Journal of Experimental Psychology: Human Perception and Performance, 20*, 1197–1211.

Coltheart, V., Avons, S.E., Masterson, J., & Laxon, V.J. (1991). The role of assembled phonology in reading comprehension. *Memory and Cognition, 19*, 387–400.

Coltheart, V., Patterson, K., & Leahy, J. (1994). When a ROWS is a ROSE: Phonological effects in written word comprehension. *Quarterly Journal of Experimental Psychology,47A*, 917–955.

Jared, D., & Seidenberg, M.S. (1991). Does word identification proceed from spelling to sound to meaning? *Journal of Experimental Psychology: General, 120*, 1–37.

Lukatela, G., & Turvey, M.T. (1991). Phonological access of the lexicon: Evidence from associative priming with pseudohomophones. *Journal of Experimental Psychology: Human Perception and Performance, 17*, 951–966.

Lukatela, G., & Turvey, M.T. (1993). Similar attentional, frequency, and associative effects for pseudohomophones and words. *Journal of Experimental Psychology: Human Perception and Performance, 19*, 166–178.

Lukatela, G., & Turvey, M.T. (1994a). Visual lexical access is initially phonological: 1. Evidence from associative priming by words, homophones, and pseudohomophones. *Journal of Experimental Psychology: General, 123*, 107–128.

Lukatela, G., & Turvey, M.T. (1994b). Visual lexical access is initially phonological: 2. Evidence from phonological priming by homophones and pseudohomophones. *Journal of Experimental Psychology: General, 123*, 331–353.

Meyer, D.E., & Gutschera, K.D. (1975). *Orthographic versus phonemic processing of printed words*. Paper presented at the meeting of the Psychonomic Society, Denver, November.

Monsell, S., Patterson, K.E., Graham, A., Hughes, C.H., & Milroy, R. (1992). Lexical and sublexical translation of spelling to sound: Strategic anticipation of lexical status. *Journal of Experimental Psychology: Learning, Memory and Cognition, 18*, 452–467.

Patterson, K.E., & Shewell, C. (1987). Speak and spell: Dissociations and word class effects. In M. Coltheart, G. Sartori, & R. Job (Eds.), *The cognitive neuropsychology of language* (pp. 273–294). London: Lawrence Erlbaum Associations Ltd.

Patterson, K., Suzuki, T., & Wydell, T.N. (1996). Interpreting a case of Japanese phonological alexia. *Cognitive Neuropsychology, 13*, 803–822.

Pollatsek, A., Lesch, M., Morris, R., & Rayner, K. (1992). Phonological codes are used in integrating information across saccades in word identification and reading. *Journal of Experimental Psychology: Human Perception and Performance, 18*, 148–162.

Sasanuma, S., Ito, H., Patterson, K., & Ito, T. (1996). Phonological alexia in Japanese: A case study. *Cognitive Neuropsychology, 13*, 823–848.

Seidenberg, M.S., & McClelland, J.L. (1989). A distributed developmental model of word recognition and naming. *Psychological Review, 96*, 523–568.

Van Orden, G.C. (1987). A ROWS is a ROSE: Spelling, sound and reading. *Memory and Cognition, 15*, 181–198.

Van Orden, G.C. (1991). Phonologic mediation is fundamental to reading. In D. Besner & G. Humphreys (Eds.), *Basic processes in reading: Visual word recognition* (pp. 77–103). Hillsdale, NJ: Lawrence Erlbaum Associates Inc.

Van Orden, G.C., Johnston, J.C., & Hale, B.L. (1988). Word identification in reading proceeds from spelling to sound to meaning. *Journal of Experimental Psychology: Learning, Memory and Cognition, 14*, 371–386.

Van Orden, G.C., Pennington, B.F., & Stone, G.O. (1990). Word identification in reading and the promise of a subsymbolic psycholinguistics. *Psychological Review, 97*, 488–522.

Van Orden, G.C., Stone, G.O., Garlington, K.L., Markson, L.R., Pinnt, G.S., Simonfy, C.M., & Brichetto, T. (1992). "Assembled" phonology and reading: A case study in how theoretical perspective shapes empirical investigation. In R. Frost & L. Katz (Eds.), *Orthography, phonology, morphology and meaning* (pp. 249–292). Amsterdam: Elsevier Science Publishers BV.

Wydell, T.N., Patterson, K.E., & Humphreys, G.W. (1993). Phonologically mediated access to meaning for KANJI: Is a ROWS still a ROSE in Japanese KANJI? *Journal of Experimental Psychology: Learning, Memory and Cognition, 19*, 491–514.

How Many Levels of Processing Are There in Lexical Access?

Alfonso Caramazza
Harvard University, Cambridge, USA

The patterns of semantic errors in speaking and writing are used to constrain claims about the structure of lexical access mechanisms in speech and written language production. It is argued that it is not necessary to postulate a modality-neutral level of lexical representation (lemma) that is intermediate between lexical-semantic representations and modality-specific lexical representations. A dual-stage access model is proposed in which the first stage involves the selection of semantically and syntactically specified, modality-specific lexical forms, and the second stage involves the selection of specific phonological (orthographic) content for the selected lexemes.

INTRODUCTION

How are words accessed in language production? Theories of speech production are in agreement on two fundamental points: (1) semantic, syntactic, and lexical form information constitute independent levels of representation, and (2) these levels of representation are probably accessed sequentially in the course of language production. The dominant view is that lexical access involves at least two distinct stages of processing. The first stage involves the selection of a semantically and syntactically specified lexical representation or lemma; the second stage involves the selection of its corresponding lexical-phonological representation or lexeme (e.g. Bock, 1982; Bock & Levelt, 1994; Burke, MacKay, Worthley, & Wade, 1991; Butterworth, 1989; Dell, 1986; Fay & Cutler, 1977; Fromkin, 1971; Garrett, 1975, 1980; Harley, 1984; Kempen &

Requests for reprints should be addressed to Alfonso Caramazza, Cognitive Neuropsychology Laboratory, Department of Psychology, William James Hall, Harvard University, 33 Kirkland St., Cambridge, MA 02138, USA (email: caram@wjh.harvard.edu).

The work reported here was supported by NIH grants NS22201 to AC. A version of this paper was presented at the Fourteenth European Workshop on Cognitive Neuropsychology, Bressanone, January 1996. I am grateful to Michele Miozzo and Jennifer Shelton for many helpful comments on earlier versions of this paper.

Huijbers, 1983; Levelt, 1989; MacKay, 1987; Roelofs, 1992; Stemberger, 1985)[1]. But this is where the agreement ends. On almost everything else, from the nature of the information represented at each stage or level of processing, to the overall number of processing stages, to the manner in which representations are selected, there are substantial disagreements among models. Thus, for example, models differ on whether they assume discrete or interactive stages of processing, whether they assume componential or holistic representations for meaning, whether they assume localist versus distributed representations, and whether or not they assume morphological composition.

Despite, or perhaps because of, the many disagreements, this is a vibrant area of research, and there are a number of active research programmes directed at articulating the structure and content of lexical-phonological representations and their associated access mechanisms (see, for example, Dell, 1986; Dell & O'Seaghdha, 1991; Garrett, 1988; Levelt, 1989; Levelt et al., 1991; MacKay, 1987; Martin, Weisberg, & Saffran, 1989; Meyer, 1990; Shattuck-Hufnagel, 1987; Starreveld & La Heij, 1996; Stemberger, 1990)[2]. Many fewer programmatic efforts have focused specifically on the nature of lemma-level representations, perhaps because semantic theory is not nearly as well developed as phonological theory, and/or perhaps because it is difficult to address questions about the syntactic properties of words by means of the single-word processing tasks typically used in psycholinguistic experiments. Nevertheless, in the last few years a number of efforts have been made to formulate explicit claims about the content and the processing structure of lemma-level representations and to provide experimental evidence on these issues (Bock & Eberhard, 1993; Bock & Levelt, 1994; Jescheniak & Levelt, 1994; Levelt, 1989; Roelofs, 1992, 1993; Schriefers, 1993; see also Garrett, 1992, for a recent review of neuropsychological evidence on this issue).

In this paper, I address the relationship among semantic, syntactic, and word form representations. I address this issue principally from the perspective of

---

[1] A similar distinction has been made in the neuropsychological literature in order to explain the dissociation between disorders of lexical-semantic processing and disorders of lexical form retrieval. Most models of the lexical system assume a two-stage retrieval process in which the first stage involves accessing a lexical-semantic representation and the second stage involves accessing modality-specific lexical forms (e.g. Caramazza & Hillis, 1990; Ellis, 1985; Howard & Franklin, 1988; Humphreys, Riddoch, & Quinlan, 1988). This view should not be confused with a superficially similar proposal that distinguishes between cognitive and lexical form systems (e.g. Allport, 1985; Allport & Funnell, 1981). On the latter view, lexical access only involves one stage: The retrieval of lexical forms from nonlinguistic conceptual information.

[2] Although on a much smaller scale, in recent years there have also been a number of attempts to articulate the structure and content of lexical-orthographic representations (see, for example, Badecker, Hillis & Caramazza, 1990; Caramazza & Miceli, 1989, 1990; Jonsdottir, Shallice, & Wise, 1996; Kay & Hanley, 1994; Link & Caramazza, 1994; McCloskey, Badecker, Goodman-Schulman, & Aliminosa, 1994).

cognitive neuropsychology—that is, by considering the language production performance of brain-damaged subjects—but I will also discuss some experimental evidence from normal speech production when relevant. The paper is organised as follows. After a brief review of the arguments and evidence for the distinction between lemma and lexeme levels of representation, I discuss the most influential proposal about the nature of lemma representations. A review of recent experimental evidence concerning the relationship between syntactic features and semantic and phonological information reveals several problems with current formulations of lemma-level representations. The principal part of the paper follows, and it concerns the analysis of semantic errors in naming, reading, and writing tasks by brain-damaged subjects. A crucial aspect of the argument presented here rests on the relationship between phonological and orthographic lexical forms—the principal issue under consideration in this special issue of *Cognitive Neuropsychology*. The implications of the distribution of semantic errors in speaking and writing for the relationship among semantic, syntactic, and word form representations are explored. Finally, I present a model of lexical access that can better account for the major results on lexical access.

THE DISTINCTION BETWEEN LEMMA AND LEXEME LEVELS OF REPRESENTATION

There are compelling arguments and empirical evidence for distinguishing between at least two levels of lexical representation. For example, the distinction between lemma and lexeme representations provides a natural account for the existence of homonyms: Words that are phonologically and orthographically identical but which differ in meaning and/or grammatical class (e.g. to watch/the watch; the bank [money]/the bank [river]). The relevant distinctions between these words are not at the level of lexical form (since they are identical) but at the level of semantic and syntactic properties. Thus, if we are to capture the lexical distinctions between the members of homonym pairs it has to be at a level other than that of phonological (orthographic) content of the word pairs. But arguments from the structure of language can only take us so far. A processing model will have to be based on empirical evidence concerning language use. Here, too, there is ample evidence in support of a dual-stage model of lexical access (for reviews see Bock & Levelt, 1994; Butterworth, 1989; Dell, 1986; Garrett, 1988, 1992; Levelt, 1989).

Various sorts of data have been cited in support of the lemma/lexeme distinction, including naturally occurring and experimentally induced speech errors or slips of the tongue (e.g. Dell, 1990; Dell & Reich, 1981; Fay & Cutler, 1977; Fromkin, 1971; Garrett, 1975, 1976; Stemberger, 1985). These data are the most extensive and the earliest evidence proffered in support of the two-stage model of lexical access. For example, Garrett (1975, 1976) noted that the elements that enter in word and sound exchange errors, such as the examples shown in Table 1, are subject to different distributional constraints: Word exchanges tend to involve words of the same grammatical class and occur between phrases, whereas sound exchanges tend to occur in words of different grammatical classes within a phrase. Furthermore, sound exchanges but not word exchanges are usually phonologically similar elements and occur in similar phonological environments. The fact that word exchanges are constrained by grammatical features and not by phonological properties, and the fact that sound exchanges are constrained by phonological and not semantic or syntactic properties, has been taken to indicate that separate lexical access stages are involved in speech production: the first stage retrieves a semantically and syntactically specified representation; the second stage retrieves a phonologically specified representation. This conclusion, aside from debates about whether the two stages are independent or interactive (e.g. Dell & O'Seaghdha, 1991; Levelt et al., 1991), has remained a constant of all models of speech production.

Other evidence cited in support of the lemma/lexeme distinction includes the reaction time data in naming and lexical decision experiments (e.g. Jescheniak & Levelt, 1994; Kempen & Huijbers, 1983; Levelt & Maassen, 1981; Levelt et al., 1991; Schriefers, Meyer, & Levelt, 1990) and the pattern of hesitation phenomena in normal and aphasic speech (Butterworth, 1979, 1980; Butterworth & Beatty, 1978). Perhaps the most intuitively appealing evidence for the lemma/lexeme distinction is the tip-of-the-tongue (TOT) phenomenon—the feeling of knowing a word that is momentarily inaccessible for production (R. Brown & McNeill, 1966; Burke et al., 1991; Jones & Langford, 1987; Kohn et al., 1987; Koriat & Lieblich, 1974; Perfect & Hanley, 1992; Rubin, 1975; and see A.S. Brown, 1991, for review). This phenomenon has been interpreted as reflecting the failure to retrieve a lexeme in the context of successful retrieval of its lemma. And, of course, there is the evidence from aphasia, which shows there are word production disorders that can be attributed to a deficit in lexical-semantic processing (e.g. Gainotti, 1976; Hillis, Rapp, Romani, & Caramazza, 1990; Warrington, 1975) and production disorders for which the deficit can clearly be localised at the level of retrieval of lexical forms

TABLE 1
Examples of Word and Sound Exchange Errors

Word exchange errors:	They *left* and *forgot* it behind (Garrett, 1988)
	I left the *briefcase* in my *cigar* (Garrett, 1980)
	... writing a *mother* to my *letter* (Dell & Reich, 1981)
Sound exchange errors:	She's a real *r*ack *p*at ... (Garrett, 1988)
	It comes down to a choice of *s*tummer *s*ipends ... (Garrett, 1980)
	... *l*orck *y*ibrary ... (Dell & Reich, 1981)

in the face of spared lexical-semantic processing (e.g. Caramazza & Hillis, 1990; Howard & Franklin, 1989; Kay & Ellis, 1987). Thus, there is a wide spectrum of evidence consistent with the two-stage model of lexical access.

Although there appears to be substantial agreement among researchers of speech production on the distinction between a lemma and a lexeme level of lexical representation, the content and processing dynamics of lemma representations remain relatively unspecified. Although everyone agrees that lemmas are modality-independent, semantically and syntactically specified lexical representations, there are different ways in which one can implement the distinction between lexical form representations (phonological and orthographic) and modality-independent, semantic, and syntactic representations.

THE STRUCTURE OF LEMMA REPRESENTATIONS

The clearest proposal concerning the processing structure of lemma representations is to be found in a paper by Roelofs (1992) and subsequently adopted by Bock and Levelt (1994) and Jescheniak and Levelt (1994). Their model distinguishes among three levels of representation (see Fig. 1): the conceptual, the lemma, and the lexeme levels. The conceptual level represents lexical concepts as unitary nodes in a conceptual network. The meaning of a word is given by the set of labeled connections between a concept node and other nodes in the network. Each lexical concept node is connected to a lemma node; lemma nodes are modality-independent units that are connected to a set of syntactic nodes specifying such properties as grammatical class (Noun, Verb, etc.), gender, and auxiliary type (be or have). Each lemma node is connected to a lexeme node which, through its connections to segmental nodes, specifies the phonological (and orthographic) form of a word. In Fig. 1, the lexical concept [TIGER] is connected to its Italian lemma node {tigre}, which is connected to the category node N(oun) and the gender feature F(eminine), and, in turn, the lemma node is connected to its lexeme /tigre/. Lexical access in this model is represented by the sequential selection of lemma (and hence the syntactic features that define a word) and lexeme nodes through spreading activation emanating from the lexical concept node.

Several properties of this model should be stressed for present purposes. First, word meaning is represented by unitary concept nodes, with each node connected to only one lemma node. Spreading activation from the concept node only activates its corresponding lemma node. However, spreading activation within the conceptual level from the concept node to connected nodes (e.g. ANIMAL, STRIPES, WILD, etc.) will result in the partial activation of the latter nodes and, consequently, the weak activation of their corresponding lemma nodes. Second, the selection of a word's lemma node is tantamount to the selection of the syntactic nodes/features that define that word. And, third, the selection of a lexeme is mediated by the selection of the word's grammatical

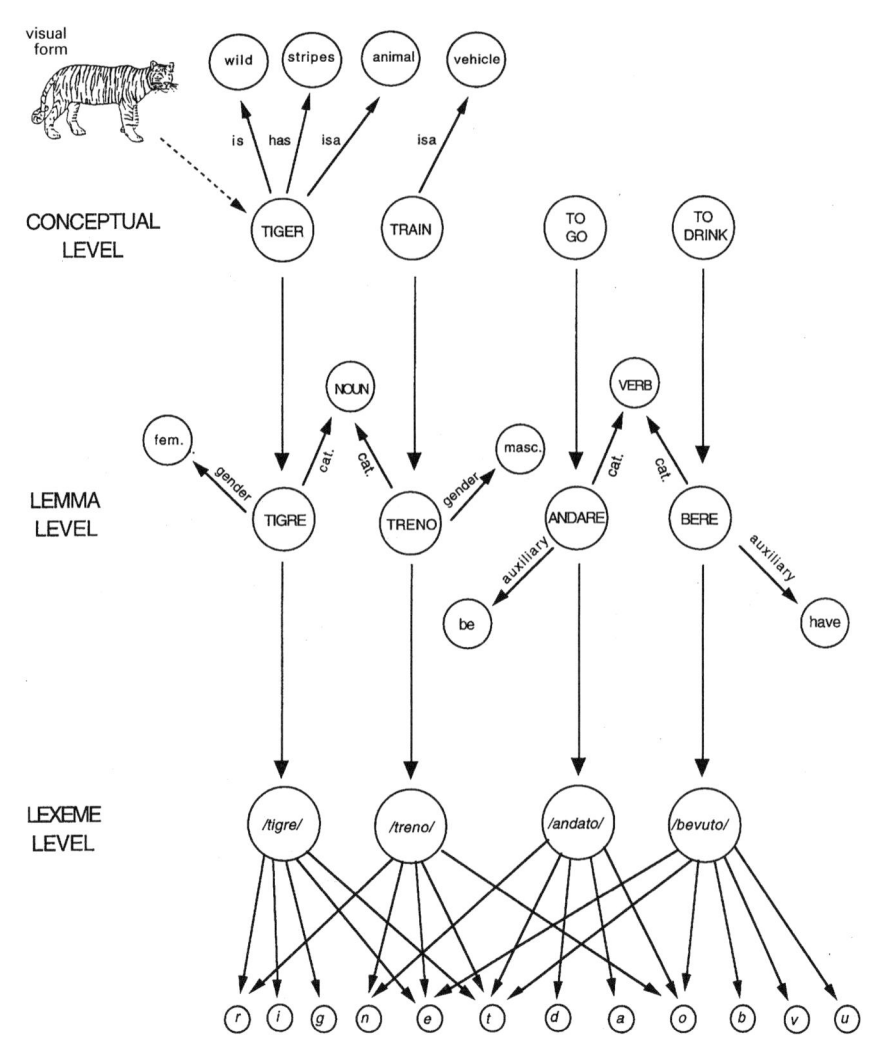

FIG. 1. Part of the lexical system showing the relation between lemma and other levels of lexical representation: The "Syntactic Mediation" hypothesis (see text). The lemma and lexeme levels show the Italian words for the lexical concepts TIGER, APPLE, TO GO, and TO DRINK. (Adapted from Bock & Levelt [1994], Jescheniak & Levelt [1994], and Roelofs [1992].)

features. Given the centrality of syntactic information in defining the structure of lemmas and in accessing lexemes, I will call this model of the structure of lemmas the "syntactic mediation" (SM) hypothesis.

In various papers, Dell (1986, 1990; Dell & O'Seaghdha, 1991) has proposed an interactive network model with a very similar hierarchy of lexical levels to that proposed by Bock and Levelt (1994), Jescheniak and Levelt (1994), and

Roelofs (1992). Dell (1990, pp. 331–332) draws a similar distinction among semantic, lemma, and lexeme representations: "The lemma node represents the lexical item as a syntactic/semantic entity. It corresponds to Dell's (1986) 'word node' and is assumed to connect directly to conceptual structure and to syntactic information. Below that, the lexeme node is a single unit representing the phonological form of the word. This corresponds roughly to the morpheme node and/or to the set of syllable nodes in Dell (1986) and MacKay (1982). The lexeme node connects to phonological segments (. . .)." However, this model differs from that of Levelt and collaborators on at least two crucial points: (1) in Dell's model, word meanings are represented in componential form, and (2) the stages of lexical processing are not discrete but interactive. Nonetheless, for present purposes, the two models make a common assumption: There is a level of representation, lemma, that is distinct from lexical-semantic and from lexical-phonological information[3].

The modality-neutral lemma hypothesis—a hypothesis shared by Roelof's discrete stage model and Dell's interactive model—predicts that retrieval of syntactic information is necessary for the successful retrieval of lexemes. However, reviews of experimental results with normal subjects in tasks requiring access to syntactic and word form information and of the performance of brain-damaged subjects with selective deficits in word production raise considerable difficulties for this hypothesis. I will argue that there are grounds for rejecting the hypothesis that a modality-neutral lemma node intervenes between lexical-semantic representations and word forms. However, I will also argue that there are equally compelling grounds for the autonomy of syntactic information from semantic and word form representations. These seemingly conflicting conclusions will be reconciled in a new model of the processing structure and organisation of lexical knowledge.

THE INDEPENDENCE OF SYNTACTIC FROM SEMANTIC AND WORD FORM INFORMATION

The neuropsychological literature is replete with evidence about the crucial role of syntactic information in the organisation of lexical knowledge. The most celebrated dissociation is that between closed- and open-class words (or function and content words). Although principally discussed in the context of agrammatic and paragrammatic speech performance (e.g. Buckingham & Kertesz, 1976; Goodglass, 1976), the dissociation can also be seen in single-

---

[3] Parenthetically, it should be noted that it is not obvious that Dell can maintain both that there are interactions between semantic and phonological levels, which he needs to explain the results showing that word substitutions are affected by both semantic and phonological similarity (Dell & Reich, 1981), and that there is a modality-neutral level of representation, lemma, intervening between lexical-phonological and semantic representations.

word processing tasks in the context of diverse clinical pictures (Andreewsky & Seron, 1975; Caramazza, Berndt, & Hart, 1981; Gardner & Zurif, 1975; see also papers in Coltheart, Patterson, & Marshall, 1980). Thus, for example, two acquired dyslexic subjects—RG (Beauvois & Dérouesné, 1979) and AM (Patterson, 1982)—could read most (>92%) content words correctly, including abstract words, but showed considerable difficulty (only 70% correct) in reading function words.

The other major grammatical class dissociation is between nouns and verbs (e.g. Berndt, Mitchum, Haendiges, & Sandson, 1997; Caramazza & Hillis, 1991; Damasio & Tranel, 1993; Daniele, Giustolisi, Silveri, Colosimo, & Gainotti, 1994; De Renzi & di Pellegrino, 1995; Hillis & Caramazza, 1995; Kremin & Basso, 1993; McCarthy & Warrington, 1985; Miceli, Silveri, Villa, & Caramazza, 1984; Miceli, Silveri, Nocentini, & Caramazza, 1988; Zingeser & Berndt, 1988). There are a number of reports of brain-damaged subjects who show a selective difficulty in producing nouns in the context of relatively spared ability to produce verbs, and those who show the opposite pattern of relative difficulties with these two classes of words. Thus, for example, De Renzi and di Pellegrino (1995) have described a subject with a frontotemporal lesion who showed a selective *sparing* of verbs. For example, in an oral spelling task he correctly produced over 93% of verbs but only about 45% of nouns and 40% of function words. His difficulties with words of other grammatical classes could not be ascribed to a deficit in processing concrete words (Breedin, Saffran, & Coslett, 1994; Warrington, 1975) because he showed no advantage for this type of words within grammatical classes. And function words, which are at least as abstract as any verb, fared no better than concrete nouns. It would seem that the effect is purely grammatical in nature.

The existence of these grammatical class dissociations implies that syntactic information is one of the dimensions along which the lexical system is organised. However, they do not establish precisely where in the lexical system syntactic information is represented, nor do they clearly specify the relation of syntactic to semantic and word form representations. Particularly relevant for the latter purpose is the performance of brain-damaged subjects who show selective difficulties in producing words of one grammatical class in only one modality of output (Caramazza & Hillis, 1991; Hillis & Caramazza, 1995; Rapp & Caramazza, 1997; Rapp, Benzing, & Caramazza, 1995). For example, subject SJD showed severe difficulties writing the very verbs that she could easily produce orally. In written and oral production tasks with homonyms (e.g. to watch/the watch) she correctly produced both the noun and verb forms in speaking but was only able to write the noun forms correctly (Caramazza & Hillis, 1991). Other examples of modality-specific grammatical class effects include subjects who show double dissociations of grammatical class by modality. Thus, EBA (Hillis & Caramazza, 1995) showed a selective deficit in recognising written forms of verbs, but a selective difficulty in producing nouns orally; KSR (Rapp et al., 1995) was selectively impaired in producing nouns in speaking, but verbs in writing; and PW (Rapp & Caramazza, 1997) has difficulties producing closed-class words in writing and open-class words in speaking. The striking commonality in these cases is the remarkable specificity of the disorder—the deficit involves words of a specific grammatical class in only one modality of output (or input).

These selective grammatical class deficits, restricted to either oral or written production, provide the evidence we need to argue that syntactic knowledge is represented independently of both lexical-semantic and word form information. We reason as follows: The fact that the deficit is restricted to one modality of output implies that the lexical-semantic system is intact; furthermore, given that the lexical-semantic system is intact and given that the impairment in these subjects is limited to one grammatical class, jointly imply that the deficit must concern a syntactic level of representation. Thus, we are led to conclude that lexical-semantic and syntactic information are represented independently.

Evidence for the autonomy of syntactic from word form information is found in the performance of anomic subjects who are able to provide information about the syntactic features of words they are unable to produce. Thus, for example, Henaff Gonon, Bruckert, and Michel (1989) described a French-speaking anomic patient who could correctly provide the grammatical gender (13/14 correct) of the nouns he failed to produce in various naming tasks. A more systematic investigation of this type of dissociation has recently been reported by Badecker, Miozzo, and Zanuttini (1995). These investigators described the performance of an anomic subject, Dante, who despite his inability to produce the names of objects, or even guess the first or last phoneme in a two-phoneme, forced-choice task, was virtually always able to recall their gender correctly. In a more recent investigation of the same subject (Miozzo & Caramazza, in press b), the dissociation between the retrievability of syntactic and word form information has been extended to verbs. Dante was shown to be able to provide correctly the auxiliary form of a verb (be or have) he was unable to retrieve: He correctly recalled the auxiliary of verbs he could not name in 99% of the trials, but was exactly at chance level in guessing the initial phoneme of the word. These results clearly show that a word's syntactic features are represented independently of its form, thereby permitting their independent access. However, they leave unanswered the question of how syntactic features are activated and how they are related to semantic and phonological information. Thus, for example, do syntactic features mediate between semantic and phonological information as proposed by the SM hypothesis? Tentative answers to this question are provided by normal subjects' ability to retrieve gender and phonological information in TOT states.

In a series of experiments (Caramazza & Miozzo, 1997; Miozzo & Caramazza, in press a), we addressed the question of whether the availability of syntactic and phonological information are correlated in TOT states. For this purpose we compared subjects' relative ability to retrieve grammatical gender and the initial phoneme of words in TOT states. Grammatical gender is a syntactic feature of nouns that, in Italian, is not deducible from their meaning. In several experiments, we were able to show that subjects are able to retrieve both the grammatical gender and the initial phoneme of words in TOT states with well above chance-level accuracy but that performance for the two features is uncorrelated. These results demonstrate that, contrary to the SM hypothesis, access of a word's phonological features does not strictly depend on the prior access of its syntactic features[4].

Converging evidence in support of the claim that access of a lexeme representation does not require successful access of its syntactic features can be found in a recent series of experiments by Jescheniak and Levelt (1994). In a study designed to explore the locus of the frequency effect in speech production, they had Dutch subjects either name a picture (Expt. 1) or make a gender decision about the name of the picture (Expt. 4). The results of the experiments are very clear: The frequency effect remains over repeated trials in the naming condition, but is not sustained in the gender decision task. In the gender condition they obtained a clear "priming" effect: It appears that once gender is retrieved, its subsequent retrieval is independent of the word's frequency. For present purposes, the important result concerns a further manipulation introduced by Jescheniak and Levelt. They wanted to determine whether the gender priming effect they observed in Expt. 4 depended on the retrieval of the lexeme or whether the direct retrieval of gender information was required. Clearly, if retrieval of a word's lexeme requires the prior selection of (all) its syntactic features, then the retrieval of the lexeme should lead to gender priming because gender, too, has been selected. To address this issue, they carried out the following two experiments. In Experiment 5a, they first gave subjects two blocks of naming trials followed by two blocks of a gender decision task with the same items; in Experiment 5b, they had the same arrangement of blocks of naming and gender decision trials but this time the naming task required subjects to produce the full noun phrase (article + noun)

---

[4] This conclusion may be too strong. It is entirely possible that there are fundamental differences in the way in which different grammatical features of a word are represented and accessed. Thus, for example, we might want to distinguish between what I will call "intrinsic" and "extrinsic" grammatical features. The former, intrinsic features, refers to those properties that are inherently associated with a word (e.g. grammatical class and gender); the latter, extrinsic features, refers to those grammatical properties that are contextually determined (e.g. number and tense). And within the set of intrinsic features, we may want to distinguish between the more and the less arbitrary features: "gender" is a purely arbitrary feature; "noun" is not nearly as arbitrary given the meaning of the word. It may turn out that the accessibility of the different types of grammatical features for any one word is not uniform.

in naming objects. Facilitation in the gender task was only obtained in Experiment 5b. That is, facilitation in the gender decision task was only obtained when the preceding trials required subjects to retrieve gender information explicitly; the mere retrieval of a word's lexeme (Expt. 5a) did not facilitate access to its gender information. These results suggest that phonological information can be accessed "independently" of grammatical information, and may even imply, contrary to the interpretation preferred by Jescheniak and Levelt, that the selection of a lemma does not lead "automatically" to the activation of its associated grammatical features.

There is also indirect evidence from the spontaneous speech of brain-damaged subjects that is consistent with the claim that lexemes can be accessed without correct access to their gender features. These subjects make syntactic agreement errors despite their ability to retrieve the phonological form of words. For example, the Italian speaker, FS (Miceli & Caramazza, 1988) produced utterances such as the following: "Poi io ascolto *il* (masculine singular) *televisione* (fem. singular)—then I listen [to] the television"; " . . . perché *il* (masc. sing.) *giornate* (fem. plural) [sono] *lungo* (masc. sing.)— . . . because the days are long." In this example, FS correctly retrieved the lexemes *televisione* and *giornate* but not the gender information needed to select the correct article (*la* and *le*, respectively) and the proper inflection on the adjective (*lunghe*, in this case). These examples suggest the possibility that the retrieval of lexemes may be spared in the face of damage to grammatical features.

A similar case has been described by Cubelli and Perizzi (1996). They report a patient who produced utterances such as "Il nonno è seduto *sul* (masc. sing.) *panchino* (neologism)"—the grandfather is seated on the bench—instead of "Il nonno è seduto *sulla* (fem. sing.) *panchina* (fem. sing.)"; and "La palla è sotto *il* (masc. sing.) *sedio* (neologism)"—the ball is under the chair—instead of "La palla è sotto *la* (fem. sing.) *sedia* (fem. sing.)." This case, too, clearly demonstrates that the phonological representation of a word (albeit deformed) can be accessed despite access of the wrong syntactic features.

The final example I will consider here concerns a subject who made article/noun agreement errors involving the mass/count distinction (Semenza, Mondini, & Cappelletti, 1995). This subject produced utterances such as "Nella cucina c'è sempre *una panna*"—In the kitchen there's always one cream; instead of "Nella cucina c'è sempre *della panna*"—In the kitchen there's always some cream; and "*Una farina* nel sacco (. . .) "—one flour in the bag . . . ; instead of "*La farina* nel sacco (. . .) "—The flour in the bag . . . . These examples demonstrate that the subject could correctly access the phonological representation of words despite the occasional failure to access (some of) their syntactic features.

In short, the agreement errors produced by the three cases briefly reviewed here suggest that access of a word's syntactic features is not required in order to activate its lexeme.

INTERIM SUMMARY

There is ample evidence in support of two-stage models of lexical access. None of the results I have reviewed challenges this view of the lexical system. To the contrary, the results further confirm the validity of distinguishing between a level of processing where word forms are represented and a level or levels of processing where lexical-semantic and syntactic information are represented. However, the evidence also indicates that access to a word's lemma level does not automatically lead to access of its syntactic features (Jescheniak & Levelt, 1994; Miozzo & Caramazza, in press a). Although the latter results are problematic for the view that syntactically specified lemma representations mediate access of lexical forms, a seemingly simple modification of the model could easily accommodate the recalcitrant results we have reviewed.

The proposed modification may be readily understood by considering the schematic representation of the model shown in Fig. 1. The model postulates the existence of autonomous lemma nodes that are directly activated by their corresponding lexical concept nodes; the lemma nodes, in turn, activate their corresponding lexeme nodes. In the original formulation of the model, the activation of the lemma node automatically spreads to its associated syntactic nodes. In this model, selection of a lemma node entails the selection of a set of syntactic features. If one drops the assumption that the selection of the lemma node implies the selection of its syntactic features and assumes instead that the selection of the lemma node merely makes it possible for the subsequent, but not necessary, selection of syntactic features, then, it might be possible to accommodate the observation that access of a word's phonological features does not presuppose access of its syntactic features. The modification entertained here essentially argues that selection of lemma is formally independent of the selection of its syntactic features. This move saves the syntactic mediation hypothesis but renders the motivation for postulating an autonomous lemma node less than compelling. The original motivation for assuming an autonomous lemma level was to capture at once the autonomy of syntactic information and the dependence of lexeme representations on their syntactically specified lexical representations. If one were to abandon the assumption that access to the lemma node entailed the automatic selection of its syntactic features, it would be unclear why one would want to have such a node in the first place—its role would have been reduced to a contentless waystation to syntactic and phonological representations: The lemma node would have been rendered superfluous.

Putting aside these considerations and granting for the moment the plausibility of the new formulation of the organisation and processing structure of the lemma level, there are empirical reasons for rejecting the postulation of a contentless lemma node. The evidence comes from the contrasting patterns of lexical production errors in speaking and writing. These data have not previously been given due consideration in the development of models of lexical access (but see an excellent review in Garrett, 1992). But, as I hope to show in what follows, the analysis of the contrasting patterns of performance in the selection of phonological and orthographic lexical forms in brain-damaged subjects can help reduce the range of plausible theories of lexical access.

In order to use lexical access performance in spelling tasks to constrain claims about the processing structure of the lemma and lexeme levels of representation, it must first be established that the relation of lemma to orthographic word forms is direct and *not* mediated by access of their corresponding phonological forms. In other words, it must first be demonstrated that access of orthographic lexemes (O-lexemes) occurs independently of access of phonological lexemes (P-lexemes) (see Fig. 2 for a schematic representation of the two hypotheses). The reason for this preliminary step in evaluating the evidence from written language production is simple: If spelling is mediated by phonology, then spelling performance will not directly reflect the interaction between lemma and lexical form access, but the complex interaction between lemma and P-lexemes and between P-lexemes and O-lexemes. However, if it could be established that access of O-lexemes is not mediated by the prior access of their associated P-lexemes, then we would be able to use lexical errors in written production to inform theories of the relation between lemma and lexeme levels of representation[5].

THE AUTONOMY OF LEXICAL-ORTHOGRAPHIC REPRESENTATIONS

Arguably, the clearest evidence for the autonomy of orthography in language production comes from the neuropsychological literature. If written production is phonologically mediated, we would expect that damage to the phonological system should necessarily result in deficits in written language production. However, it has been observed repeatedly that the ability to spell is often preserved even though phonological production is severely impaired (e.g. Alajouanine & Lhermitte, 1960; Assal, Buttet, & Jolivet, 1981; Basso, Taborelli, & Vignolo, 1978; Caramazza, Berndt, & Basili, 1983; Ellis, Miller, & Sin, 1983; Hanley & McDonnell, this issue; Hier & Mohr, 1977; Lecours & Rouillon, 1976; Lhermitte & Dérouesné, 1974; Patterson & Shewell, 1987; Shelton & Weinrich, this issue). Although this dissociation has often been interpreted as sufficient evidence for the hypothesis of phonologically unmediated (direct) access of O-lexemes (e.g. Allport & Funnell, 1981), this conclusion would only be warranted if it could be shown that the deficit in speech

---

[5] This conclusion does not entail that the relation between the lemma level and the corresponding P-lexeme and O-lexeme levels must be identical. However, it is more parsimonious to begin with this assumption.

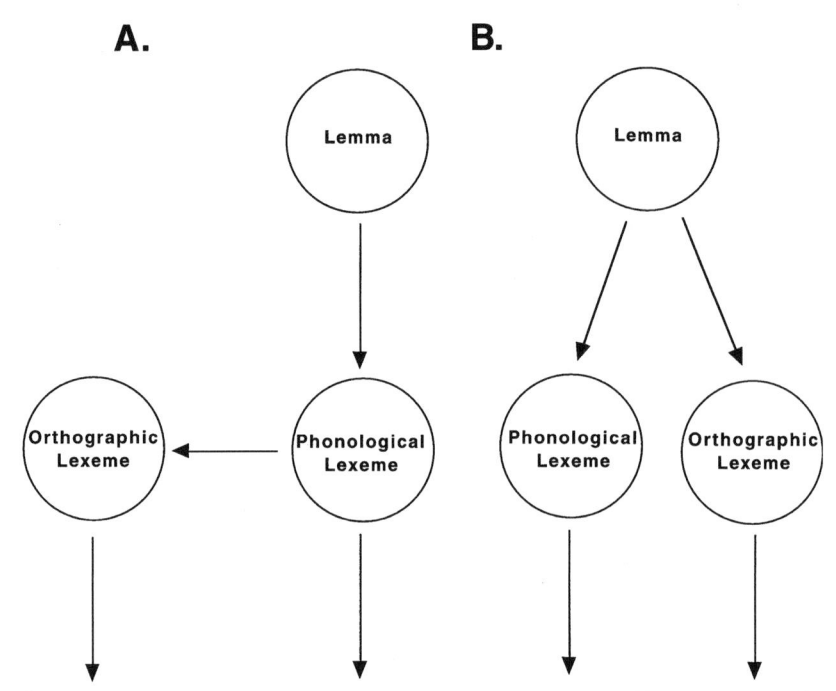

FIG. 2. Schematic representation showing the relation between lemma and lexeme representations. Panel A shows the phonological mediation hypothesis; panel B shows the orthographic autonomy hypothesis.

production was not the result of damage to post-lexical phonological processes but of damage directly to the phonological lexicon. Otherwise, it could be argued that O-lexeme access is mediated by P-lexeme access and that the observed impairment in speech production was merely the result of damage to post-lexical phonological processes. However, there are a number of results that are not subject to these reservations. The clearest examples are those where brain-damaged subjects make semantic errors in oral naming but not in written naming (e.g. subjects RGB and HW: Caramazza & Hillis, 1990) or semantic errors in written naming but not in oral naming (e.g. subject SJD: Caramazza & Hillis, 1991). The production of lexical (semantic) errors indicates a lexical as opposed to a post-lexical process as the locus of damage; the fact that the semantic errors occur in only one modality of output indicates that P-lexemes and O-lexemes are activated independently by their lemma-level representations. In other words, the fact that subjects RGB and HW were able to retrieve the correct lexical form in writing despite the production of semantic errors in speaking demonstrates that access of O-lexemes is not mediated by prior access of P-lexemes (see also Hanley & McDonnell, this issue; Shelton & Weinrich, this issue; and Rapp & Caramazza, 1997, for discussion of other relevant evidence).

One other type of evidence in support of the orthographic autonomy hypothesis is the observation of different oral and written semantic errors in response to the same object in double, sequential naming tasks. WMA (Miceli, Benvegnù, Capasso, & Caramazza, this issue) and PW (Rapp, Benzing, & Caramazza, this issue) produced semantic errors both in speaking and in writing. Crucially for present purposes, in double naming tasks they produced inconsistent lexical responses in oral and written naming of the same picture—for example, they might produce a correct response in writing followed by a "don't know" or a semantic error in oral naming—and they occasionally produced different semantic errors in oral and written naming. For example, in response to a picture of tweezers, PW orally named it "pliers," wrote "needle," and then orally named it again "pliers." Similarly, the Italian subject WMA, in response to a picture of a cook (cuoco) said "pietanza" (dish) but wrote "forchette" (forks), and in response to a picture of peppers (peperoni) wrote "tomato" (pomodoro) but said "carciofo" (artichoke). These patterns of performance undermine the phonological mediation hypothesis of written language production, and they suggest instead that lemma representations independently activate their associated O-lexeme and P-lexeme representations. Thus, we can safely proceed to interpret the implications of contrasting patterns of P-lexeme and O-lexeme selection errors for models of lexical access and, more specifically, for theories of the structure of lemma-level representations.

DISPENSING WITH THE CONTENTLESS LEMMA NODE

The evidence that will be used for this purpose is the pattern of dissociations of lexical errors in speaking and writing. There are several steps to the argument. I begin by briefly summarising the relevant facts.

As already noted, there are brain-damaged subjects who make semantic errors in only one modality of output. The deficit in these patients can be located unambiguously in the language production system at a stage beyond the lexical-semantic level. Especially convincing in this regard is the fact that when subjects were asked to read aloud and define words, they often made semantic errors in oral reading but invariably went on to provide the correct definition (Caramazza & Hillis, 1990). For example, HW read the word pirate as "money" but then went on to define the word she was supposed to read as "Has a thing over its eye . . . I would say that they don't have any anymore, but they do in business. He wants your money and your gold." And RGB read pharmacist as "drugs" and went on to define the stimulus as "He gives you your prescriptions." Observations such as these, together with the fact that subjects performed virtually flawlessly in various comprehension tasks, confine the deficit to output processes. More important for present purposes is the observation that semantic errors were restricted to one modality of output. This implies that lemma-level representations were correctly activated. That is, since subjects could consistently select the correct lexemes in one modality of output it follows that their associated lemmas must have been correctly accessed, or it would not have been possible to produce the correct lexemes in the first place. A further relevant observation is that their semantic errors occurred in the context of unimpaired post-lexical processes. Thus, for example, HW only occasionally produced an articulatory error; RGB spoke fluently and without phonological or articulatory errors; and SJD only rarely made spelling errors. In all three cases, their errors consisted of fluently produced semantic substitutions. These facts rule out a post-lexical deficit as a determinant of the contrasting patterns of performance in oral and written naming. Thus, the locus of damage in these subjects is at a point between the correctly selected lemma-level representations and their modality-specific lexeme representations.

Having confined the possible locus of damage in subjects HW, RGB, and SJD to a point between the lemma and the lexeme levels of representation, we are confronted with a puzzle: If the correct lemma has been selected, how can the inaccessibility of a modality-specific lexeme result in a *semantic* error? It is not immediately apparent how models that postulate a "contentless" node between lexical-semantic and lexeme levels of representation can account for the occurrence of semantic errors in a single modality of output. That is, it is not clear what happens when a correctly selected lemma node fails to activate either its P- or O-lexeme. Since the lemma node has a discrete, one-to-one relationship to its P- and O-lexemes, the expectation ought to be that failure to activate one of its modality-specific lexemes would result in the absence of a response and not in the production of a semantic error. Nonetheless, although it does not flow naturally from its basic architecture, the lemma-as-abstract-node hypothesis could be made to account for the modality-specific semantic errors as follows.

It could be argued that damage to the connections between lemma and lexemes in one modality leads to the reselection of another lemma because of spreading activation within the conceptual system. The chain of events might be as follows: the correctly selected lexical concept activates the correct lemma, leading to its selection; the correctly selected lemma activates its associated P- and O-lexemes; if one of these lexemes cannot reach threshold because of damage within that level of representation, a different lexical-concept node is selected from among the set of nodes that have become activated by the spreading activation from the originally selected lexical-concept node; the newly selected lexical-concept node will activate its associated lemma node, and so on. The way in which the abstract lemma hypothesis can motivate the reselection of another lemma is by proposing that this process is undertaken whenever the appropriate lexeme node does not reach threshold.

This account is further strained when we consider the performance of subjects WMA (Miceli et al., this issue) and PW (Rapp et al., this issue), who make different oral and written semantic errors in naming the same object. Here the story would take the following form: The reason a semantic error is made in one modality is, as previously discussed, because the target lexeme in that modality could not reach threshold and therefore a new cycle of lexical selection beginning with a related lexical-concept node would have to be undertaken. To explain the production of a semantic error in the other modality we would have to argue that in that modality, too, the target lexeme could not reach threshold and therefore yet another cycle of lexical selection would have to be undertaken for production in that modality. What has to be explained, however, is why a different lexical concept is selected the second time. We know that the reason for this is not because the process of selection of alternative lexical concepts from one trial to another is random. This is shown by the fact that consecutive responses in the same modality always resulted in the same response—it was only across modalities that different lexical responses were produced to the same stimulus. Thus, the selection of a different semantically related lexeme must be due to the failure to select successfully the other modality lexeme of the previously selected lemma. An example should make this clear. Subject PW produced the following sequence of responses to a picture of tweezers: "pliers," "needle," and "pliers," in oral, written, and oral production respectively. To explain this performance we would have to assume that the P-lexeme representation /tweezers/ could not reach threshold and consequently the next lexical-concept node selected was "pliers." This cycle could be brought to completion because the P-lexeme /pliers/ could reach threshold and was selected. We would then have to argue that in trying to write the name of tweezers, PW again selected the lexical-concept node correctly and proceeded as before, only to encounter difficulty in selecting the O-lexeme for tweezers. At this point we would expect that the same alternative lexical-concept node as the one selected in the previous trial (pliers) would again be selected (as in within-modality consecutive trials). But since the subject produced a different semantic error in writing, we must assume that the O-lexeme for "pliers" could not reach threshold and therefore a completely new cycle of lexical selection had to be undertaken. In the new cycle the lexical-concept node "needle" was selected and this time the cycle could be brought to completion.

The two cases considered here do not constitute knock-down arguments against the abstract lemma hypothesis. And it might even be argued that it has been shown that the abstract lemma hypothesis is able to account for the supposedly recalcitrant results. However, the way in which the model has been forced to account for the results provides the most compelling argument against the hypothesis. The explanation proposed for the contrasting patterns of semantic errors across modalities of output gives absolutely no role to the abstract lemma node. Had we completely omitted all mention of this node, we would have produced a formally equivalent argument. That is, the burden of explanation for the existence of contrasting semantic errors in oral and written naming was completely carried by the "interaction" between lexical-semantic and lexeme representations. Thus, once again, we find that the notion of an abstract lemma node may be quite superfluous.

To this point I have presented various results and arguments against the lemma-as-abstract-node hypothesis. Singly, each observation or argument may be insufficient to reject this hypothesis since each observation may be challenged or alternative interpretations offered. However, the combined weight of all the evidence is not easily dismissed on one pretext or another, and is sufficient to raise profound scepticism about the explanatory value of the hypothesis. This scepticism about the validity of the syntactic mediation hypothesis of lemma-level representation encourages the consideration of alternative forms of organisation of the lexical system. One such possible alternative is considered next.

THE INDEPENDENT NETWORK MODEL OF LEXICAL ACCESS

The Independent Network (IN) model of the lexicon assumes that lexical knowledge is organised in sets of independent networks connected to each other by a *modality-specific lexical node*. The lexical-semantic network represents word meanings as sets of semantic properties, features, or predicates. The lexical-syntactic network represents a word's syntactic features such as grammatical category, gender, auxiliary type, tense, and so on. The nodes in this network are organised in subnetworks corresponding to the different syntactic functions. Thus, there is a subnetwork consisting of category nodes (N, V, etc.); one consisting of gender nodes (M, F); one consisting of auxiliary types (be, have); and so on. Nodes within a subnetwork have inhibitory links since they are in competition. The P- and the O-lexeme networks consist of the modality-specific representations of lexical items (more specifically, lexical stems). Nodes in these networks are also linked inhibitorily since they are in competition.

The production of a word involves the following sequence of events. A selected lexical-semantic representation propagates activation toward the lexical-syntactic and the P- and O-lexeme networks[6]. Not all syntactic features can be activated by the semantic network. For example, with the exception of

---

[6] The lexical-syntactic network also receives input from outside the lexical system—from sentence generation mechanisms. However, these inputs will not be considered here.

natural, gender-marked words (e.g. uomo [man] in Italian), gender features do not receive activation from the semantic network. However, grammatical category and verb tense features, for example, do receive activation from the semantic network (see footnote 4, p. 186). Under normal circumstances the activation of syntactic nodes from the semantic network[7] is *not* sufficient for a grammatical feature to reach threshold. Selection of the full set of grammatical features of a word requires the prior activation and selection of the modality-specific lexical node.

Activation and selection of a modality-specific lexical form (P- and O-lexemes) results in activation of its associated phonological and orthographic properties. Thus, in this model, the selection of grammatical features typically occurs temporally prior to the selection of the specific phonological and orthographic content of a word[8]. However, since the selection of the lexeme node does not depend on the prior selection of its associated syntactic features, the phonological and orthographic content of the lexeme nodes may, under special circumstances (e.g. TOT states, brain damage), become available independently of their grammatical features. A schematic representation of the IN model is shown in Fig. 3.

The IN model shares many properties with other models of the lexical system: lexical-semantic information is represented independently of syntactic and word form representations as in the models proposed by Bock and Levelt (1994), Dell (1990), and Roelofs (1992); lexical-semantics is componential as in Butterworth (1989) and Dell (1986), but unlike Garrett (1992), Jescheniak and Levelt (1994), and Roelofs (1992); it is a forward activation model as in Butterworth (1989) and Roelofs (1992), but unlike Dell (1986) and Stemberger (1985); however, unlike all previous models, the activation from the selected lexical-semantic representation spreads simultaneously and independently to the lexical-syntactic and the word-form networks. Furthermore, unlike these earlier models it does not postulate a modality-neutral lemma representation; instead, it only postulates direct links between lexical-semantic representations and modality-specific (phonological and orthographic) lexical representations. The latter representations may be called phonological lexemes (P-lexemes) and orthographic lexemes (O-lexemes), if we wanted to stress the modality-specific nature of the representations, but they could also be called phonological lemma (P-lemma) and orthographic lemma (O-lemma), if we wanted to stress the fact

---

[7] We can think of the effect of the activation propagated from the semantic network to the syntactic feature network as a form of priming of the target features that will eventually be selected when additional activation is provided by the lexeme node.

[8] The fact that the model assumes that syntactic nodes reach threshold before lexeme-level representations does not mean that subjects should be able to "report" syntactic information more rapidly than word form information. Whereas the production of word forms is a natural function of the lexical system, the metalinguistic task of reporting syntactic features may be quite difficult and slow.

```
                    SEMANTIC
                 REPRESENTATION
                      (  )
                    /  |  \
                   /   |   \
                  /    |    \
                 ↓     ↓     ↓
        ORTHOGRAPHIC  SYNTACTIC  PHONOLOGICAL
          LEXEMES  →  FEATURES ← LEXEMES
             |                      |
             ↓                      ↓

                    PANEL A
```

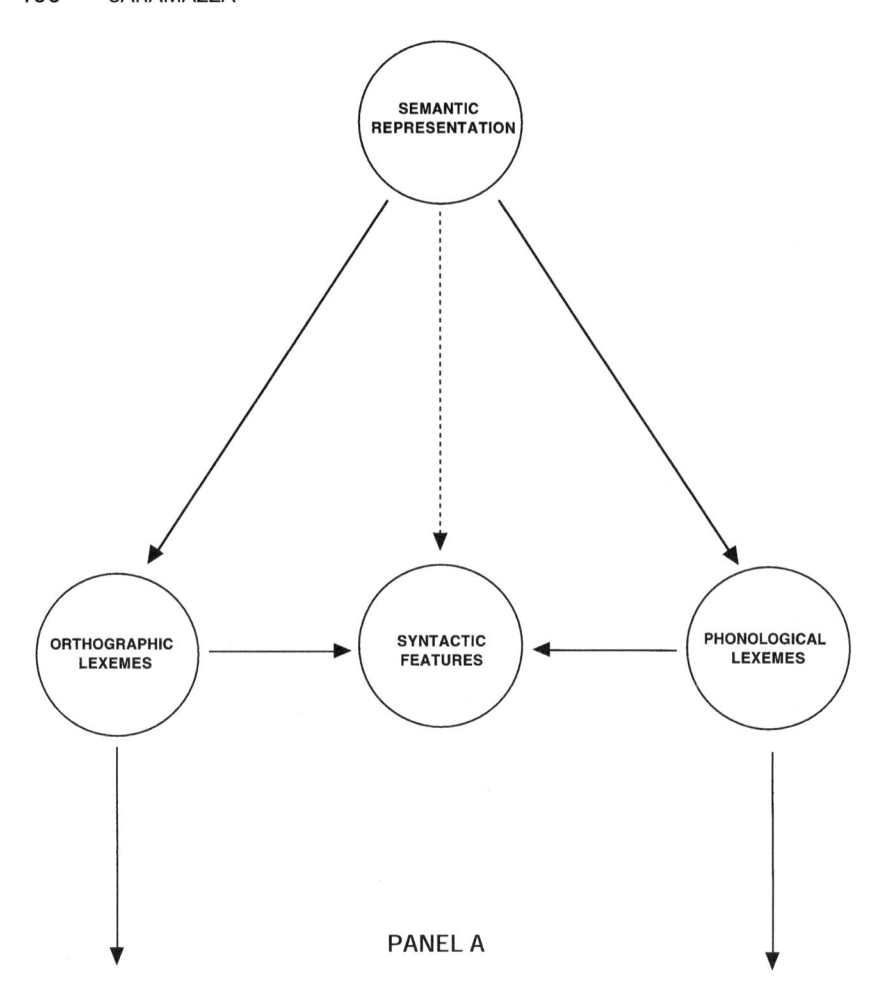

FIG. 3A. Panel A (see also Panel B, Fig. 3B, opposite) presents a schematic representation of the Independent Network model showing the relation among semantic, syntactic, and lexical form representations.

that they are semantically and syntactically specified lexical representations. I will use the terms P-lexeme and O-lexeme.

The IN model can readily account for the results we have reviewed in this paper. It accounts for the contrast between word exchanges and sound exchanges by assuming that lexical access occurs in two separate stages: the first stage involves the selection of a modality-specific, syntactically and semantically specified representation; the second stage involves the selection of the lexeme's phonological (orthographic) content. The general features of the TOT phenomenon are also explained by assuming that lexical access occurs in two

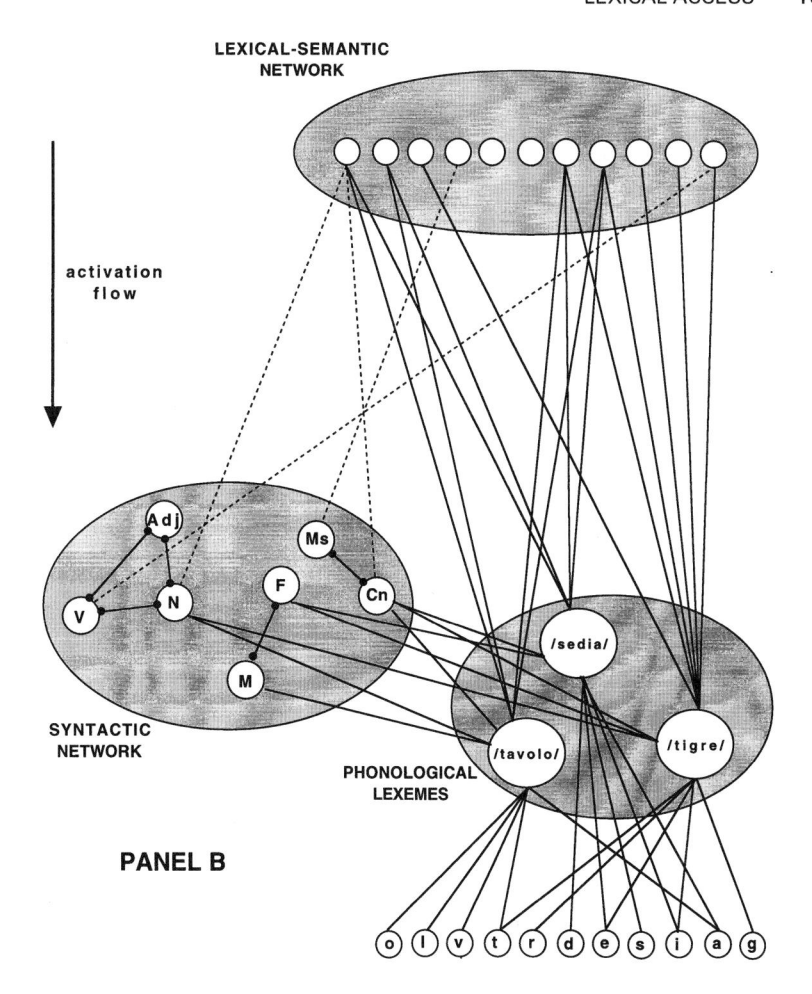

FIG. 3B. Panel B (see also Panel A, Fig. 3A, opposite) shows a more detailed representation of the model. The O-lexeme network is not shown in this figure to avoid excessive crowding. The flow of information is from semantic to lexeme and syntactic networks and then on to segmental information. N=noun; V=verb; Adj=adjective; M=masculine; F=feminine; CN=count noun; Ms=mass noun. Dotted lines indicate weak activation. Links within a network are inhibitory.

stages. The more specific results concerning the nondependence of phonological information on the prior retrieval of syntactic features (Caramazza & Miozzo, 1997; Miozzo & Caramazza, in press a) follow naturally from the assumption that the selection of a lexeme does not guarantee the selection of the full set of its associated syntactic features. And the results of Miozzo and his collaborators (Badecker et al., 1995; Miozzo & Caramazza, in press) concerning the performance of Dante, which showed that gender and auxiliary type information was consistently available in the face of a complete inability to provide information about the phonological features of inaccessible noun and verb lexemes, are explained by assuming a deficit in accessing the phonological content of the correctly selected lexeme representations.

The IN model naturally accounts for the pattern of dissociations and associations of semantic errors across modalities of output. Semantic errors can arise either from damage to the lexical-semantic level or from damage in accessing lexeme representations. As for the other models considered here, in the IN model, damage to the lexical-semantic level should result in quantitatively and qualitatively similar semantic errors in all lexical processing tasks. This pattern of performance has been documented in subjects with dementing disorders (e.g. Chertkow & Bub, 1990; Warrington, 1975) as well as in subjects who have sustained extensive focal brain damage (e.g. Hillis et al., 1990).

More pertinent to the present discussion are those cases of semantic errors restricted to one modality of output. This pattern of performance follows naturally from two characteristics of the IN model: the assumption that meanings are componential, and the assumption that a selected lexical-semantic representation activates in parallel the lexemes of all words that share semantic features with the selected meaning (Caramazza & Hillis, 1990; Dell, 1986; Hillis & Caramazza, 1995). A consequence of these assumptions is that under normal circumstances the cohort of activated lexemes is defined semantically—all the entries that share semantic features. In the eventuality of a problem in accessing the target lexeme, either because of damage directly at the lexeme level or because of damage to the connections from the semantic network to the lexeme level, the lexeme with the highest activation will be selected. This lexeme has a high probability of being semantically related to the target response.

The proposed structure of semantic/lexeme interaction in the IN model also naturally explains the pattern of contrasting semantic errors across oral and written naming in some brain-damaged subjects. On the assumption of damage to both the P- and O-lexeme networks, resulting in the temporary inaccessibility of some lexemes (typically low-frequency items), the most active lexeme in each network will be produced in response to the activation from the selected lexical-semantic representation. The selected lexemes will be semantically related to the target response. However, since the lexeme networks are activated independently of each other, and directly from the selected lexical-semantic representation, there is no expectation that the selected lexemes in the two networks will always be the same (although they are more likely than not to be the same if such factors as frequency and semantic similarity determine the selection of the lexeme). In other words, a natural consequence of the functional architecture and processing dynamics of the IN model is precisely the pattern of performance observed in subjects WMA (Miceli et al., this issue) and PW

(Rapp et al., this issue) in conditions where access to the P- and O-lexeme networks is impaired.

Finally, in order for the IN model to account for the selective deficits for words of one grammatical class in only one modality of output, we must make an additional assumption about the organisation of lexical knowledge in the brain. We must assume either that syntactic information about different grammatical classes is represented in different areas of the brain or that lexeme representations are organised by grammatical class in different parts of the brain[9]. We could, then, explain the patterns of spared and impaired production of nouns, verbs, and function words as the result of selective damage to either one of the spatially segregated networks. Some similar assumption is needed by all models of lexical production.

It would seem that the IN model can readily and naturally account for the full pattern of results discussed in this paper. However a problem remains to be addressed. In the IN model, much of the burden for explaining the observed patterns of semantic errors in brain-damaged subjects is carried by the assumption that meanings are componential—it is because of the componentiality assumption that a semantic representation activates multiple lexemes. This assumption has not gone unchallenged over the years (e.g. Fodor, Garrett, Walker, & Parkes, 1980). Levelt (1989, 1992) has recently raised a further objection in the form of what he calls the "hyperonym" problem: Why don't people speak in hyperonyms (i.e. produce "animal" instead of "dog," "furniture" instead of "table," "artefact" instead of "furniture," and so on) if meanings are componential? This is a non-trivial problem that must be addressed by proponents of componential theories of meaning. Indeed, as Levelt (1992) has correctly noted, a simple, unadorned componential theory of lexical semantics is fatally flawed. Here I propose a solution to this problem within a parallel activation, componential theory of meaning.

A SOLUTION TO THE HYPERONYM PROBLEM

Levelt (1992, p. 6) states the hyperonym problem as follows: "When lemma A's meaning entails lemma B's meaning, B is a hyperonym of A. If A's conceptual conditions are met, then B's are necessarily also satisfied. Hence if A is the correct lemma, B will (also) be retrieved." Thus, if a speaker intended to produce "dog," the set of semantic features selected at the level of the semantic network would fully satisfy not only the word "dog" but also "animal." Why, then, don't speakers say animal when they intend to say dog?

Levelt (1992) has proposed two solutions. One solution, within a componential account of meaning, is to adopt what he has called the "principle of

---

[9] An implication of the latter assumption is that there are independent lexeme representations for homonyms such as to play/the play (the position that was taken in Caramazza & Hillis, 1991).

specificity." This principle states that given that the activation conditions for multiple lexemes are satisfied by the selected lexical-semantic representation, speakers select the most specific lexeme. Thus, speakers intending to say "table" will select "table" instead of "furniture"; and speakers intending to say "furniture" will select "furniture" instead of "artefact." However, as Levelt notes, it is not obvious how to implement such a principle in current network models of language production.

The other solution proposed by Levelt is to give up altogether the assumption of componentiality and adopt a holistic conception of semantics, where word meanings are represented by lexical-concept nodes and the set of labelled connections among the concept nodes (e.g. Collins & Quillian, 1969). On this view, there is a node in conceptual memory corresponding to every lexical entry in the language. These nodes are directly connected to their corresponding lemma representation in a one-to-one fashion (as already discussed). Thus, the conceptual node DOG would be connected to its lemma "dog," and the conceptual node ANIMAL would be connected to its lemma "animal." This solution to the hyperonym problem may face other problems, however (see Bierwisch & Schreuder, 1992, for discussion).

There is another solution possible within the IN model that does not require the implementation of the "principle of specificity." The solution is quite simple, and follows naturally from the assumptions of componentiality and parallel activation that form part of the basic structure of the IN model. All that needs to be assumed is that the amount of activation passed onto the next level by any one "feature" is a weighted proportion of the number of selected features. So, for example, if the meaning of a word is represented by 10 features, the amount of activation passed on by each feature is (roughly) 1/10th of the amount of activation propagated from the lexical-semantic network to the lexeme level[10]. A further assumption is that the amount of activation normally needed by the activated lexemes to reach threshold is the full unit of activation propagated from the lexical-semantic network. Consequently, the lexeme most likely to reach threshold (ignoring other factors such as resting state levels of different lexemes) will be the one that receives activation from *all* the selected semantic features—the only one that receives the full complement of activation propagated from the lexical-semantic level. The hyperonym lexeme will, by definition, receive activation from only a fraction of the selected features and therefore not enough to reach threshold (see example in Fig. 4). On this view, it is not even necessarily the case that the most active alternative lexeme to the target lexeme will be the hyperonym; a very similar co-hyponym (e.g. dog, given that cat has been selected at the lexical-semantic level) could reach a greater level of activation than the hyperonym (animal).

---

[10] I say roughly because the amount of activation propagated by each feature may also be weighted by its importance to the meaning of the word.

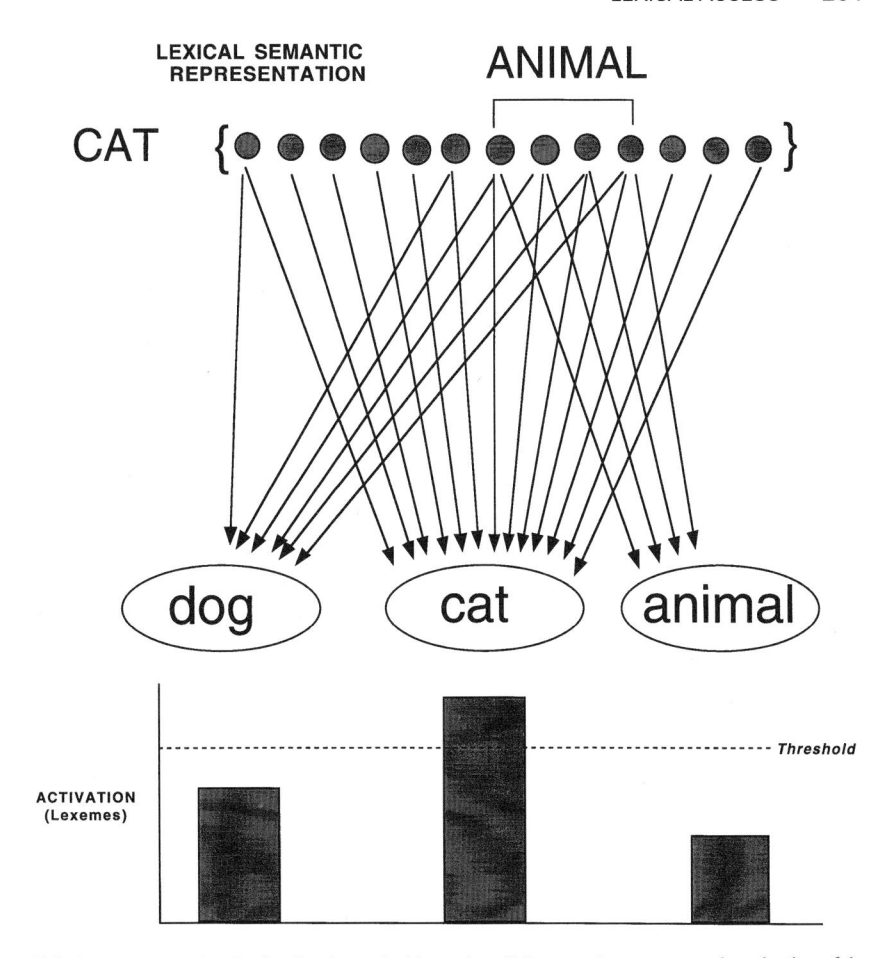

FIG. 4. Example of activation levels reached by various P-lexemes in response to the selection of the semantic representation CAT.

The proposed solution to the hyperonym problem does not solve the inverse problem also associated with componential theories of meaning—the "hyponym problem." If people intend to say "animal," why don't they sometimes say "dog" or "elephant" instead? The solution proposed for the hyperonym problem could lead to hyperonym errors—producing "dog" instead of "animal"—since the amount of activation reaching the hyponym (dog) would be the same as that reaching the intended target (animal). So, why don't people regularly make hyponym errors? To solve this problem we must make an additional assumption: The maximum amount of activation contributed by a single link to a node is a direct function of the number of links that feed into the node. Specifically, we assume that the maximum activation contributed by any one connecting link to a lexeme node that has N links feeding into it will be 1/Nth the total activation needed for selection of a lexeme node (or some other arbitrary value just greater than threshold). In this way, the activation reaching the lexeme "dog" when the semantic representation ANIMAL has been selected will necessarily be smaller than the activation reaching the lexeme "animal."

CONCLUSION

In this paper I have been concerned with whether it is necessary to postulate a modality-neutral level of lexical representation (lemma) that is intermediate between lexical-semantic representations and modality-specific lexical representations. I have argued that there is no compelling reason for postulating such a level of representation and that, in fact, its postulation has undesirable empirical consequences. I have also attempted to articulate a hypothesis about the relations among lexical-semantic, syntactic, and word form representations that is compatible with the facts of cognitive neuropsychology, normal speech errors and experimental evidence with normal subjects.

Two facts, in particular, have been stressed in this criticism of the lemma-as-abstract-node hypothesis: the existence of brain-damaged subjects with selective grammatical class deficits restricted to either oral or written production, and the existence of subjects who make semantic errors only in speaking or only in writing. The reason for stressing the importance of these facts is because the peculiar nature of these dissociations allows us to specify relatively precisely the locus of functional damage in these subjects. Thus, we can be confident that the locus of damage in subjects who only make semantic errors in speaking, say, must directly concern the inaccessibility of P-lexeme representations. The reason for this conclusion is simple: As the subject can produce the target response correctly in the other modality of output—writing, in this example—we must conclude that the lexical-semantic level of representation is undamaged. Furthermore, since the errors are well-formed lexical substitutions, we must conclude that lexical-phonological knowledge is also undamaged. The only remaining possible locus of damage is at the level of the connections leading to the activation of lexeme representations. And since a consequence of this damage is the production of *semantic* errors, we are invited to infer that the damaged relation concerns a mapping between meaning and lexical forms—that is, between lexical-semantic representations and P- and O-lexeme representations. This conclusion is incompatible with the syntactic mediation hypothesis of lexeme access proposed by Bock and Levelt (1994), Dell (1990), Jescheniak and Levelt (1994), and Roelofs (1992).

Another important source of evidence for the organisation of the lexical system concerns the observation that selective grammatical class deficits, such as difficulties in producing verbs, can be restricted to either oral or written production. Here again we can rule out damage to the lexical-semantic level because the subjects could produce verbs correctly in the unaffected output modality. Furthermore, the fact that the modality-specific deficit was restricted to only one class of words allows us to exclude a post-lexeme deficit as the cause of the observed impairment. We are thus invited to draw the following inferences: lexical-semantic and grammatical information are independent since we can damage one without affecting the other; and syntactic and word form information are also independent of each other for the same reason.

The two conclusions reached on the basis of the neuropsychological evidence find further support from research with neurologically intact subjects. It has been found that access to a word's lexical-semantic representation does not guarantee access to its syntactic features, and that access to the word's phonological features can occur independently of access to its syntactic features (at least for gender; Caramazza & Miozzo, 1997; Miozzo & Caramazza, in press a). Also, in a study involving the analysis of priming effects in object naming and gender decision tasks (Jescheniak & Levelt, 1994), it has been found that access of a word's lexeme facilitated a second retrieval of that lexeme but not access of its syntactic features. Thus, experimental evidence with normal subjects converges with that from neuropsychological investigations in showing that access of lexeme representations does not depend on the prior selection of (all) the grammatical features of a word.

The evidence reviewed here finds a plausible account within a model of lexical access that shares many features with current theories of the lexical system but differs from them in some important respects. The central assumptions of the Independent Network (IN) hypothesis are:

1. The lexical-semantic, syntactic, and modality-specific form representations of a word are independently stored in separate networks.
2. P-lexeme and O-lexeme representations are independently activated by semantic representations.
3. Lexical-semantics is componential and it activates in parallel the syntactic nodes and the P- and O-lexemes, but whereas the former nodes only receive enough activation to be primed, the lexeme nodes can receive enough activation for independent selection.
4. The selected lexical-semantic representation activates in parallel all the lexemes of words that share semantic features with the selected lemma.
5. Activation from selected lexeme converges on the grammatical features already primed by activation from the lexical-semantic network.

The fact that there is a direct link between the lexical-semantic and the lexeme levels provides a natural explanation for the occurrence of semantic errors only in writing or in speaking; the fact that syntactic features are represented autonomously allows a natural explanation for the occurrence of selective deficits of grammatical classes in only one modality of output.

There are several empirical and theoretical issues that have not been addressed here. For example, what is the time course of activation of different levels of representation? And, what are the dynamics (discrete vs. continuous; strictly forward vs. forward and backward propagation) of activation and selection of representations at different levels of processing? These issues are currently the focus of concerted experimental and theoretical analysis (e.g. Dell & O'Seaghdha, 1991; Levelt et al., 1991). It remains to be seen whether closer scrutiny of the IN hypothesis in light of these other issues will confirm the optimistic conclusion reached here.

REFERENCES

Alajouanine, T., & Lhermitte, F. (1960). Les troubles des activités expressives du langage dans l'aphasie. Leurs relations avec les apraxies. *Revue Neurologique, 102*, 604–629.

Allport, D.A. (1985). Distributed memory, modular systems and dysphasia. In S.K. Newman & R. Epstein (Eds.), *Current perspectives in dysphasia*. Edinburgh: Churchill Livingstone.

Allport, D.A., & Funnell, E. (1981). Components of the mental lexicon. *Philosophical Transactions of the Royal Society of London B, 295*, 397–410.

Andreewsky, E., & Seron, X. (1975). Implicit processing of grammatical rules in a classical case of agrammatism. *Cortex, 11*, 379–390.

Assal, G., Buttet, J., & Jolivet, R. (1981). Dissociations in aphasia: A case report. *Brain and Language, 13*, 223–240.

Badecker, W., Hillis, A.E., & Caramazza, A. (1990). Lexical morphology and its role in the writing process: Evidence from a case of acquired dysgraphia. *Cognition, 34*, 205–243.

Badecker, W., Miozzo, M., & Zanuttini, R. (1995). The two-stage model of lexical retrieval: Evidence from a case of anomia with selective preservation of grammatical gender. *Cognition, 57*, 193–216.

Basso, A., Taborelli, A., & Vignolo, L.A. (1978). Dissociated disorders of speaking and writing in aphasia. *Journal of Neurology, Neurosurgery, and Psychiatry, 41*, 556–563.

Beauvois, M.F., & Dérousné, J. (1979). Lexical or orthographic agraphia. *Brain, 104*, 21–49.

Berndt, R.S., Mitchum, C.S., Haendiges, A.N., & Sandson, J. (1997). Verb retrieval in aphasia. 1. Characterizing single word impairments. *Brain and Language, 56*, 68–106.

Bierwisch, M., & Schreuder, R. (1992). From concepts to lexical items. *Cognition, 42*, 23–60.

Bock, J.K. (1982). Toward a cognitive psychology of syntax: Information processing contributions to sentence formulations. *Psychological Review, 89*, 1–47.

Bock, K., & Eberhard, K.M. (1993). Meaning, sound and syntax in English number agreement. *Language and Cognitive Processes, 8*, 57–99.

Bock, K., & Levelt, W. (1994). Language production: Grammatical encoding. In M.A. Gernsbacher (Ed.), *Handbook of psycholinguistics*. San Diego, CA: Academic Press.

Breedin, S.D., Saffran, E.M., & Coslett, H.B. (1994). Reversal of the concreteness effect in a patient with semantic dementia. *Cognitive Neuropsychology, 11*, 617–660.

Brown, A.S. (1991). A review of the tip-of-the-tongue experience. *Psychological Bulletin, 109*, 204–223.

Brown, R., & McNeill, D. (1966). The "tip-of-the-tongue" phenomenon. *Journal of Verbal Learning and Verbal Behavior, 5*, 325–337.

Buckingham, H.W., & Kertesz, A. (1976). *Neologistic jargon aphasia*. Amsterdam: Swets & Zeitlinger.

Burke, D., MacKay, D.G., Worthley, J.S., & Wade, E. (1991). On the tip of the tongue: What causes word finding failures in young and older adults? *Journal of Memory and Language, 30*, 542–579.

Butterworth, B. (1979). Hesitation and the production of verbal paraphasias and neologisms in jargon aphasia. *Brain and Language, 8*, 133–161.

Butterworth, B. (1980). Evidences from pauses in speech. In B. Butterworth (Ed.), *Language production. Vol. 1: Speech and talk*. London: Academic Press.
Butterworth, B. (1989). Lexical access in speech production. In W. Marslen-Wilson (Ed.), *Lexical representation and process*. Cambridge, MA: MIT Press.
Butterworth, B., & Beatty, G. (1978). Gesture and silence as indicators of planning in speech. In R. Campbell & G.T. Smith (Eds.), *Recent advances in the psychology of language: Formal and experimental approaches*. New York: Plenum Press.
Caramazza, A. (1988). Some aspects of language processing revealed through the analysis of acquired aphasia: The lexical system. *Annual Review of Neurosciences, 11*, 395–421.
Caramazza, A., Berndt, R.S., & Basili, A.G. (1983). The selective impairment of phonological processing: A case study. *Brain and Language, 18*, 128–174.
Caramazza, A., Berndt, R.S., & Hart, J. (1981). "Agrammatic" reading. In F.J. Pirozzolo & M.C. Wittrock (Eds.), *Neuropsychological and cognitive processing in reading*. New York: Academic Press.
Caramazza, A., & Hillis, A.E. (1990). Where do semantic errors come from? *Cortex, 26*, 95–122.
Caramazza, A., & Hillis, A.E. (1991). Lexical organization of nouns and verbs in the brain. *Nature, 349*, 788–790.
Caramazza, A., & Miceli, G. (1989). Orthographic structure, the graphemic buffer and the spelling process. In C. von Euler, I. Lundberg, & G. Lennerstrand (Eds.), *Brain and reading*. London: Stockton Press.
Caramazza, A., & Miceli, G. (1990). The structure of graphemic representations. *Cognition, 37*, 243–297.
Caramazza, A., & Miozzo, M. (1997). *The relation between syntactic and phonological knowledge in lexical access: Evidence from the 'tip-of-the-tongue' phenomenon*. Manuscript, Harvard University, Cambridge, MA.
Chertkow, H., & Bub, D. (1990). Semantic memory loss in dementia of Alzheimer's type. *Brain, 113*, 397–417.
Collins, A.M., & Quillian, M.R. (1969). Retrieval time from semantic memory. *Journal of Verbal Learning and Verbal Behavior, 8*, 240–247.
Coltheart, M., Patterson, K.E., & Marshall, J. (Eds.) (1980). *Deep dyslexia*. London: Routledge & Kegan Paul.
Cubelli, R., & Perizzi, S. (1996). *Selective loss of grammatical gender of nouns in aphasia*. Paper presented at the Istituto di Psicologia del CNR, Roma, December 10.
Damasio, A.R., & Tranel, D. (1993). Nouns and verbs are retrieved with differently distributed neural systems. *Proceedings of the National Academy of Sciences of the United States of America, 90*, 4857–4960.
Daniele, A., Silveri, M.C., Giustolisi, L, Colosimo, C., & Gainotti, G. (1994). Evidence for a possible neuroanatomical basis for lexical processing of nouns and verbs. *Neuropsychologia, 32*, 1325–1341.
Dell, G.S. (1986). A spreading activation theory of retrieval in sentence production. *Psychological Review, 93*, 283–321.
Dell, G.S. (1988). The retrieval of phonological forms in production: Test of predictions from a connectionist model. *Journal of Memory and Language, 27*, 124–142.
Dell, G.S. (1990). Effects of frequency and vocabulary type on phonological speech errors. *Language and Cognitive Processes, 4*, 313–349.
Dell, G.S., Juliano, C., & Govindjee, A. (1993). Structure and content in language production: A theory of frame constraints in phonological speech errors. *Cognitive Science, 17*, 149–195.
Dell, G.S., & O'Seaghdha, P.G. (1991). Mediated and convergent lexical priming in language production: A comment on Levelt et al. (1991). *Psychological Review, 98*, 604–614.
Dell, G.S., & Reich, P.A. (1981). Stages in sentence production: An analysis of speech error data. *Journal of Verbal Learning and Verbal Behavior, 20*, 611–629.

De Renzi, E., & di Pellegrino, G. (1995). Sparing of verbs and preserved but ineffectual reading in patient with impaired word production. *Cortex, 31*, 619–636.
Ellis, A.W. (1985). The production of spoken words: A cognitive neuropsychological perspective. In A.W. Ellis (Ed.), *Progress in the psychology of language, Vol. 2*. London: Lawrence Erlbaum Associates Ltd.
Ellis, A.W., Miller, D., & Sin, G. (1983). Wernicke's aphasia and normal language processing: A case study in cognitive neuropsychology. *Cognition, 15*, 111–144.
Fay, D., & Cutler, A. (1977). Malapropisms and the structure of the mental lexicon. *Linguistic Inquiry, 8*, 505–520.
Fodor, J.A., Garrett, M.F., Walker, E.C.T., & Parkes, C.H. (1980). Against definitions. *Cognition, 8*, 263–367.
Fromkin, V.A. (1971). The non-anomalous of anomalous utterances. *Language, 47*, 27–52.
Gainotti, G. (1976). The relationship between semantic impairment in comprehension and naming in aphasic patients. *British Journal of Disorders of Communication, 11*, 57–61.
Gardner, H., & Zurif, E. (1975). *Bee* but not *be*: Oral reading of single words in aphasia and alexia. *Neuropsychologia, 13*, 181–190.
Garrett, M.F. (1975). The analysis of sentence production. In G. Bower (Ed.), *The psychology of learning and motivation: Advances in research and theory. Vol. 9*. New York: Academic Press.
Garrett, M.F. (1976). Syntactic processes in sentence production. In R. Wales & E. Walker (Eds.), *New approaches to language mechanisms*. Amsterdam: North-Holland.
Garrett, M.F. (1980). Levels of processing in sentence production. In B. Butterworth (Ed.), *Language production. Vol. 1: Speech and talk*. London: Academic Press.
Garrett, M.F. (1988). Processes in language production. In F.J. Newmeyer (Ed.), *The Cambridge survey of linguistics. Vol. 3: Biological and psychological aspects of language*. Cambridge, MA: Harvard University Press.
Garrett, M.F. (1992). Disorders of lexical selection. *Cognition, 42*, 143–180.
Goodglass, H. (1976). Agrammatism. In H. Whitaker & H.A. Whitaker (Eds.), *Studies in neurolinguistics, Vol. 1*. New York: Academic Press.
Harley, T.A. (1984). A critique of top-down independent levels of speech production. Evidence from non-plan-internal speech errors. *Cognitive Science, 8*, 191–219.
Henaff Gonon, M., Bruckert, R., & Michel, F. (1989). Lexicalization in an anomic patient. *Neuropsychologia, 27*, 391–407.
Hier, D.B., & Mohr, J.P. (1977). Incongruous oral and written naming. *Brain and Language, 4*, 115–126.
Hillis, A.E., & Caramazza, A. (1995). Representation of grammatical categories of words in the brain. *Journal of Cognitive Neuroscience, 7*, 396–407.
Hillis, A.E., Rapp, B., Romani, C., & Caramazza, A. (1990). Selective impairments of semantics in lexical processing. *Cognitive Neuropsychology, 7*, 191–243.
Howard, D., & Franklin, S. (1988). Memory without rehearsal. In T. Shallice & G. Vallar (Eds.), *The neurological impairment of short-term memory*. Cambridge: Cambridge University Press.
Howard, D., & Franklin, S. (1989). *Missing the meaning? A cognitive neuropsychological study of the processing of words by an aphasic patient*. Cambridge, MA: MIT Press.
Humphreys, G.W., Riddoch, M.J., & Quinlan, P.T. (1988). Cascade processing in picture identification. *Cognitive Neuropsychology, 5*, 67–103.
Jescheniak, J.D., & Levelt, W.J.M. (1994). Word frequency effects in speech production: Retrieval of syntactic information and of phonological form. *Journal of Experimental Psychology: Learning, Memory, and Cognition, 20*, 824–843.
Jonsdottiir, M.K., Shallice, T., & Wise, R. (1996). Phonological mediation and the graphemic buffer disorder in spelling: Cross language differences? *Cognition, 59*, 169–197.
Jones, G.V., & Langford, S. (1987). Phonological blocking in the tip of the tongue state. *Cognition, 26*, 115–122.

Kay, J., & Ellis, A. (1987). A cognitive neuropsychological case study of anomia. *Brain, 110*, 613–629.

Kay, J., & Hanley, R. (1994). Peripheral disorders of spelling: The role of the graphemic buffer. In G.D.A. Brown & N.C. Ellis (Eds.), *Handbook of spelling: Theory, process and intervention.* Chichester, UK: Wiley.

Kempen, G., & Huijbers, P. (1983). The lexicalization process in sentence production and naming: Indirect election of words. *Cognition, 14*, 185–209.

Kohn, S.E., Wingfield, A., Menn, L., Goodglass, H., Berko Gleason, J., & Hyde, M. (1987). Lexical retrieval: The tip of the tongue phenomenon. *Applied Psycholinguistics, 8*, 245–266.

Koriat, A., & Lieblich, I. (1974). What does a person in a "TOT" state know that a person in "don't know" state doesn't know. *Memory and Cognition, 2*, 647–655.

Lecours, A.R., & Rouillon, F. (1976). Neurolinguistic analysis of jargonaphasia and jargonagraphia. In H. Whitaker & H.A. Whitaker (Eds.), *Studies in neurolinguistics, Vol. 2.* New York: Academic Press.

Levelt, W.J.M. (1989). *Speaking: From intention to articulation.* Cambridge, MA: MIT Press.

Levelt, W.J.M. (1992). Accessing words in speech production: Stages of processing and representations. *Cognition, 42*, 1–22.

Levelt, W.J.M., & Maassen, B. (1981). Lexical search and order of mention in sentence production. In W. Klein & W.J.M. Levelt (Eds.), *Crossing the boundaries of linguistics. Studies presented to Manfred Bierwisch.* Dordrecht: Reidel.

Levelt, W.J.M., Schriefers, H., Vorberg, D., Meyer, A.S., Pechmann, T., & Havinga, J. (1991). The time course of lexical access in speech production: A study of picture naming. *Psychological Review, 98*, 122–142.

Lhermitte, F., & Dérousné, J. (1974). Paraphasies et jargonaphasies dans le langage oral avec conservation du langage écrit. Genèse des neologismes. *Revue Neurologique, 130*, 21–38.

Link, K., & Caramazza, A. (1994). Orthographic structure and the spelling processes. In G.A. Brown & N.C. Ellis (Eds.), *The handbook of normal and distributed spelling development: Theory, process and intervention.* Chichester, UK: Wiley.

MacKay, D.G. (1982). The problem of flexibility, fluency, and speed-accuracy trade-off in skilled behavior. *Psychological Review, 89*, 483–506.

MacKay, D.G. (1987). *The organization of perception and action: A theory for language and other cognitive skills.* New York: Springer.

Martin, N., Weisberg, R.W., & Saffran, E.M. (1989). Variables influencing the occurrence of naming errors: Implications for models of lexical retrieval. *Journal of Memory and Language, 28*, 462–485.

McCarthy, R., & Warrington, E.W. (1985). Category-specificity in an agrammatic patient: The relative impairment of verb retrieval and comprehension. *Neuropsychologia, 23*, 709–727.

McCloskey, M., Badecker, W., Goodman-Shulman, R.A., & Aliminosa, D. (1994). The structure of graphic representations in spelling: Evidence from a case of acquired dysgraphia. *Cognitive Neuropsychology, 11*, 341–392.

Meyer, A.S. (1990). The time course of phonological encoding in language production: The encoding of successive syllables of a word. *Journal of Memory and Language, 7*, 269–282.

Miceli, G., & Caramazza, A. (1988). Dissociation of inflectional and derivational morphology. *Brain and Language, 35*, 24–65.

Miceli, G., Silveri, M.C., Villa, G., & Caramazza, A. (1984). On the basis for agrammatic's difficulty in producing main verbs. *Cortex, 20*, 207–220.

Miceli, G., Silveri, M.C., Nocentini, U., & Caramazza, A. (1988). Patterns of dissociation in comprehension and production of nouns and verbs. *Aphasiology, 1*(2), 351–358.

Miozzo, M., & Caramazza, A. (in press a). The retrieval of lexical-syntactic features in tip-of-the-tongue states. *Journal of Experimental Psychology: Learning, Memory, and Cognition.*

Miozzo, M., & Caramazza, A. (in press b). On knowing the auxiliary of a verb that cannot be named: Evidence for the independence of grammatical and phonological aspects of lexical knowledge. *Journal of Cognitive Neuroscience.*
Patterson, K.E. (1982). The relation between reading and phonological coding: Further neuropsychological observations. In A.W. Ellis (Ed.), *Normality and pathology in cognitive functions.* London: Academic Press.
Patterson, K.E., & Shewell, C. (1987). Speak and spell: Dissociations and word-class effects. In M. Coltheart, G. Sartori, & R. Job (Eds.), *The cognitive neuropsychology of language.* London: Lawrence Erlbaum Associates Ltd.
Perfect, T.J., & Hanley, J.R. (1992). The tip-of-the-tongue phenomenon: Do experimenter-presented interlopers have any effect? *Cognition, 45*, 55–75.
Rapp, B., Benzing, L., & Caramazza, A. (1995). *The modality-specific representation of grammatical category.* Paper presented at the Meeting of the Psychonomic Society, Los Angeles, CA.
Rapp, B., & Caramazza, A. (1997). The modality-specific organization of grammatical categories: Evidence from impaired spoken and written sentence production. *Brain and Language, 56*, 248–286.
Roelofs, A. (1992). A spreading-activation theory of lemma retrieval in speaking. *Cognition, 42*, 107–142.
Roelofs, A. (1993). Testing a non-decompositional theory of lemma retrieval in speaking: Retrieval of verbs. *Cognition, 42*, 107–142.
Rubin, D.C. (1975). Within-word structure in tip-of-the-tongue phenomenon. *Journal of Verbal Learning and Verbal Behavior, 14*, 392–397.
Sartori, G., Job, R., & Coltheart, M. (1993). The organization of object knowledge: Evidence from neuropsychology. In D.E. Meyer & S. Kornblum (Eds.), *Attention and performance, XIV.* Hillsdale, NJ: Lawrence Erlbaum Associates Inc.
Schriefers, H. (1993). Syntactic processes in the production of noun phrases. *Journal of Experimental Psychology: Learning, Memory, and Cognition, 19*, 841–850.
Schriefers, H., Meyer, A.S., & Levelt, W.J.M. (1990). Exploring the time course of lexical access in language production: Picture-word interference studies. *Journal of Memory and Language, 29*, 86–102.
Semenza, C., Mondini, S., & Capelletti, M. (in press). The grammatical properties of mass nouns: An aphasia case study. *Neuropsychologia.*
Shattuck-Hufnagel, S. (1987). The role of word onset consonants in speech production planning: New evidence from speech error patterns. In E. Keller & M. Gopnik (Eds.), *Sensory processes in language.* Hillsdale, NJ: Lawrence Erlbaum Associates Inc.
Starreveld, P.A., & La Heij, W. (1996). Semantic interference, orthographic facilitation, and their interaction in naming tasks. *Journal of Experimental Psychology: Learning, Memory, and Cognition, 21*, 686–698.
Stemberger, J.P. (1985). An interactive activation model of language production. In A.W. Ellis (Ed.), *Progress in the psychology of language, Vol. 1.* Hillsdale, NJ: Lawrence Erlbaum Associates Inc.
Stemberger, J.P. (1990). Wordshape errors in language production. *Cognition, 35*, 123–158.
Vigliocco, G., Silverberg, N.B., Garrett, M.F., & Antonini, T. (1995). *Retrieval of grammatical information in anomia and during tip-of-the-tongue states.* Poster presented at the Academy of Aphasia Conference, San Diego, CA.
Warrington, E. (1975). The selective impairment of semantic memory. *Quarterly Journal of Experimental Psychology, 27*, 635–657.
Zingeser, L.B., & Berndt, R.S. (1988). Retrieval of nouns and verbs in agrammatism and anomia. *Brain and Language, 39*, 14–32.

Subject Index

abstract word meaning deafness 124
acquired dyslexia 4, 14, 148–9
anomia 185
auditory comprehension 43, 46, 120–21

barrier of uncertainty 138
behaviour & neurobiology 136–9

causality 134–6
context 122–5, 157

deep dyslexia 14, 148, 149
dictation deficits
  case studies 20, 21, 40, 42, 47–8, 84, 112–13, 116–17
  context 122–5
  explaining 119, 122, 124, 126
direct-access hypothesis *see* orthographic autonomy
dual-route cascaded model 172–3
dual-route hypothesis 169
dynamic systems theory 138–9
dyslexia 4, 14, 148–9

effect=structure 133–6
error types
  speech 76–80, 114, 148–9, 179–80
  spelling 21–2, 32–3, 114

feedback 155–7
flow-chart models 133, 143, 155

gender retrieval 185–7

grammatical class deficits 113–14, 120–21, 122, 183–7, 198–9, 202–3

homonyms 179
homophone judgements 5–6, 17–18, 23–4, 27
hyperonyms 199–201
hysteresis 157–8

independent network model 194–200, 203–4
interactive network model 182–3

language processing models 36, 106–7, 177–8, 195
  dual-route cascaded 172–3
  flow-chart 133, 143, 155
  independent network 194–200, 203–4
  interactive network 182–3
  recurrent feedback 139, 140–45, 146–8, 149–50, 151, 153–61
  syntactic mediation 181, 188
lemmas & lexemes 36, 177, 178–83, 188–9, 191–4

metastability 137–8, 158–60
models 36, 106–7, 177–8, 195
  dual-route cascaded 172–3
  flow-chart 133, 143, 155
  independent network 194–200, 203–4
  interactive network 182–3
  nervous system 138

recurrent feedback 139, 140–45, 146–8, 149–50, 151, 153–61
syntactic mediation 181, 188
multistability 144, 155–8

name recognition 9–10
naming, written & oral differences
  case studies 20, 43–4, 47, 52–63, 83–4, 89–99, 112–13
  explaining 118–19, 125, 126, 150–51, 153, 190–91, 192–3, 198
nervous system models 138
neurobiology & behaviour 136–9
1/f noise 158–60
nonlinear systems 137–8
nonword reading deficits 4, 13–14
nonword writing deficits 20, 109, 117, 119
noun deficits 113–14, 120–21, 122, 184

oral reading deficits 10–14, 40, 42, 47–8, 117, 191
orthographic autonomy 73, 96, 169
  evidence for 37–8, 51–2, 56–8, 64–5, 81, 91, 101, 110, 189–91
  strong & weak versions 65–7

phonological coherence 142, 144
phonological dyslexia 4
phonological mediation 3–4, 72–3, 105–6, 143–4

SUBJECT INDEX

evidence against 4–5, 55–7, 78, 81, 91, 98, 99, 126, 127
impoverished 98–9
instability of 91, 96–7
obligatory or optional? 6, 73, 99–101
reading 3–6, 15–18, 27, 110, 126–7, 139–40, 167–73
spelling & writing 6–7, 22–6, 28, 51–2, 63–4, 106–9, 126, 139–40, 173, 189
picture naming, written & oral differences
case studies 20, 43–4, 47, 52–63, 83–4, 89–99, 112–13
explaining 118–19, 125, 126, 150–51, 153, 190–91, 192–3, 198
processing models 36, 106–7, 177–8, 195
dual-route cascaded 172–3
flow-chart 133, 143, 155
independent network 194–200, 203–4
interactive network 182–3
recurrent feedback 139, 140–45, 146–8, 149–50, 151, 153–61
syntactic mediation 181, 188
pseudohomophones 15–16, 117, 172, 173

reading
hearing the words while 100

phonological mediation 3–6, 15–18, 27, 110, 126–7, 139–40, 167–73
& spelling 145–8
reading aloud deficits 10–14, 40, 42, 47–8, 117, 191
reading comprehension 110, 126–7, 167–73
recurrent feedback model 139, 140–45, 146–8, 149–50, 151, 153–61
regularisation errors in dyslexia 148, 149–50
repetition deficits 40, 42–3, 48, 117–18, 125–6
rhyme recognition 16–17, 23

semantic errors in dyslexia 149
sensorimotor neurons 137
single word comprehension 85, 119–23, 167–9
single word production 83–4, 111–19
slips of the pen 100–101
slips of the tongue 179–80, 195–6
sound exchanges 179–80, 195–6
speech deficits 4–5, 22–3
case studies 8, 83
error types 76–80, 114, 148–9, 179–80
localising 85–6
slips of the tongue 179–80, 195–6
& spelling 37–9, 73, 76–80
speech perception 157
speech production 177–8, 194–5

& spelling 37–9, 73, 76–80
spelling see also writing
phonological mediation 6–7, 22–6, 28, 51–2, 63–4, 139–40, 173, 189
& reading 145–8
& speech 37–9, 73, 76–80
spelling deficits 8–9, 19–22, 23–4 see also dictation deficits; writing deficits
error types 21–2, 32–3, 114
surface dyslexia 148
syntactic mediation 181, 188

tip-of-the-tongue 180, 185–6, 196

verb deficits 113–14, 120–21, 122, 184
visual word recognition 6, 18

word exchanges 179–80, 195–6
word meaning deafness 124
word–picture matching 46, 120
word recognition 6, 18
writing see also spelling
hearing oneself while 99–100
phonological mediation 106–9, 126
writing deficits see also dictation deficits; spelling deficits
localising 87
slips of the pen 100–101